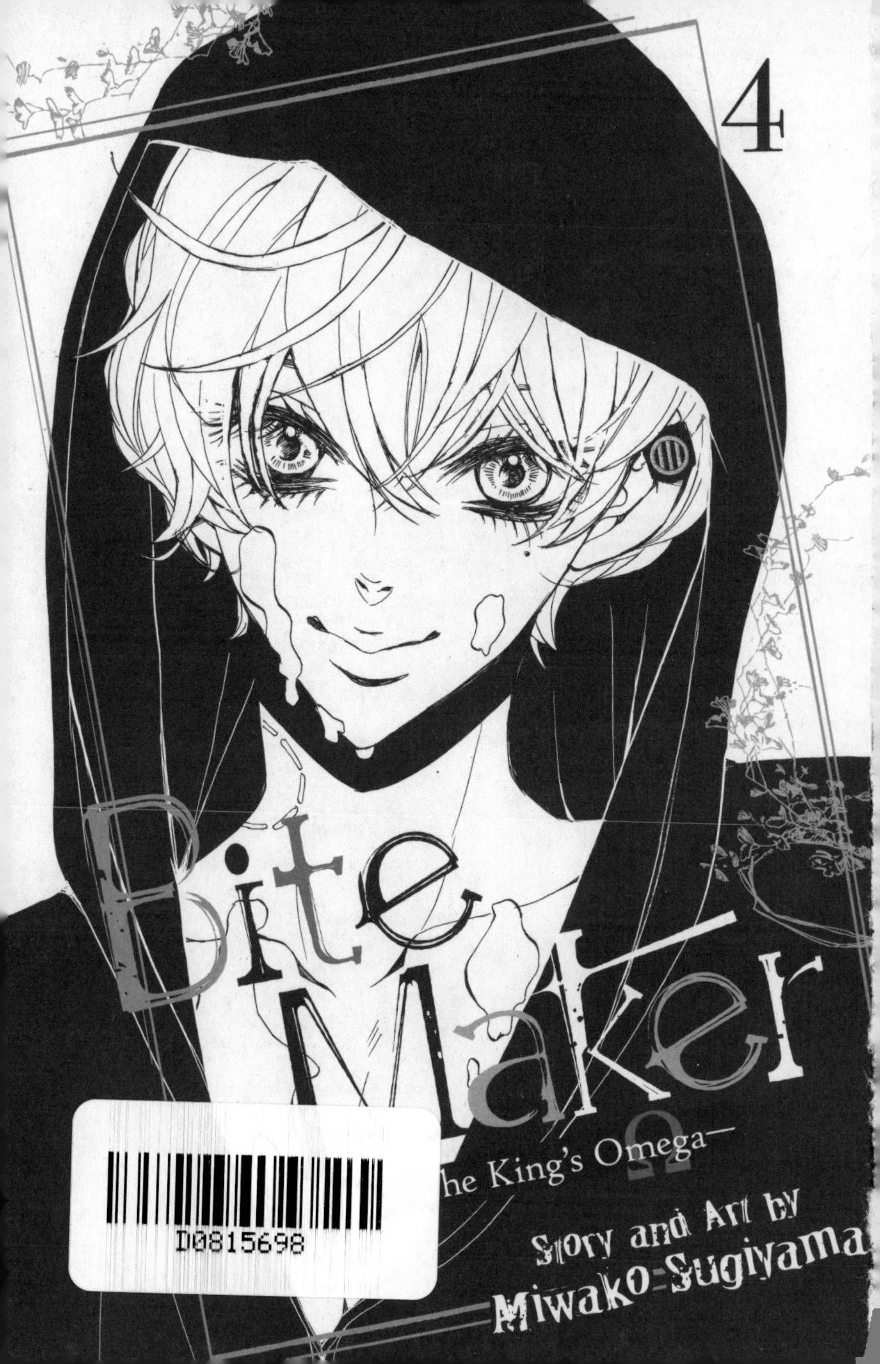
4
Bite Maker
Ω
he King's Omega—
Story and Art by
Miwako Sugiyama

Characters

National Azuchi Momoyama Gakuin Upper School

Many outstanding students attend this prestigious school, including Nobunaga, Hideyoshi, and Yukimura, who rule it as Numbers.

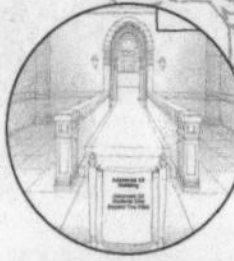

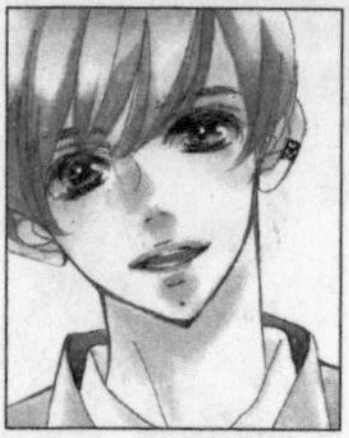

Asagi Yukimura
(alpha)

Appears to be laid-back but is actually quite ambitious. Possesses a special oral power which he can use to manipulate others when they come in contact with his saliva.

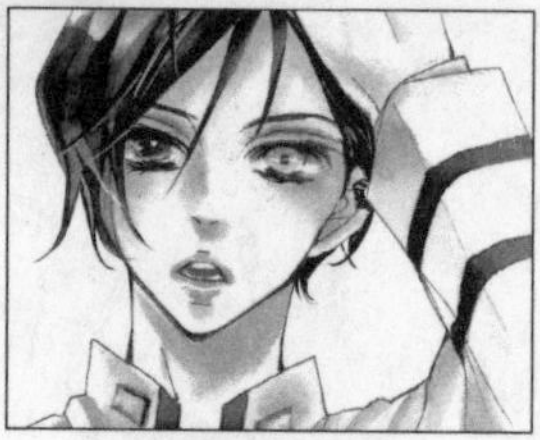

Suou Nobunaga
(alpha)

The attractive, powerful, and self-absorbed Absolute King. Possesses a special ocular power, which he can use to steal someone's heart and manipulate them.

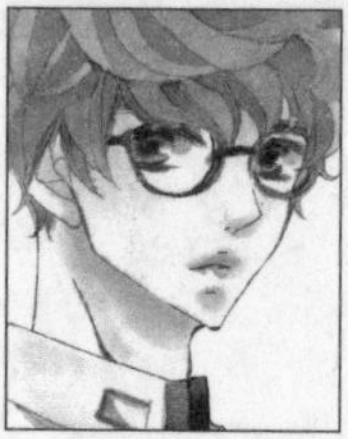

Aoni Hideyoshi
(alpha)

The most level-headed and logical of the Numbers, Hideyoshi loathes his sexual instincts. Possesses a special nasal power, which he can use to trace scents across long distances and sniff out lies.

Servants

※By rule, each alpha has three Servants.

Nobunaga's Servants

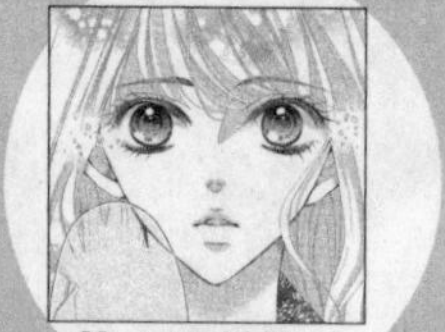

Mamesaki Noel
(omega)

She was transferred to Azuchi Momoyama Academy by Nobunaga. She became his servant while concealing her identity as an omega.

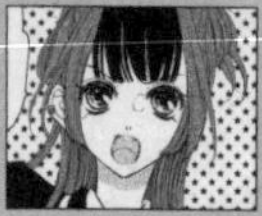

Ran
(beta)

Yukimura's Servants

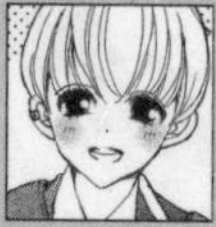

Yukiya
(beta)

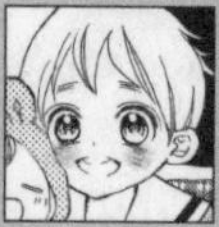

Yukito
(beta)

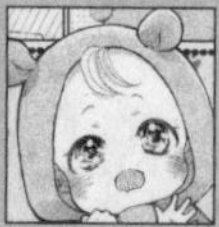

Yuki
(beta)

Hideyoshi's Servants

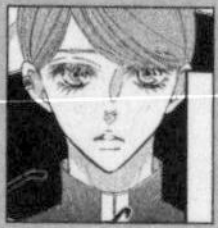

Ukon
(beta)

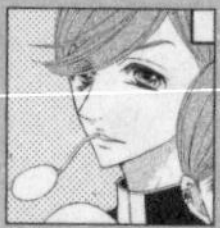

Sakon
(beta)

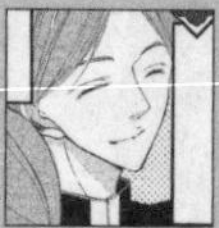

Nakaba
(beta)

Prefectural Shinjuku West High School

A typical school for average students who are mostly betas.

Noel's Friends

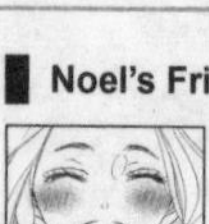

Iyo (beta)
A high school girl who loves romance.

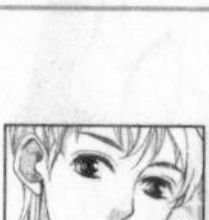

Hiro (beta)
A friendly boy who plays soccer.

The World of Bite Maker

The story takes place in the neo-futuristic city of Tokyo. Besides the typically recognized genders, others called alpha, beta, and omega exist in this world.

【 Alpha 】

α

Alphas are born with special genes, giving them exceptional looks, intelligence, and abilities. They go through periodic increases in sex drive (rut) and are sensitive to omega pheromones.

【 Beta 】

β

The most common gender; most people fall into this category. They don't release any pheromones.

【Omega】

Ω

Omegas are dedicated to breeding; they ensure the bearing of alpha children. They instinctively attract anyone with their pheromones when they're in heat. Omegas are rare and are thought to be endangered.

Suppressant

Oral Medicat
Mamesaki Noel
For:
Appetite Suppressant

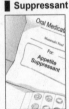

A medication that suppresses pheromones and sexual excitement. Noel takes this in order to hide her identity as an omega.

Partner

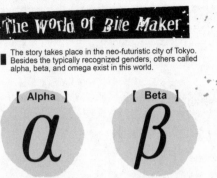

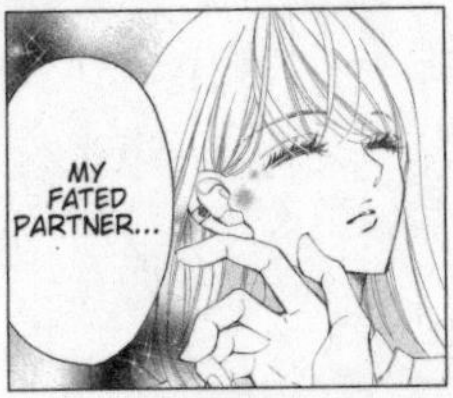

MY FATED PARTNER...

The relationship between an alpha and an omega is very strong. Fated Partners are naturally attracted to each other from the moment they meet.

Story

AN OMEGA... IS HERE.

Noel transferred to Azuchi Momoyama Academy when Nobunaga the Absolute King took an interest in her. She was introduced to the students as Nobunaga's new Servant and captured their hearts with her beauty. She quickly grew close to the reigning Numbers of the school, capturing the attention of all three, but she has managed to brush them off so far.

On a ride home from school, Nobunaga told Noel they were going on a date, something his supernatural magnetism (and apparent disinterest in love) never required him to bother with before. Noel reluctantly agreed to go.

Around the same time, Hideyoshi broke off an engagement that had been arranged to preserve his alpha bloodline. Not long after, he detected a dizzying scent he had smelled the day before! Unaware of Hideyoshi's presence, Noel and Nobunaga continue their date not far away...

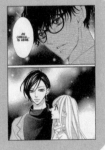

Contents

Bite Maker 4
The King's Omega

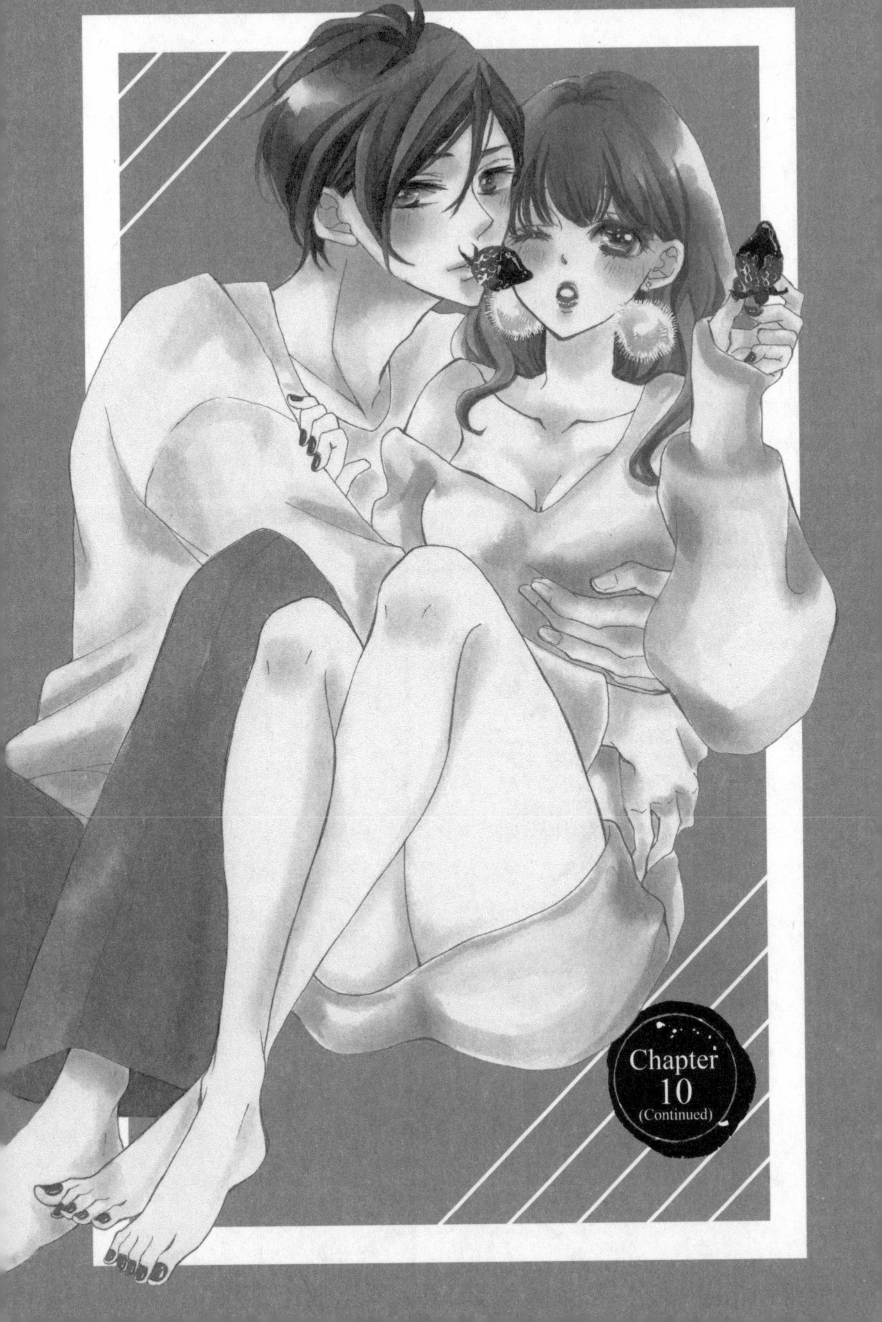
Chapter
10
(Continued)

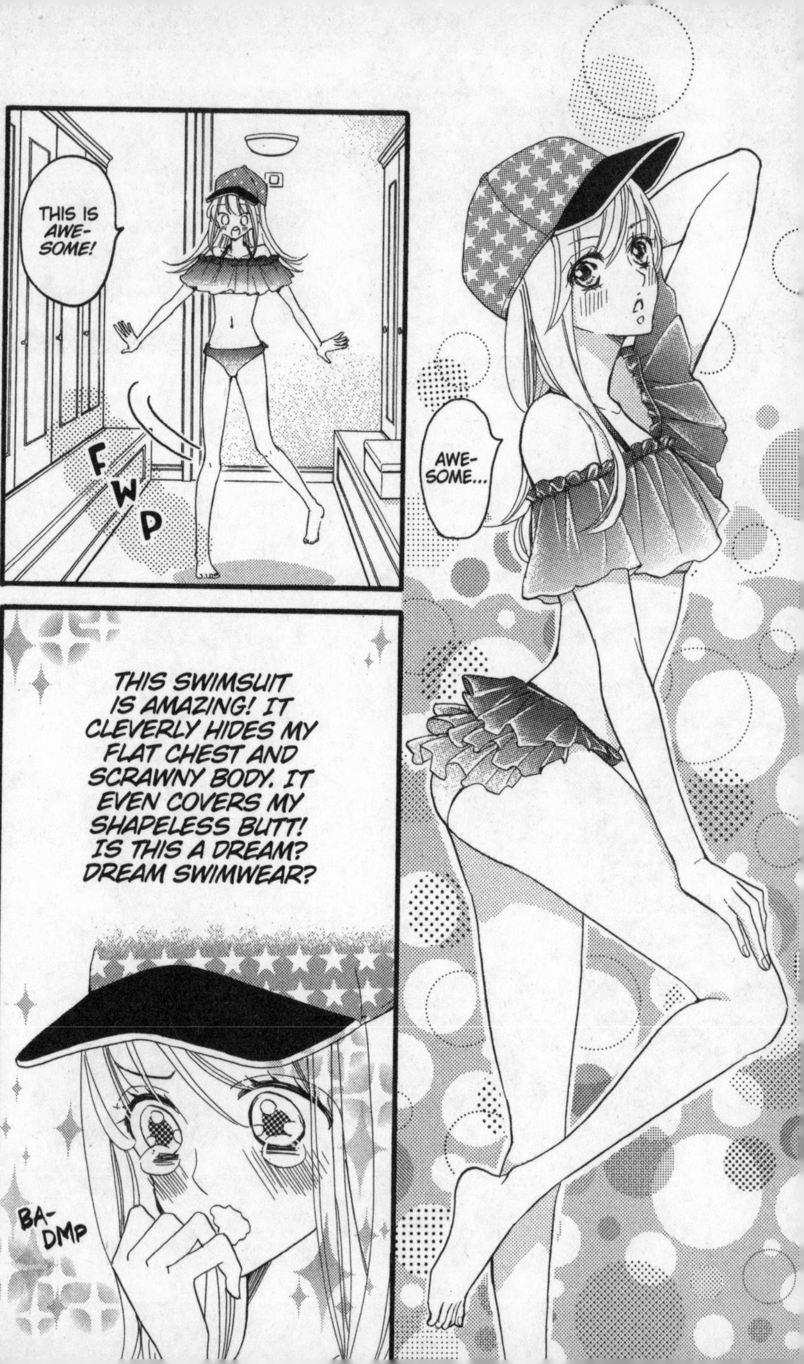
AWE-
SOME...
THIS IS AWE-SOME!
FWP
THIS SWIMSUIT IS AMAZING! IT CLEVERLY HIDES MY FLAT CHEST AND SCRAWNY BODY. IT EVEN COVERS MY SHAPELESS BUTT! IS THIS A DREAM? DREAM SWIMWEAR?
BA-DMP

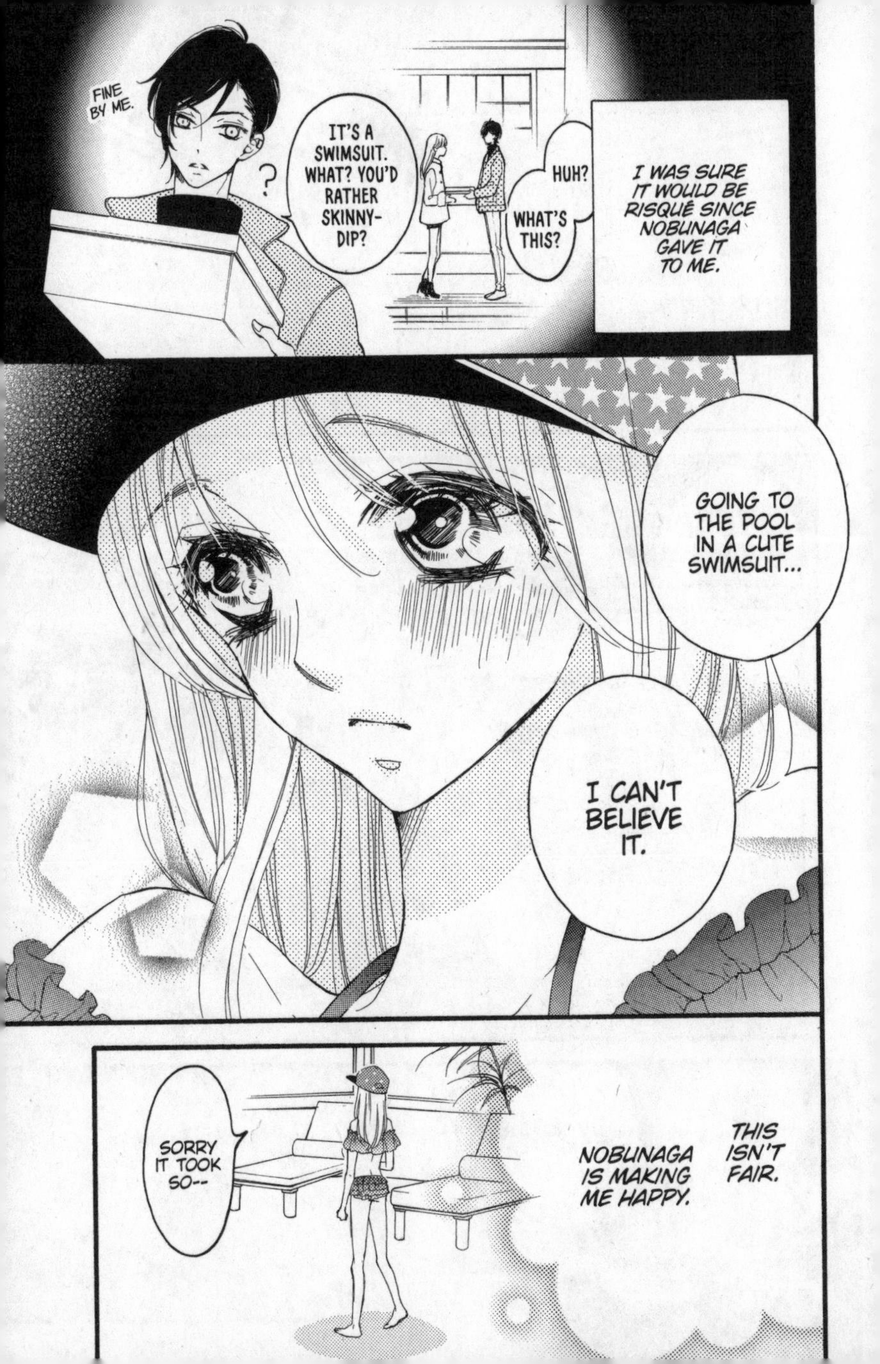
I WAS SURE IT WOULD BE RISQUÉ SINCE NOBUNAGA GAVE IT TO ME.
HUH?
WHAT'S THIS?
IT'S A SWIMSUIT. WHAT? YOU'D RATHER SKINNY-DIP?
?
FINE BY ME.
GOING TO THE POOL IN A CUTE SWIMSUIT...
I CAN'T BELIEVE IT.
THIS ISN'T FAIR.
NOBUNAGA IS MAKING ME HAPPY.
SORRY IT TOOK SO--

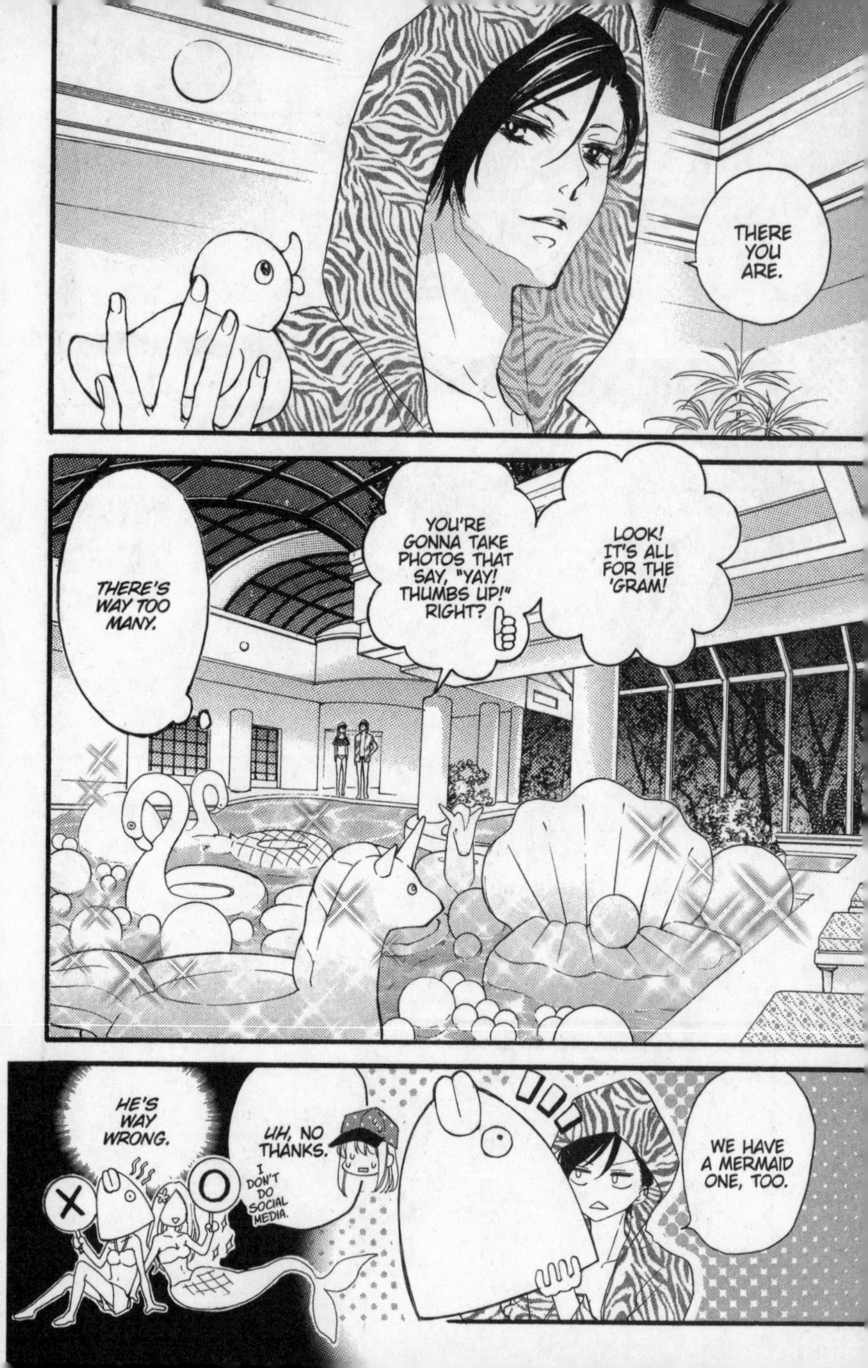
THERE YOU ARE.
LOOK! IT'S ALL FOR THE 'GRAM!
YOU'RE GONNA TAKE PHOTOS THAT SAY, "YAY! THUMBS UP!" RIGHT?
THERE'S WAY TOO MANY.
WE HAVE A MERMAID ONE, TOO.
UH, NO THANKS.
I DON'T DO SOCIAL MEDIA.
HE'S WAY WRONG.

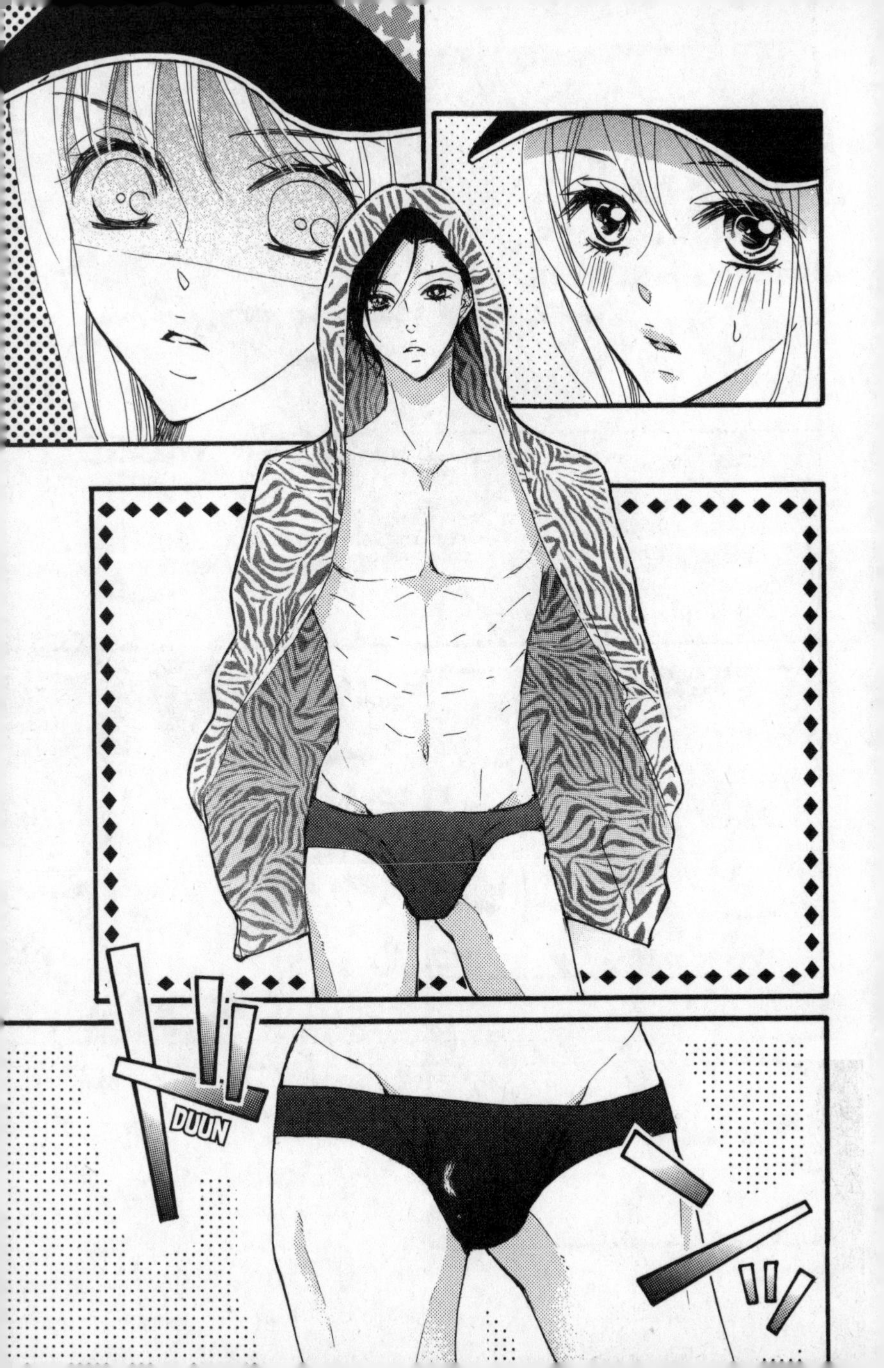
DUUN

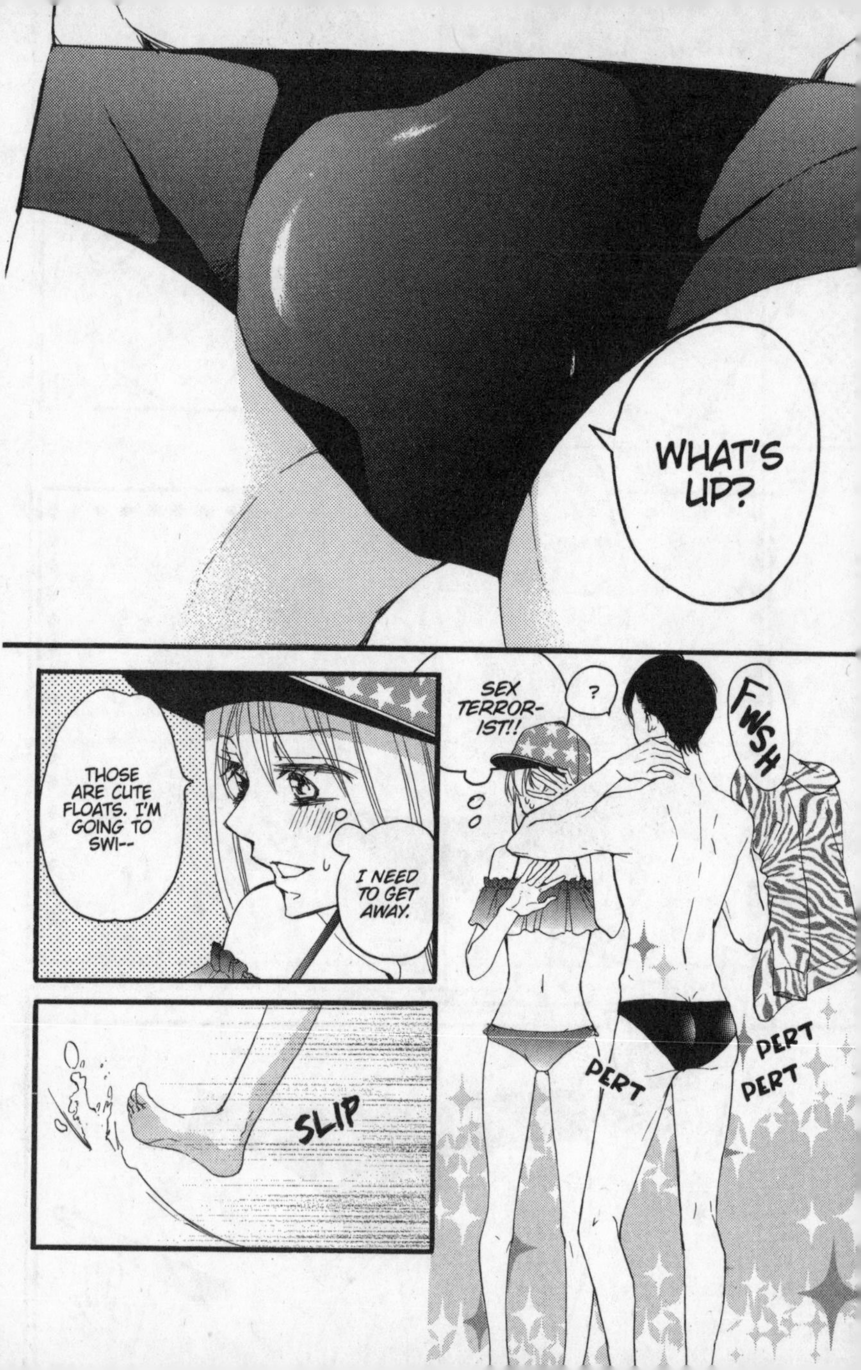
WHAT'S UP?
FWSH
?
SEX TERROR-IST!!
PERT
PERT
PERT
THOSE ARE CUTE FLOATS. I'M GOING TO SWI--
I NEED TO GET AWAY.
SLIP

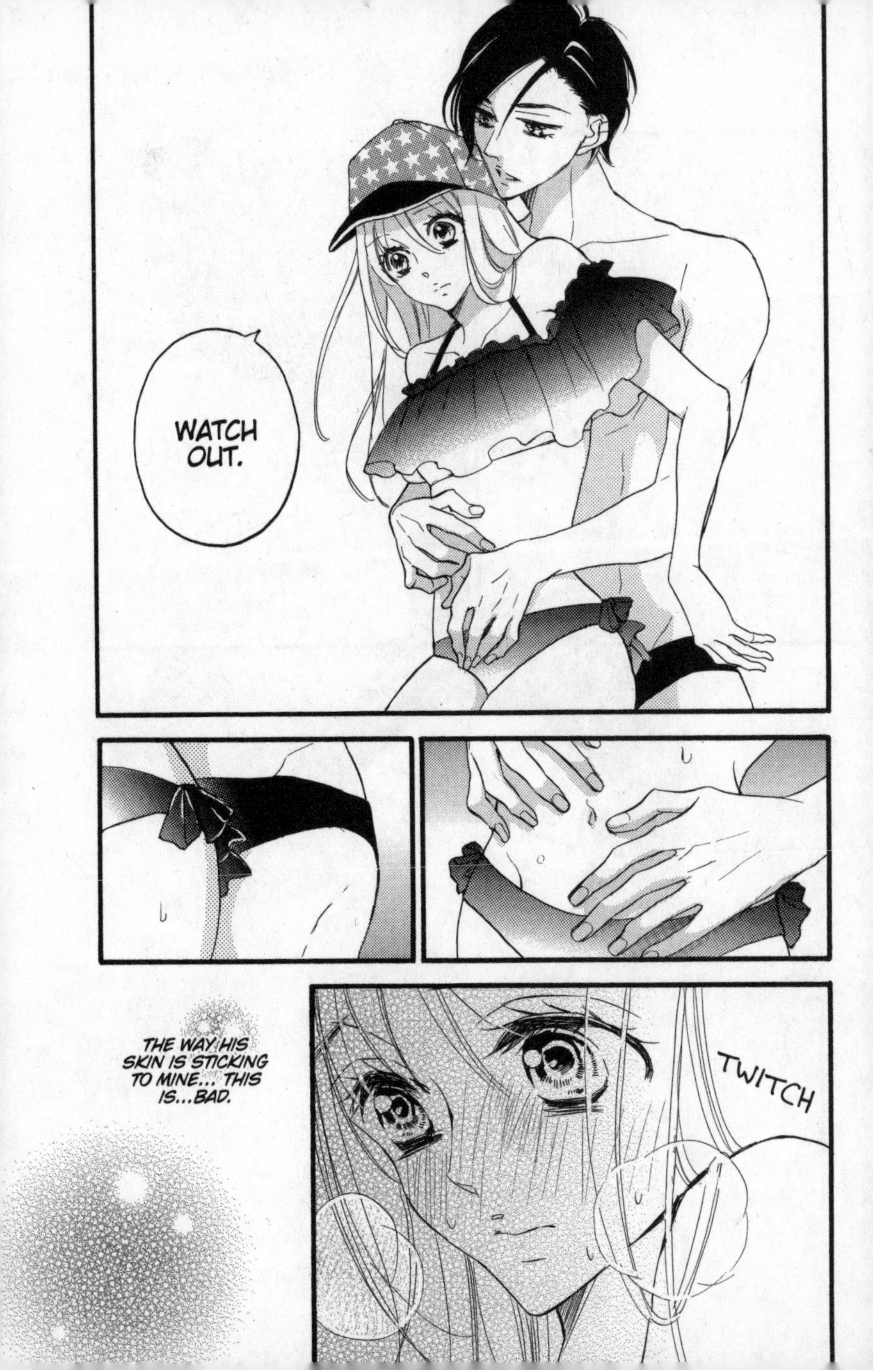
WATCH OUT.
TWITCH
THE WAY HIS SKIN IS STICKING TO MINE... THIS IS...BAD.

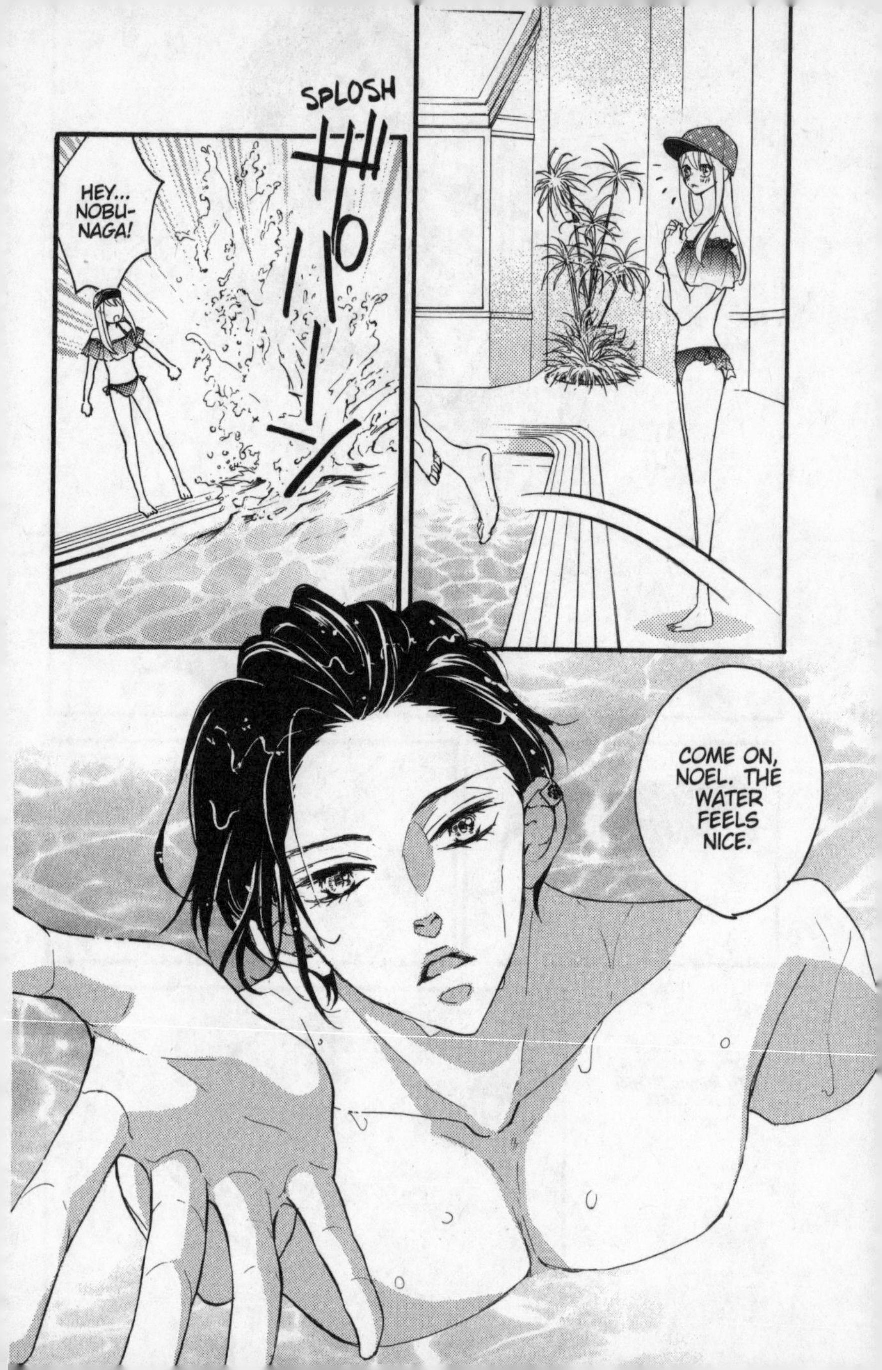
SPLOSH
HEY... NOBU-NAGA!
COME ON, NOEL. THE WATER FEELS NICE.

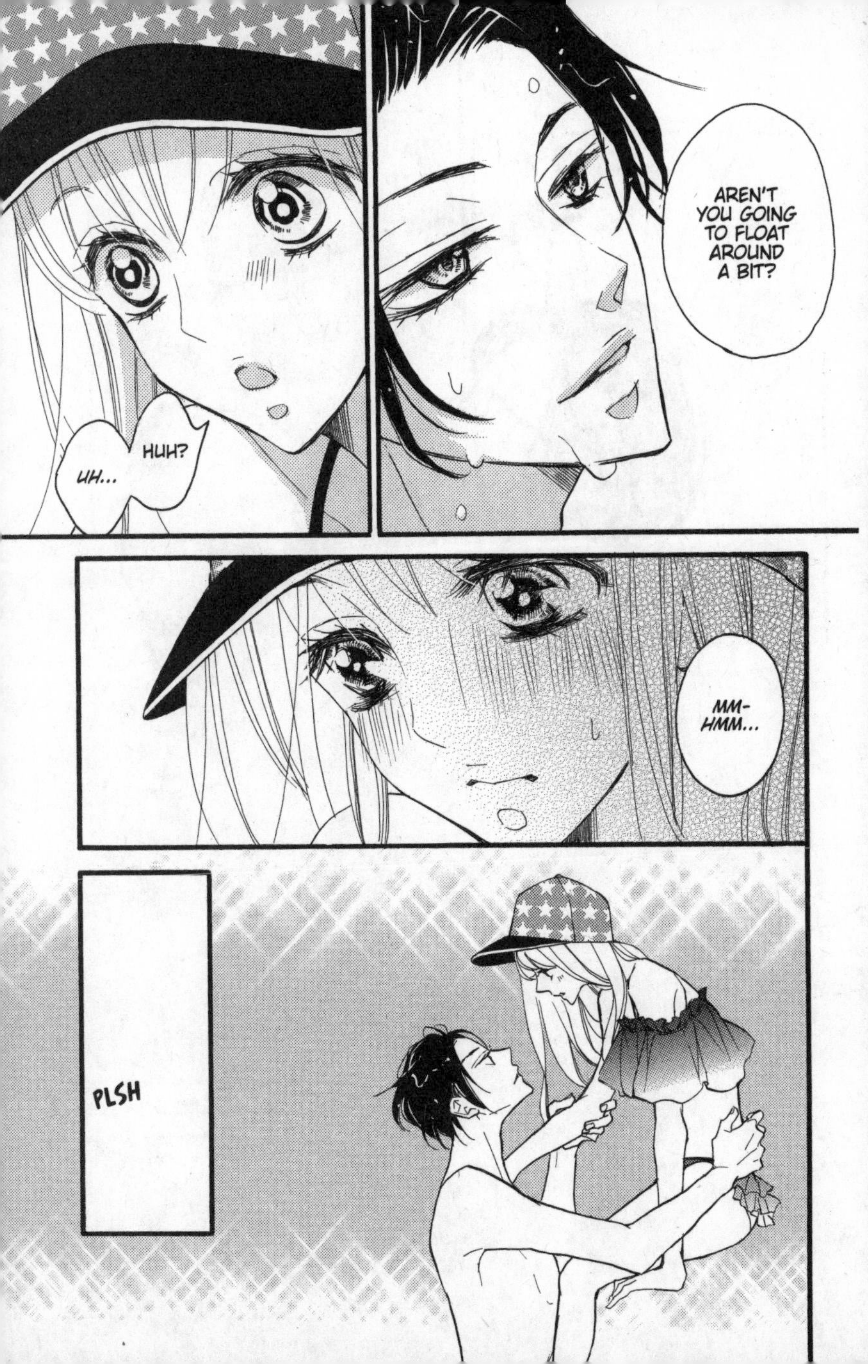
AREN'T YOU GOING TO FLOAT AROUND A BIT?
HUH?
UH...
MM-HMM...
PLSH

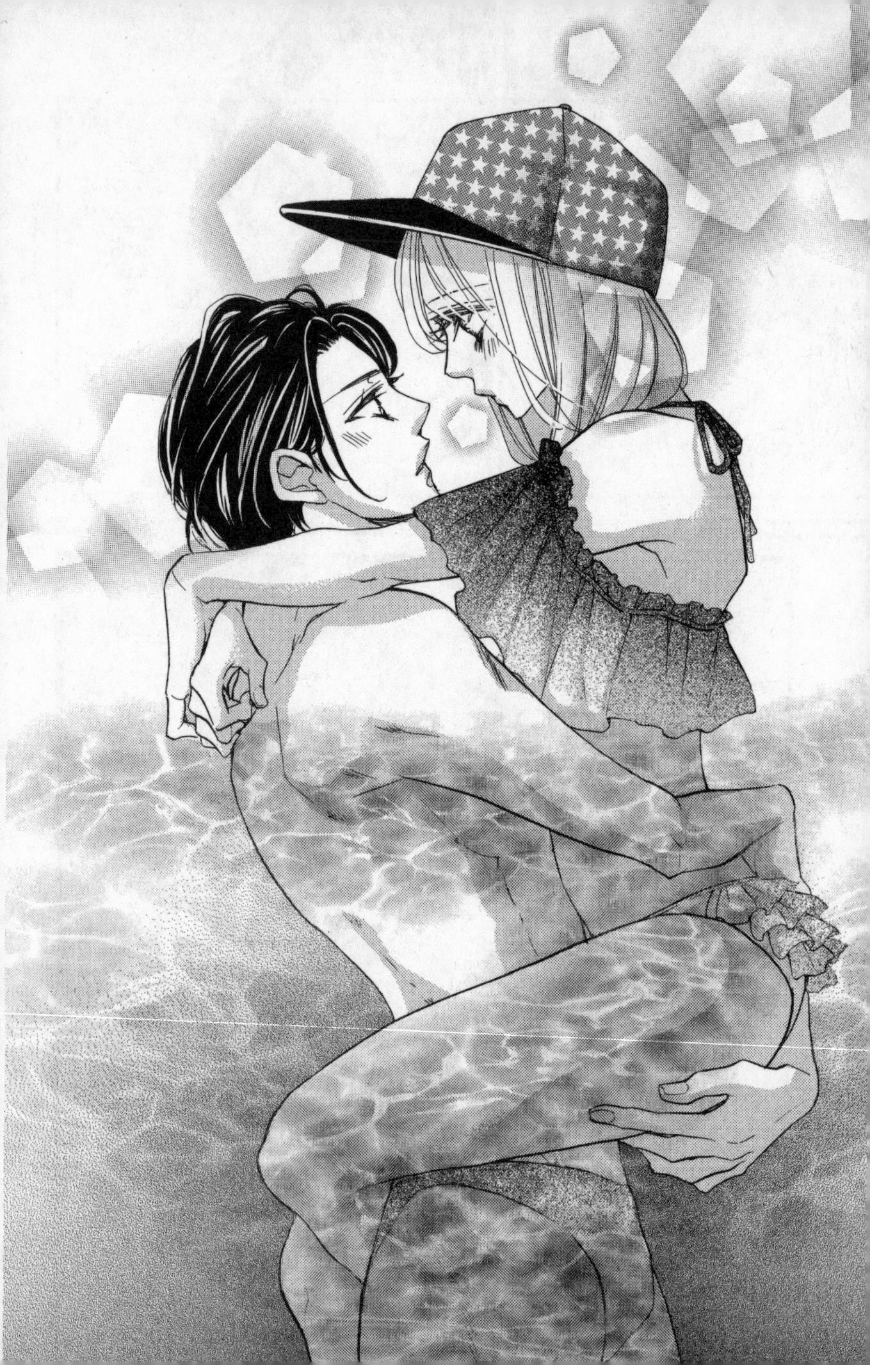

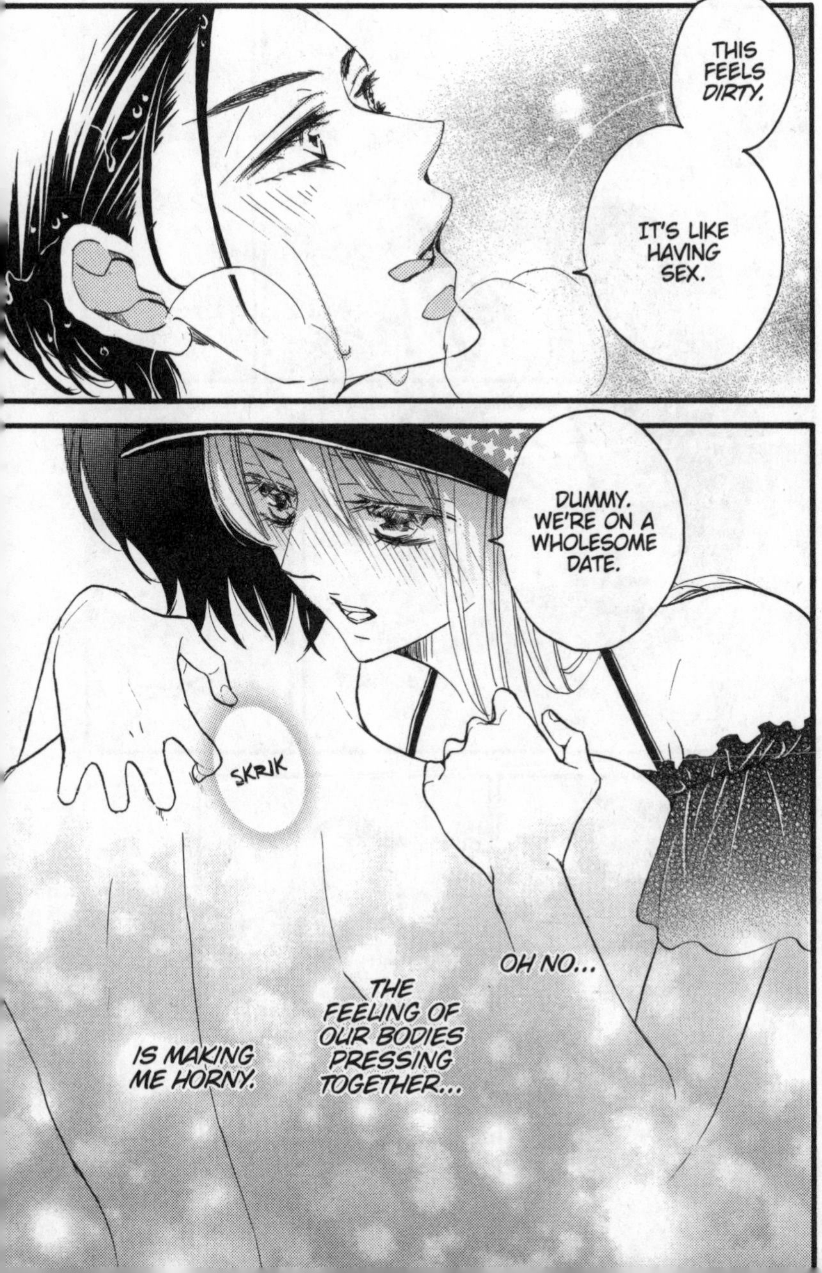
THIS FEELS DIRTY.
IT'S LIKE HAVING SEX.
DUMMY. WE'RE ON A WHOLESOME DATE.
SKRIK
OH NO...
THE FEELING OF OUR BODIES PRESSING TOGETHER...
IS MAKING ME HORNY.

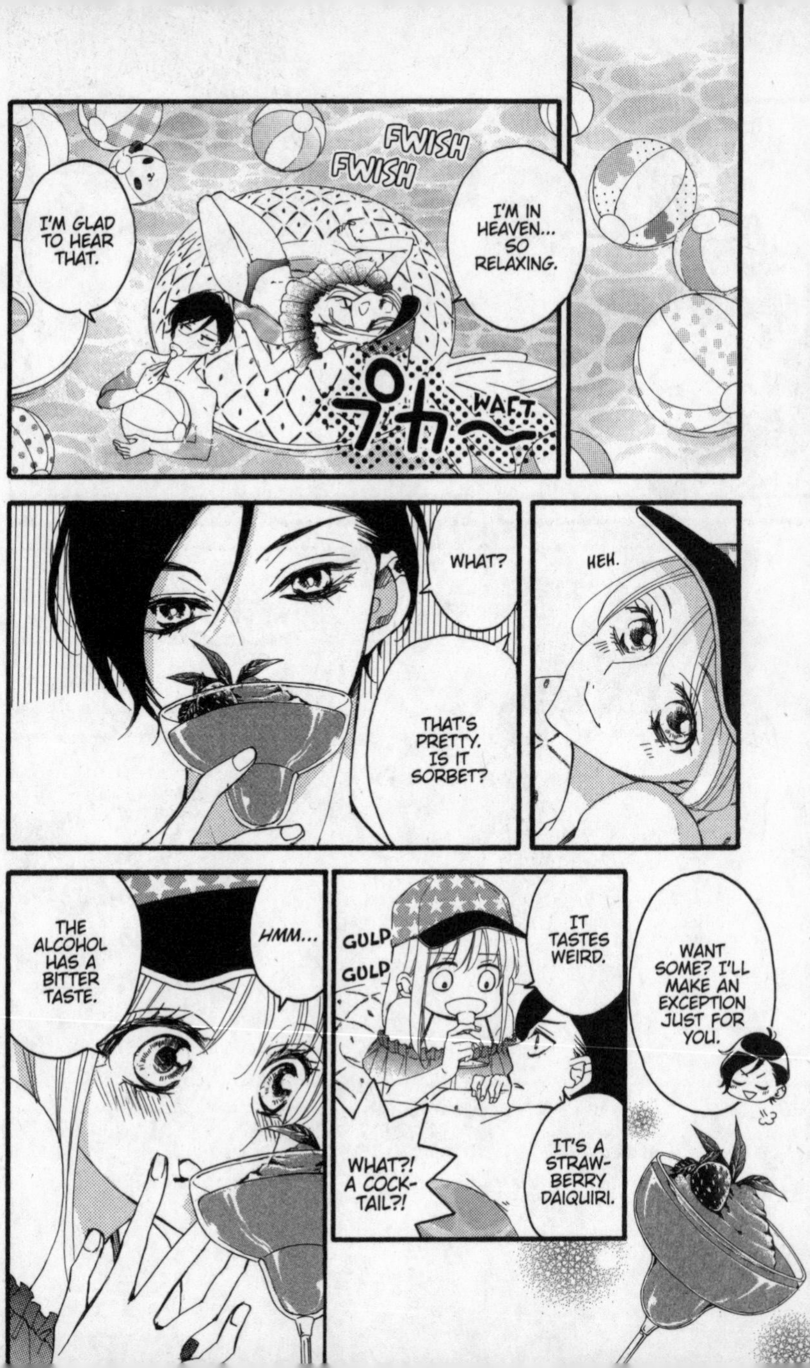
I'M IN HEAVEN... SO RELAXING.
FWISH FWISH
ぷか〜
WAFT
I'M GLAD TO HEAR THAT.
HEH.
WHAT?
THAT'S PRETTY. IS IT SORBET?
WANT SOME? I'LL MAKE AN EXCEPTION JUST FOR YOU.
IT'S A STRAW-BERRY DAIQUIRI.
IT TASTES WEIRD.
GULP GULP
WHAT?! A COCK-TAIL?!
HMM...
THE ALCOHOL HAS A BITTER TASTE.

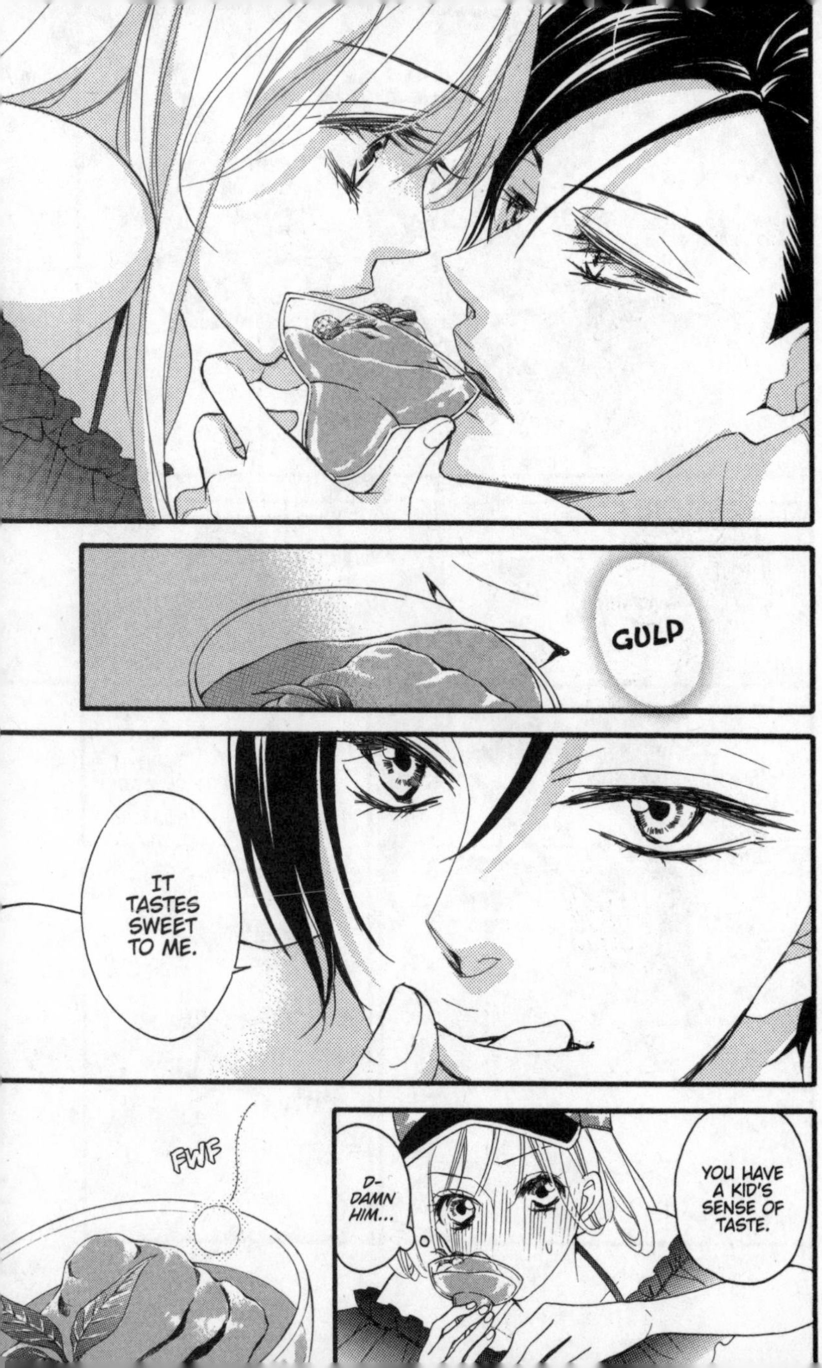
GULP
IT TASTES SWEET TO ME.
YOU HAVE A KID'S SENSE OF TASTE.
D-DAMN HIM...
FWF

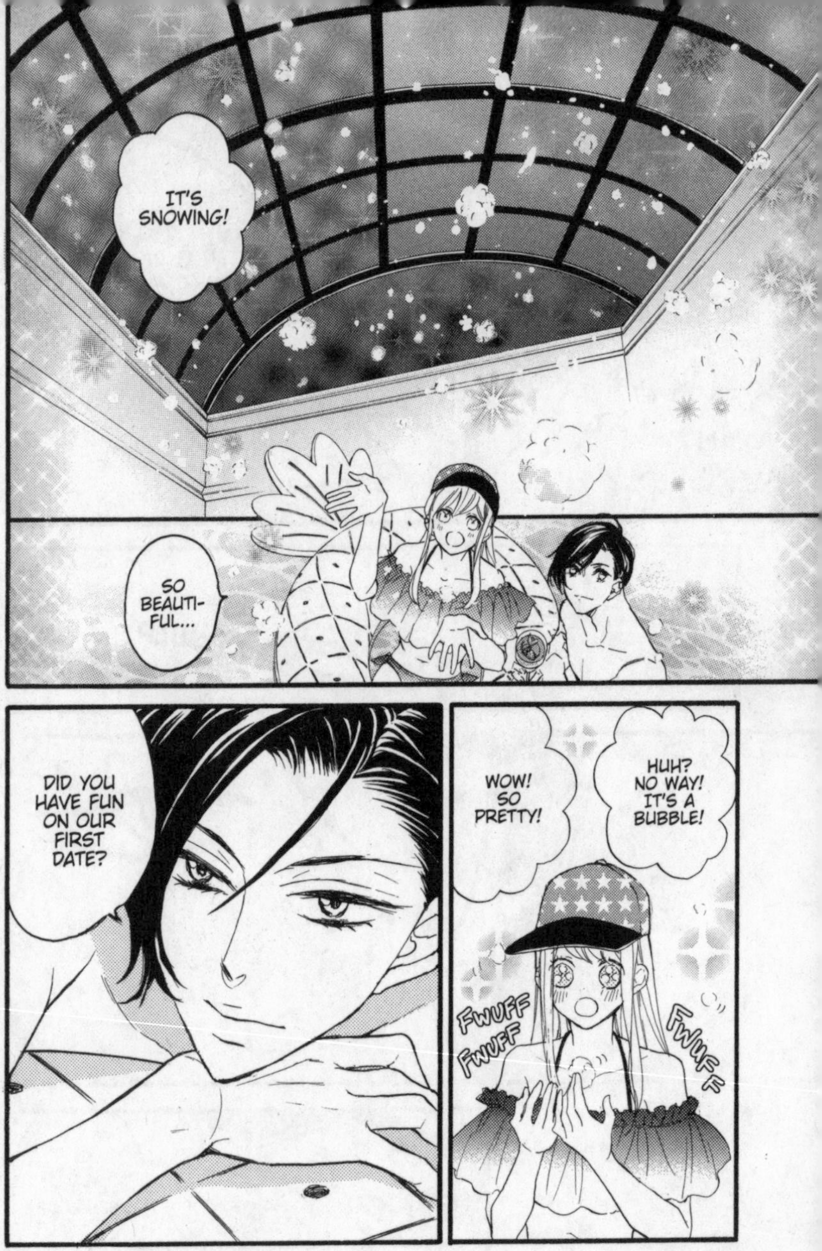
IT'S SNOWING!
SO BEAUTI-FUL...
HUH? NO WAY! IT'S A BUBBLE!
WOW! SO PRETTY!
FWUFF
FWUFF
FWUFF
DID YOU HAVE FUN ON OUR FIRST DATE?

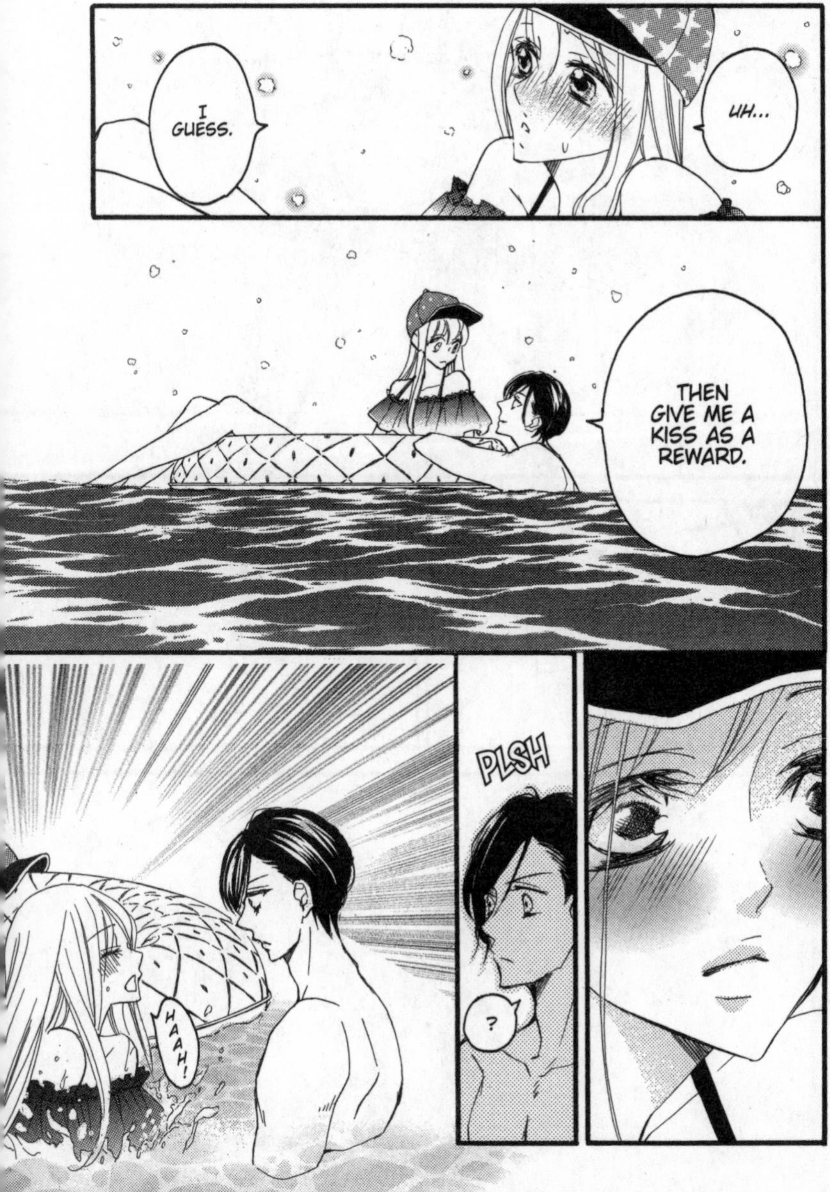
UH...
I GUESS.
THEN GIVE ME A KISS AS A REWARD.
PLSH
?
HAAH!

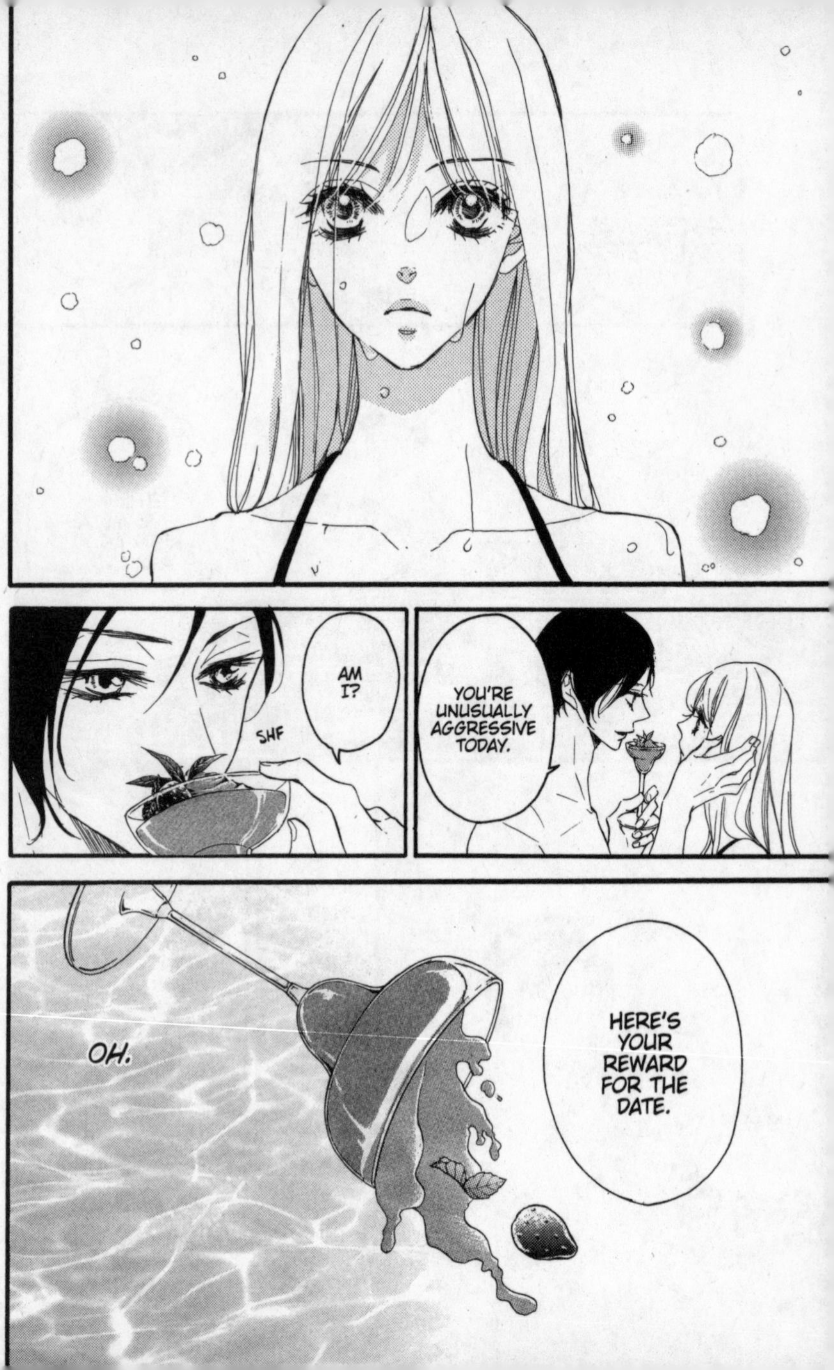
YOU'RE UNUSUALLY AGGRESSIVE TODAY.
AM I?
SHF
HERE'S YOUR REWARD FOR THE DATE.
OH.

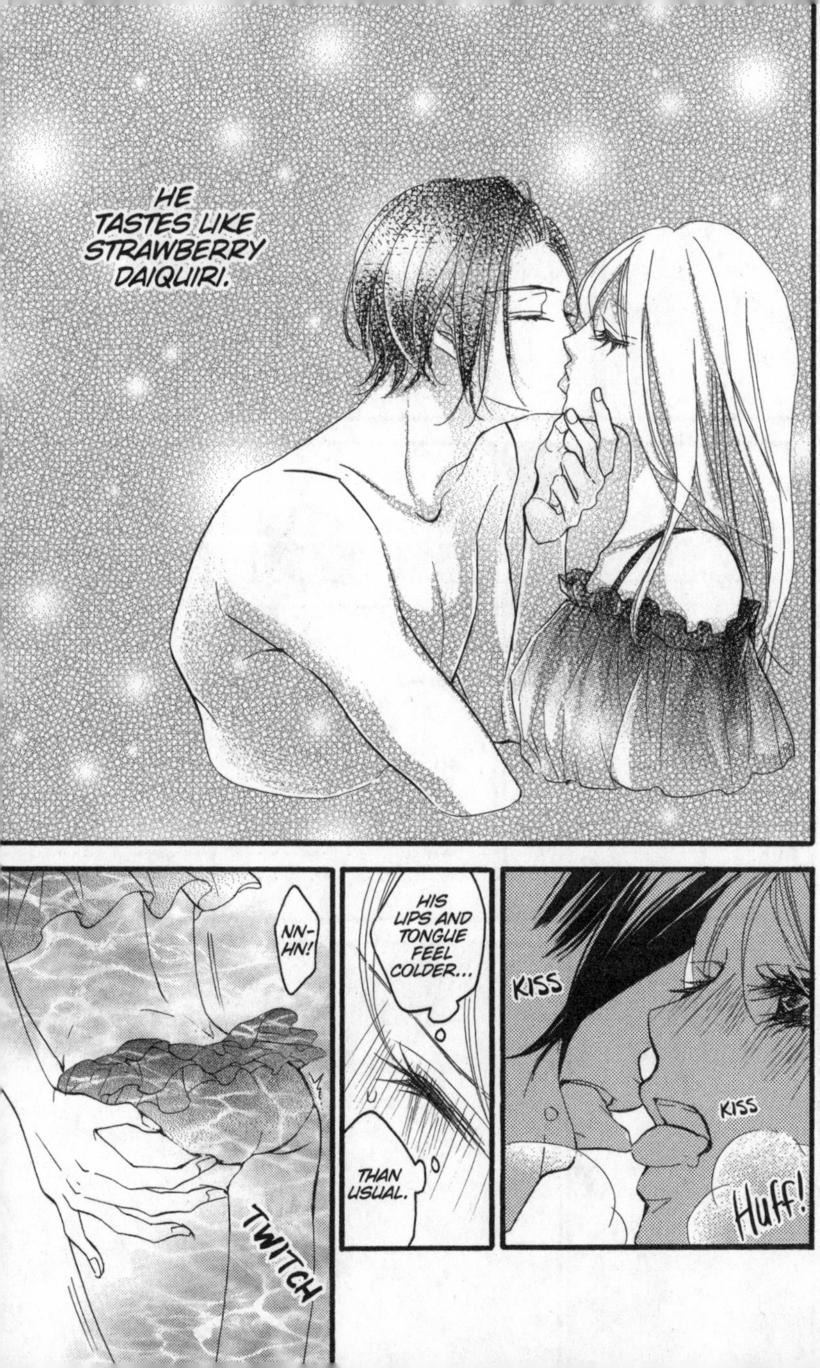
HE TASTES LIKE STRAWBERRY DAIQUIRI.
KISS
KISS
Huff!
HIS LIPS AND TONGUE FEEL COLDER...
THAN USUAL.
NN-HN!
TWITCH

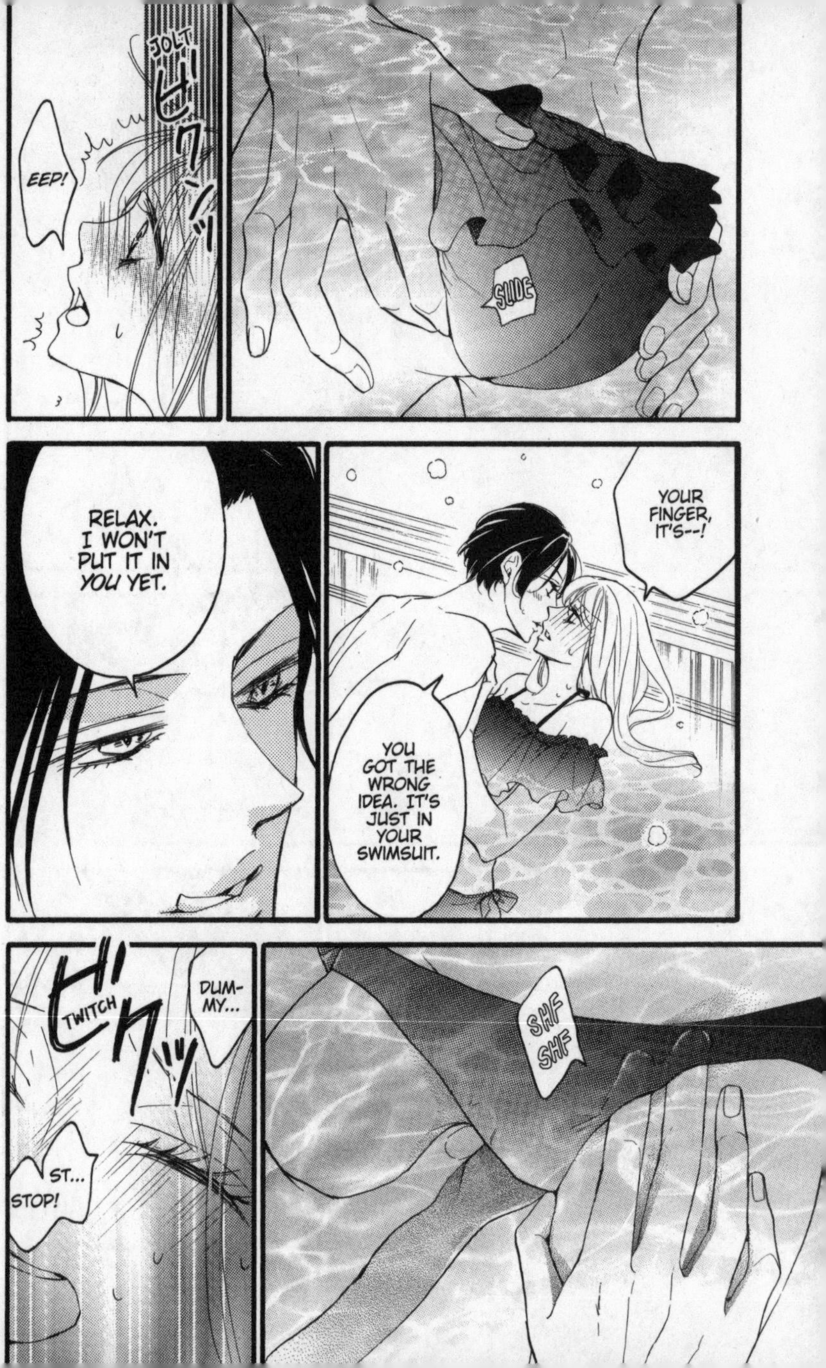
SLIDE
JOLT
EEP!
YOUR FINGER, IT'S--!
YOU GOT THE WRONG IDEA. IT'S JUST IN YOUR SWIMSUIT.
RELAX. I WON'T PUT IT IN *YOU* YET.
SHF SHF
DUM-MY...
TWITCH
ST... STOP!

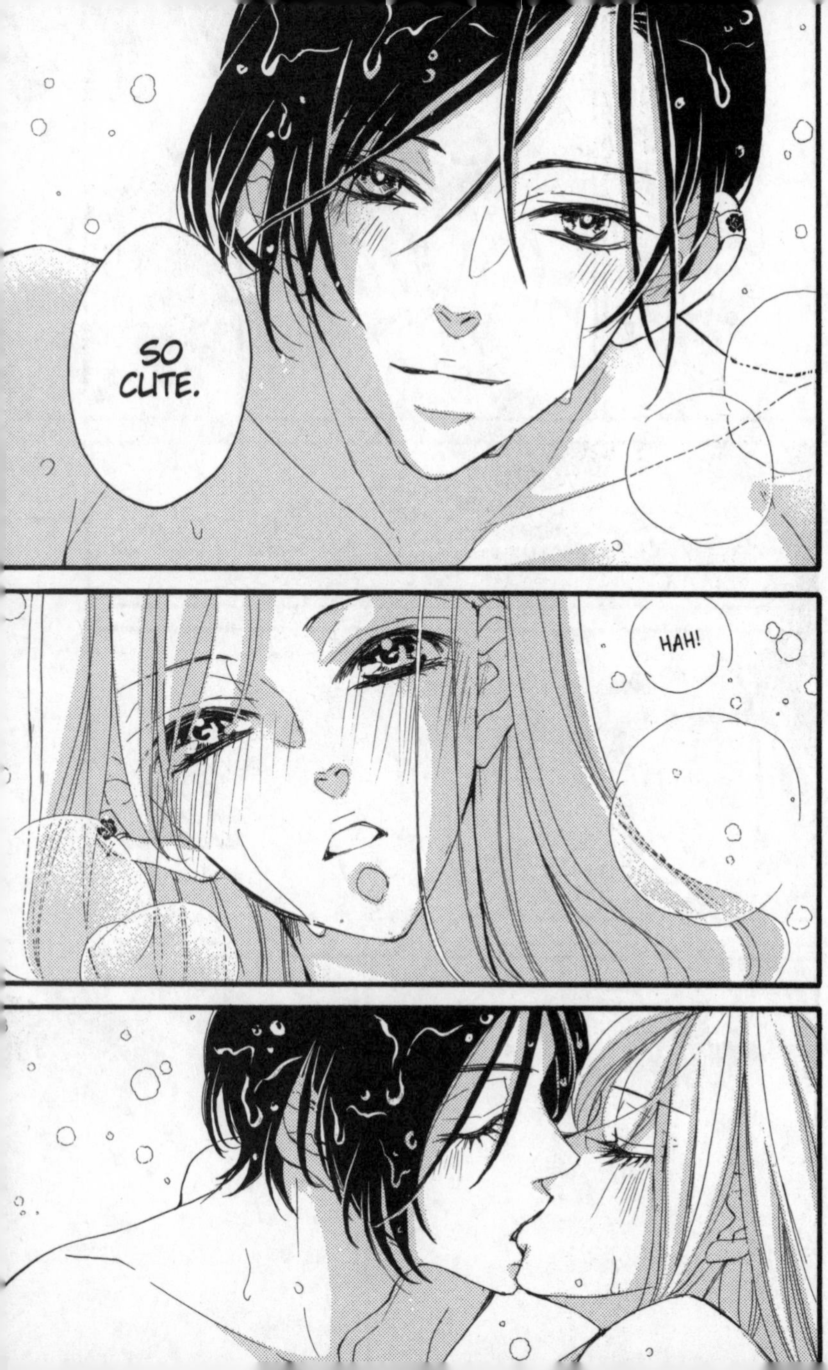
SO CUTE.
HAH!

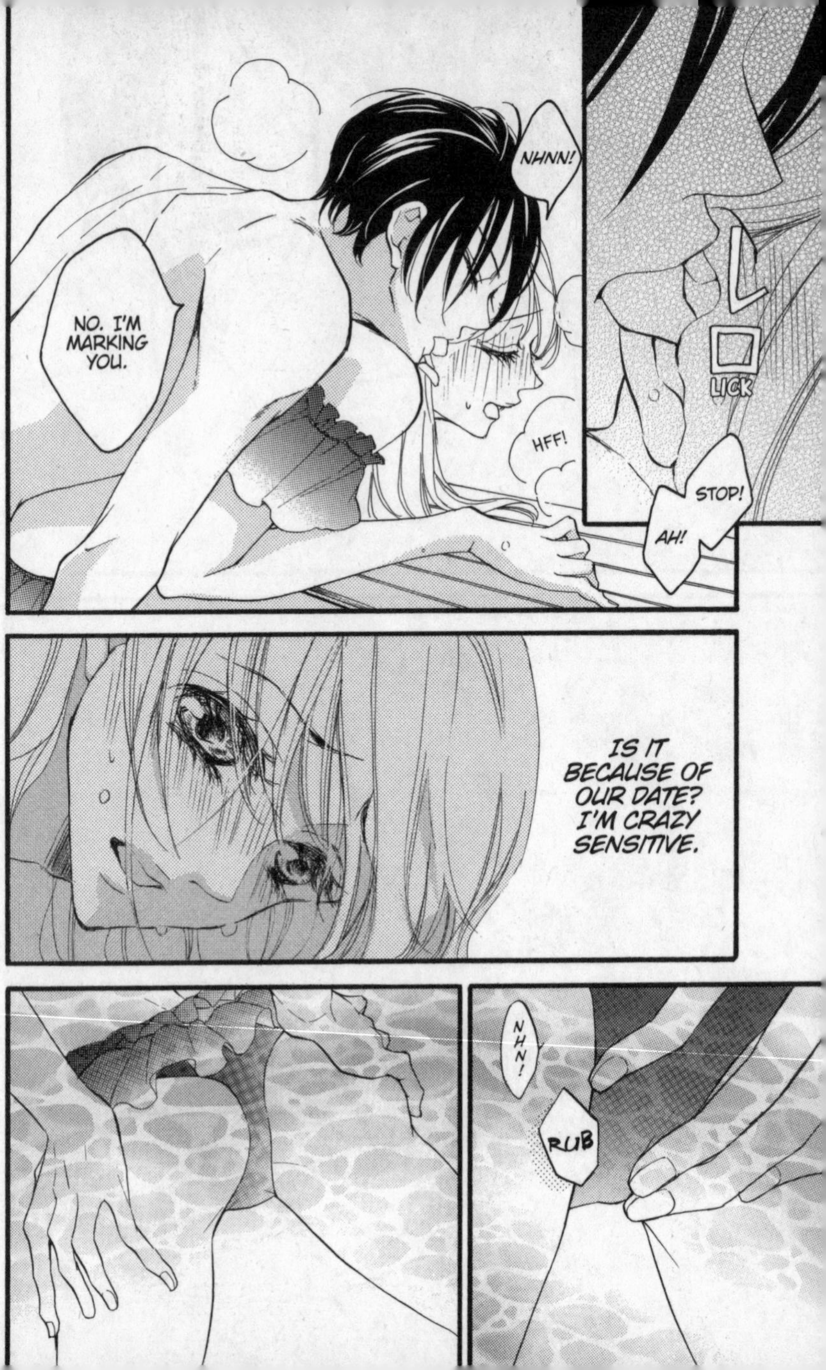
LICK
STOP!
AH!
NHNN!
NO. I'M MARKING YOU.
HFF!
IS IT BECAUSE OF OUR DATE? I'M CRAZY SENSITIVE.
NHN!
RUB

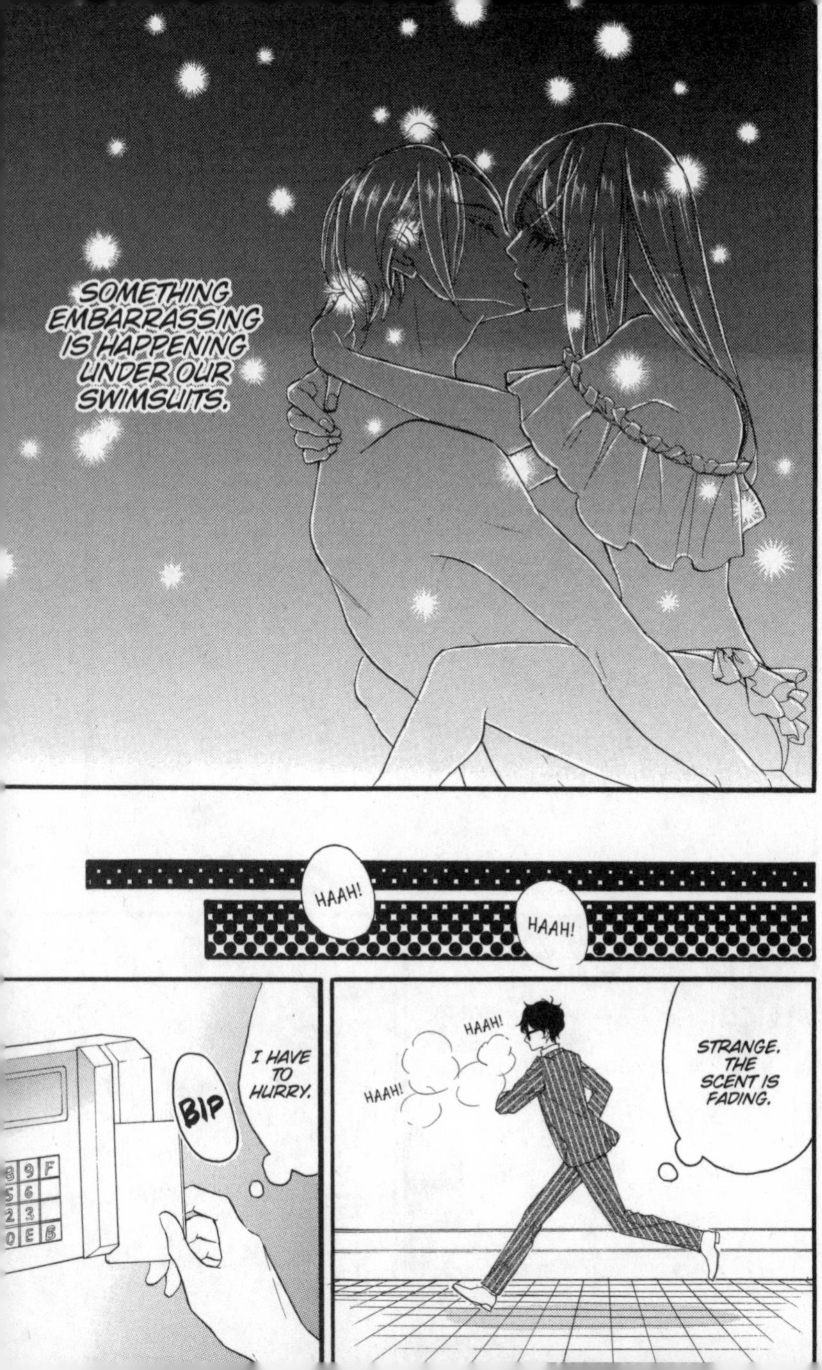
SOMETHING EMBARRASSING IS HAPPENING UNDER OUR SWIMSUITS.
HAAH!
HAAH!
STRANGE. THE SCENT IS FADING.
HAAH!
HAAH!
I HAVE TO HURRY.
BIP

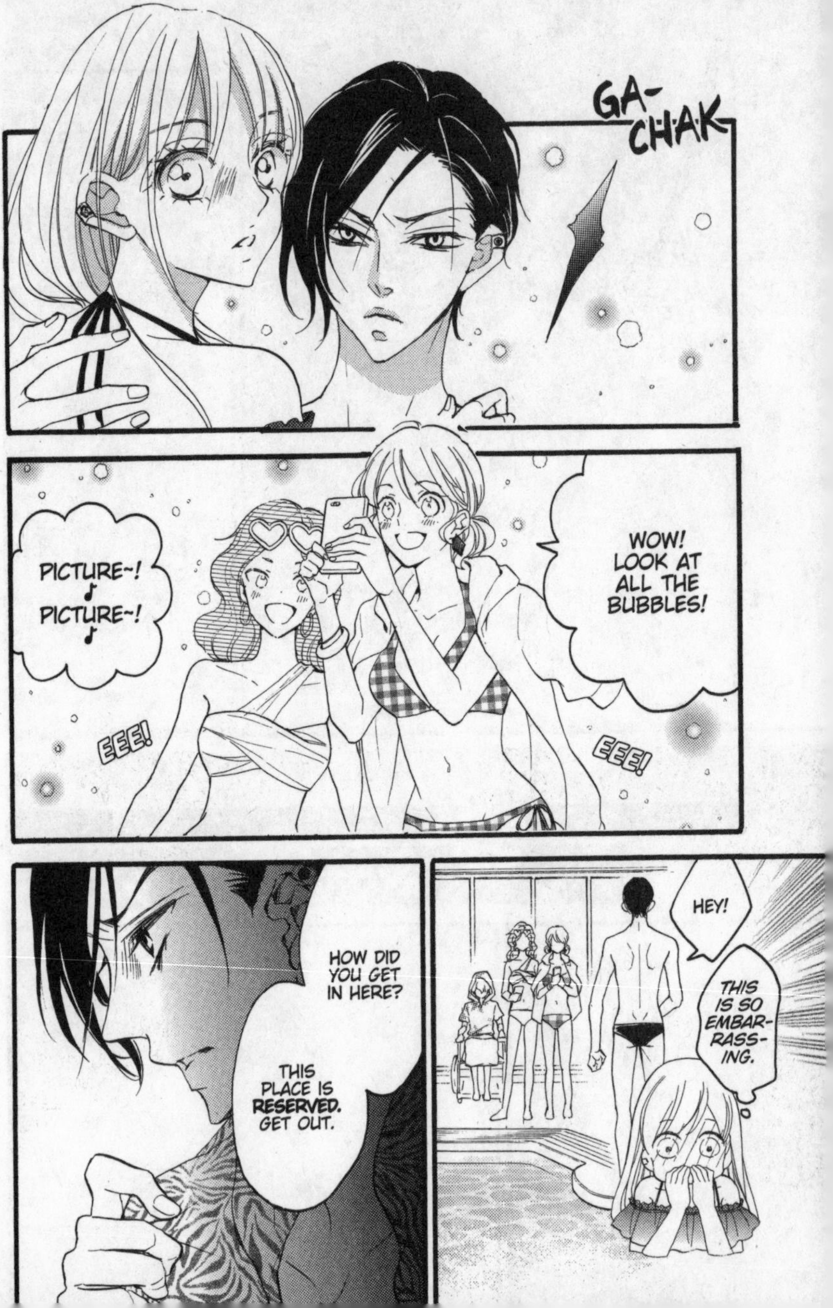
GA-CHAK
WOW! LOOK AT ALL THE BUBBLES!
EEE!
PICTURE~! ♪ PICTURE~! ♪
EEE!
HEY!
THIS IS SO EMBARRASSING.
HOW DID YOU GET IN HERE?
THIS PLACE IS RESERVED. GET OUT.

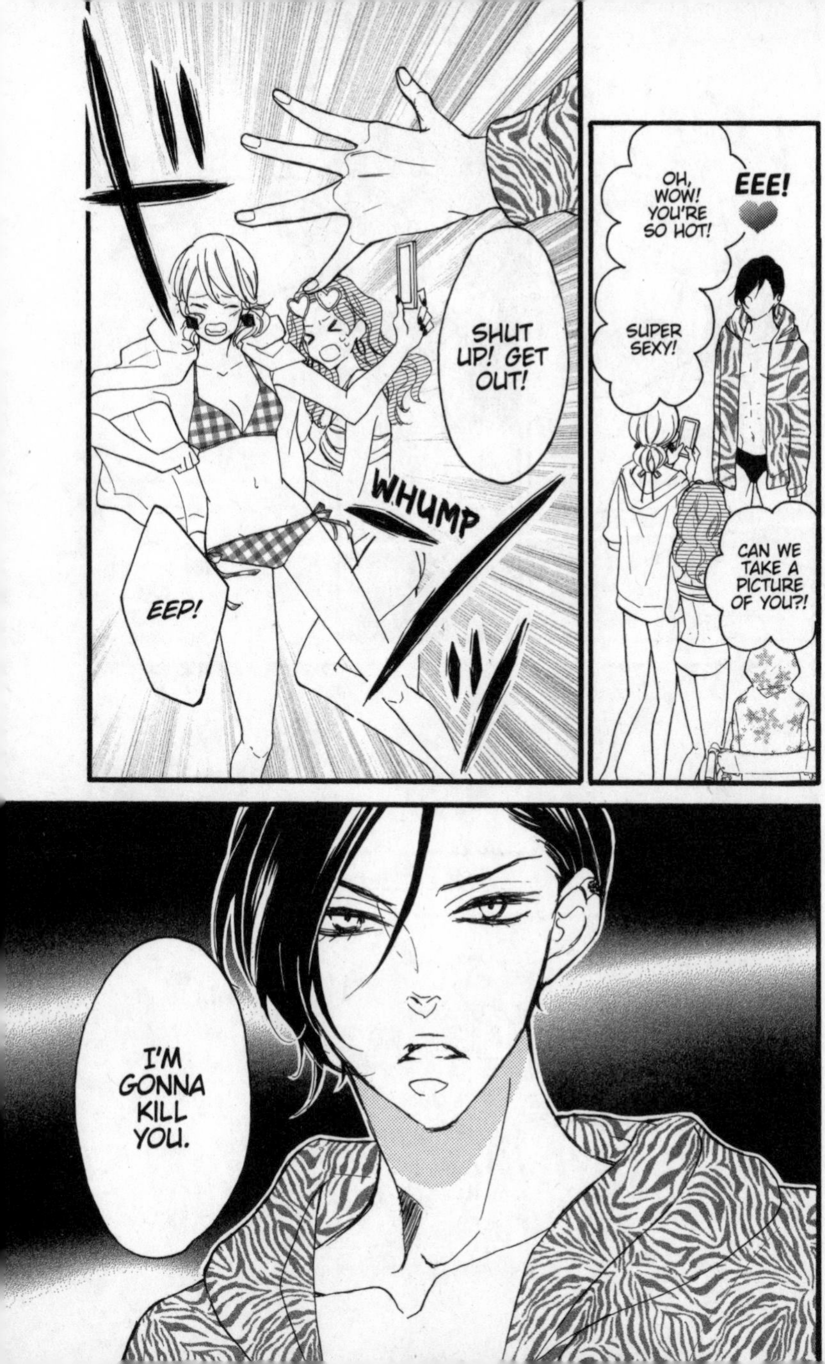
EEE!
OH, WOW! YOU'RE SO HOT!
SUPER SEXY!
CAN WE TAKE A PICTURE OF YOU?!
SHUT UP! GET OUT!
WHUMP
EEP!
I'M GONNA KILL YOU.

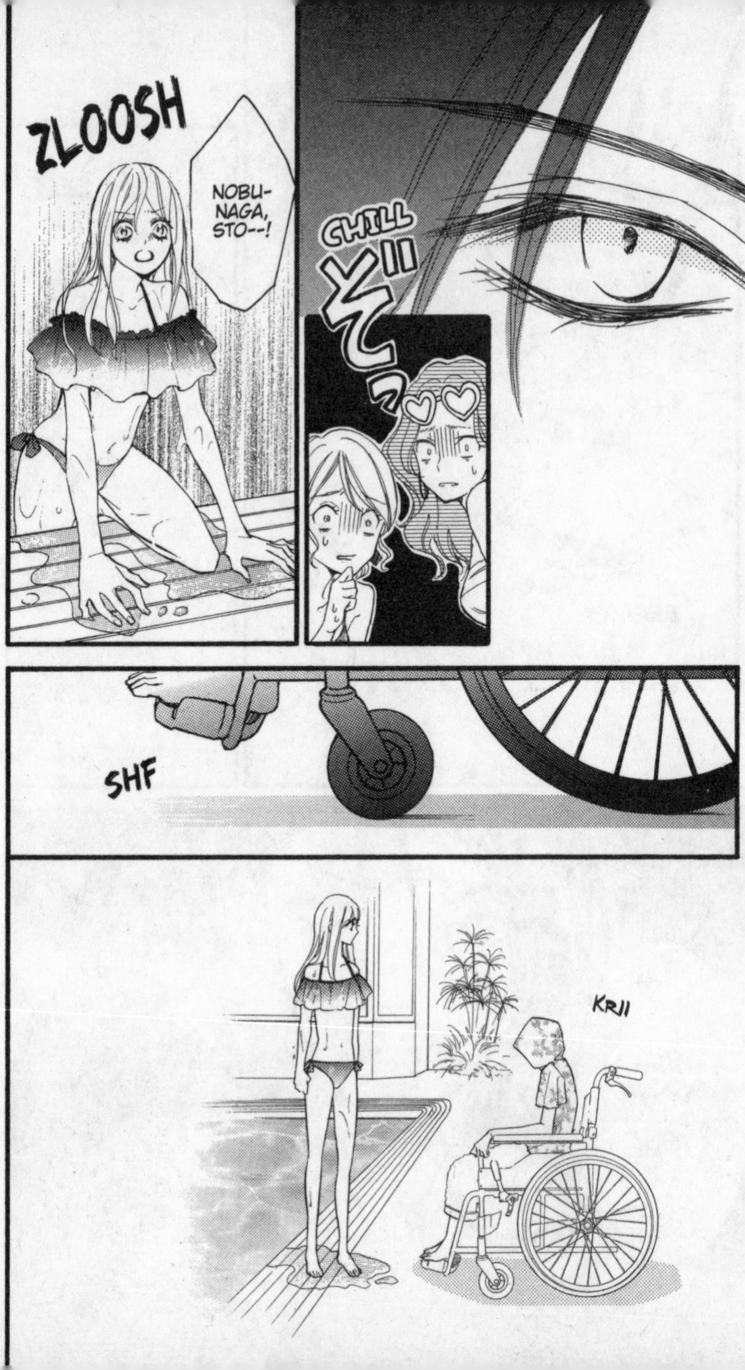
CHILL
ぞっ
ZLOOSH
NOBUNAGA, STO--!
SHF
KRII

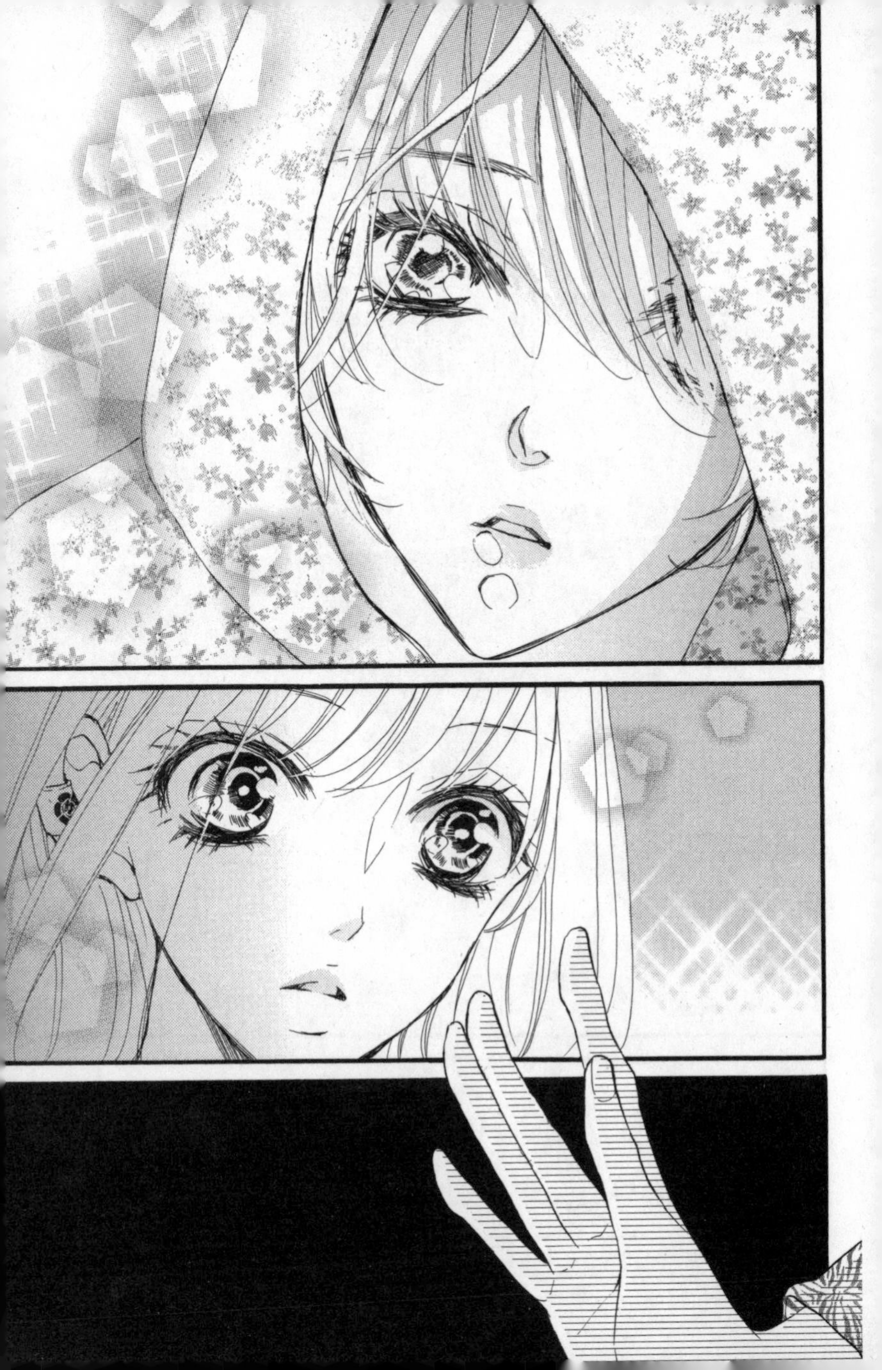

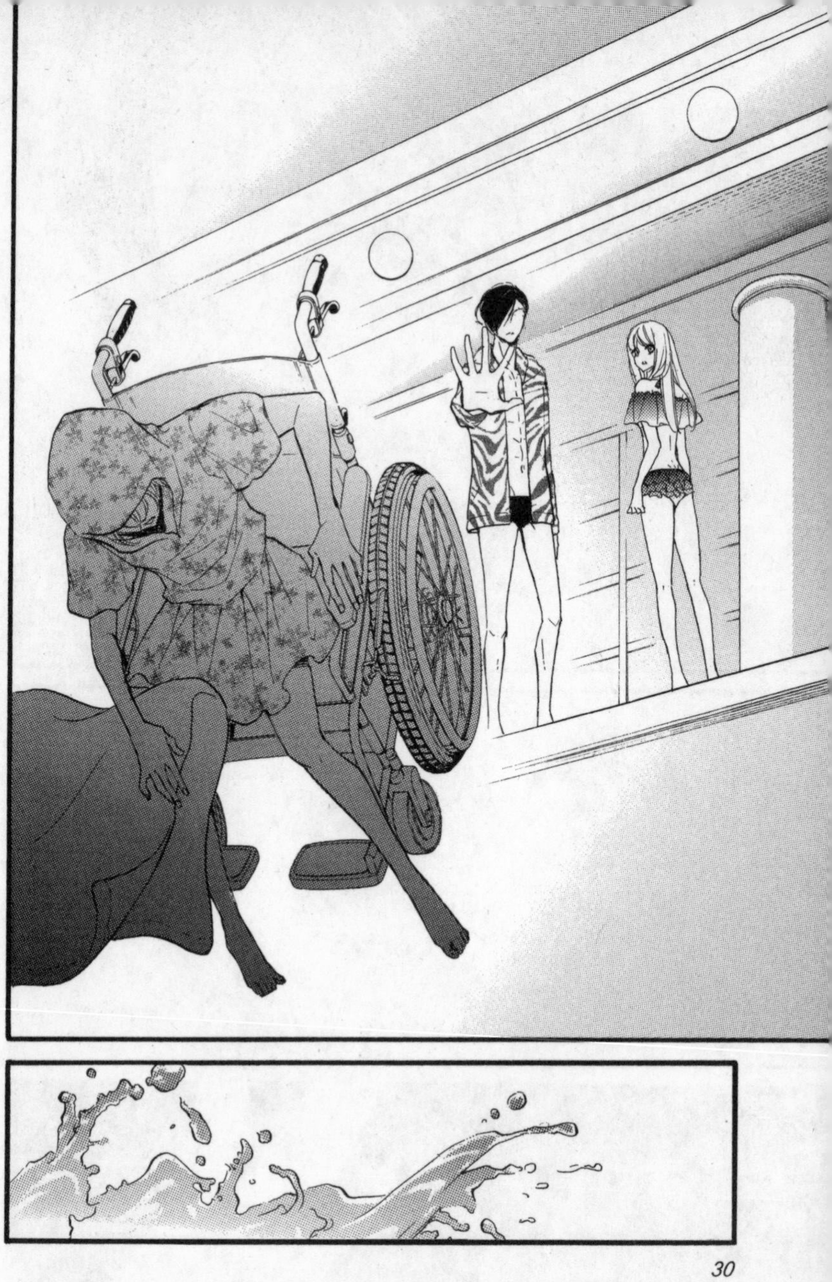

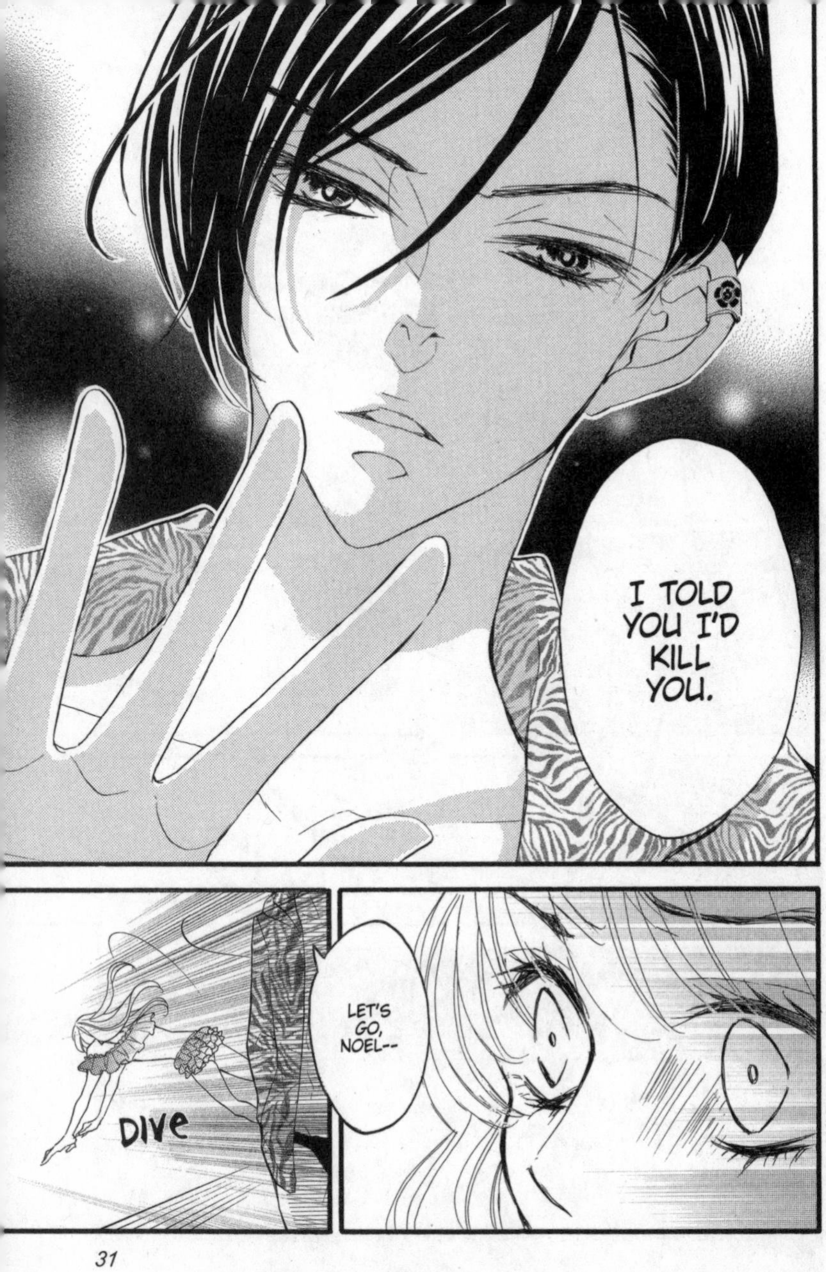
I TOLD YOU I'D KILL YOU.
LET'S GO, NOEL--
DIVE

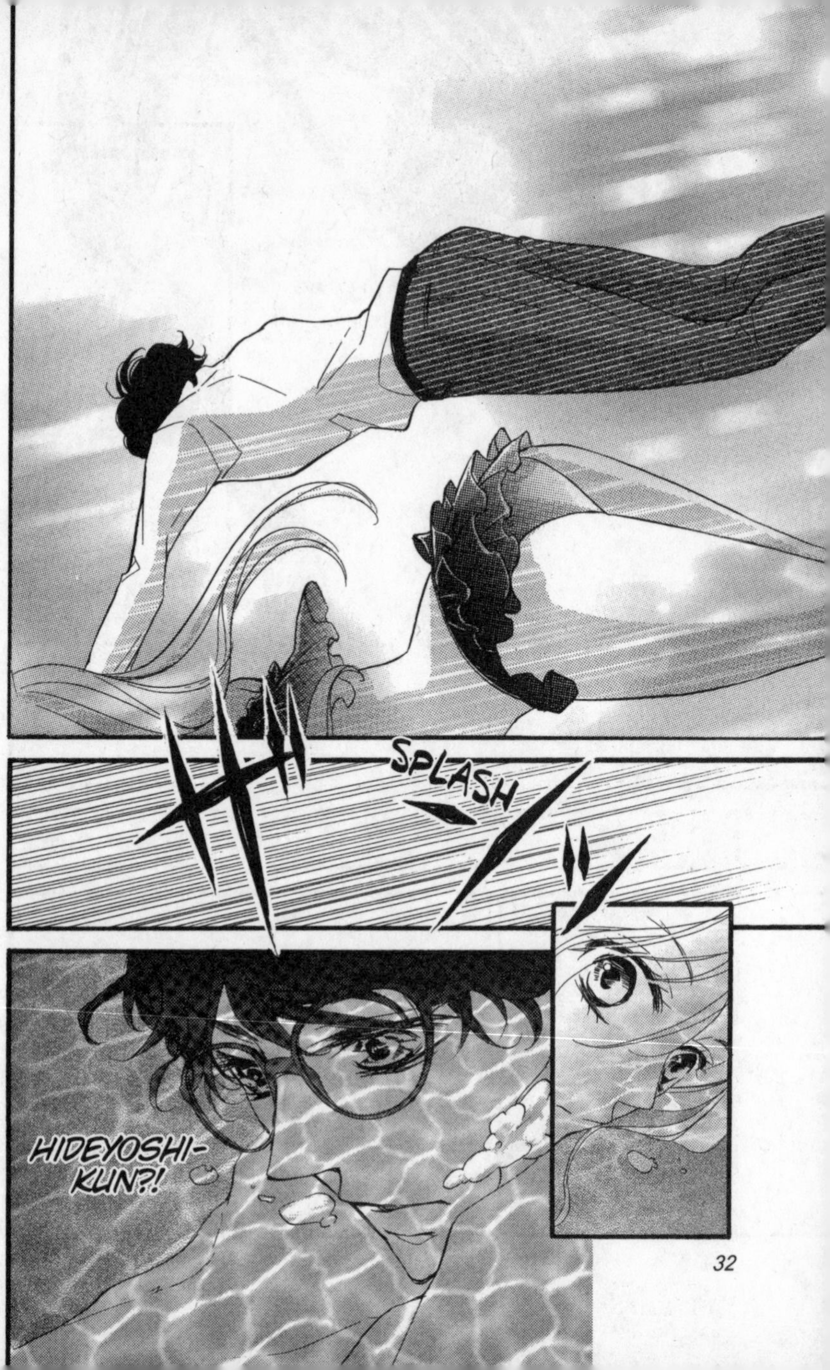
SPLASH
HIDEYOSHI-KUN?!

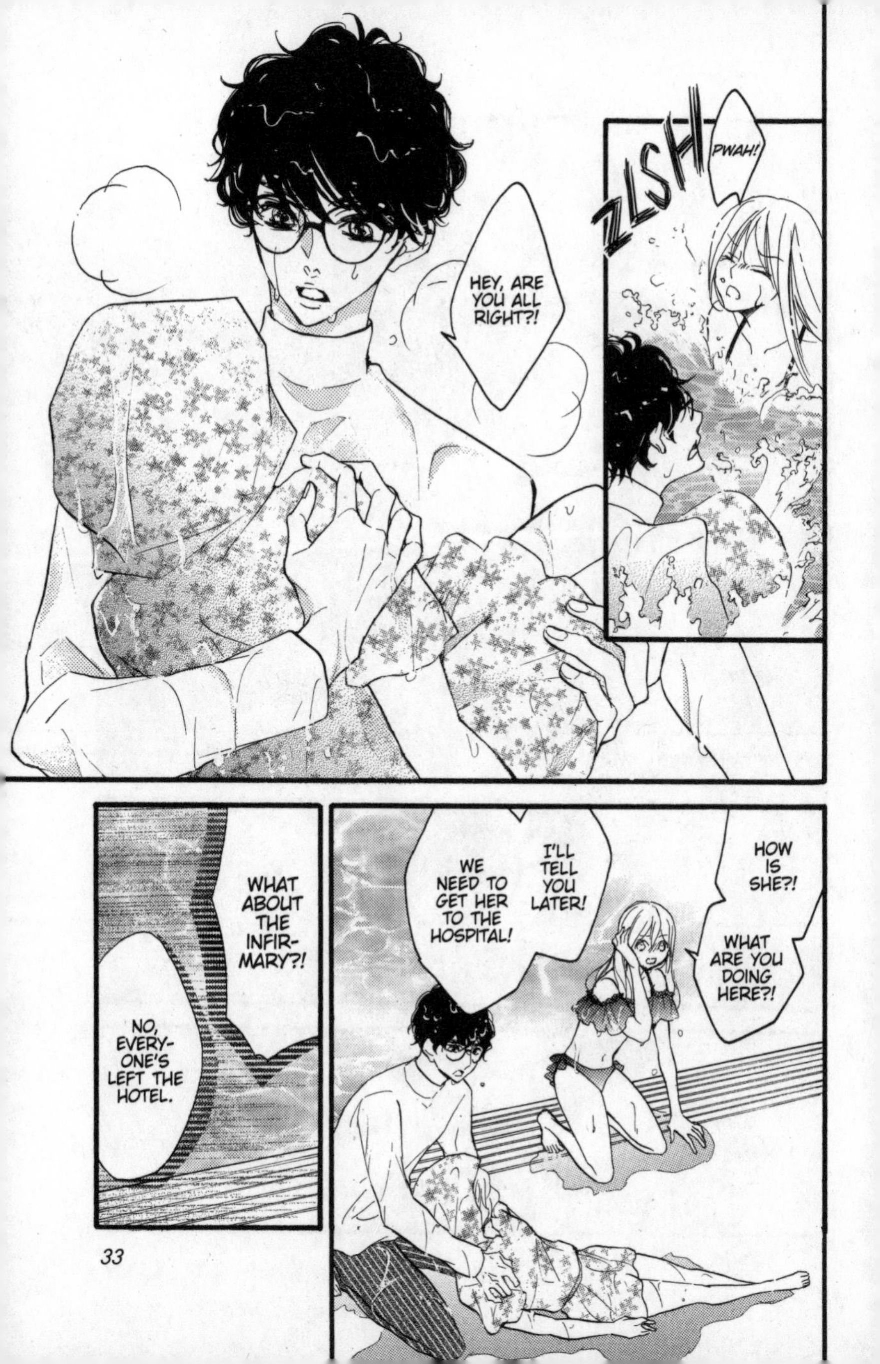
ZLSH
PWAH!
HEY, ARE YOU ALL RIGHT?!
HOW IS SHE?!
WHAT ARE YOU DOING HERE?!
I'LL TELL YOU LATER!
WE NEED TO GET HER TO THE HOSPITAL!
WHAT ABOUT THE INFIRMARY?!
NO, EVERYONE'S LEFT THE HOTEL.

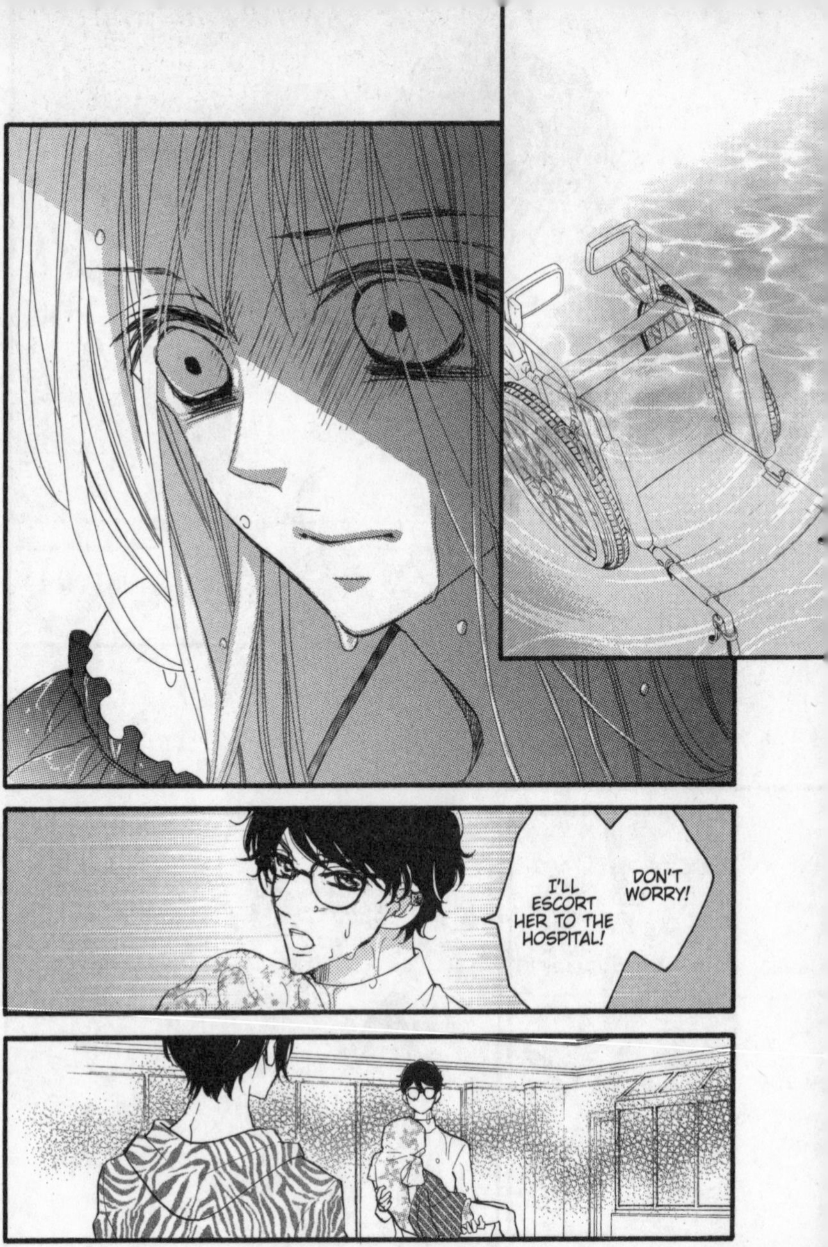
DON'T WORRY!
I'LL ESCORT HER TO THE HOSPITAL!

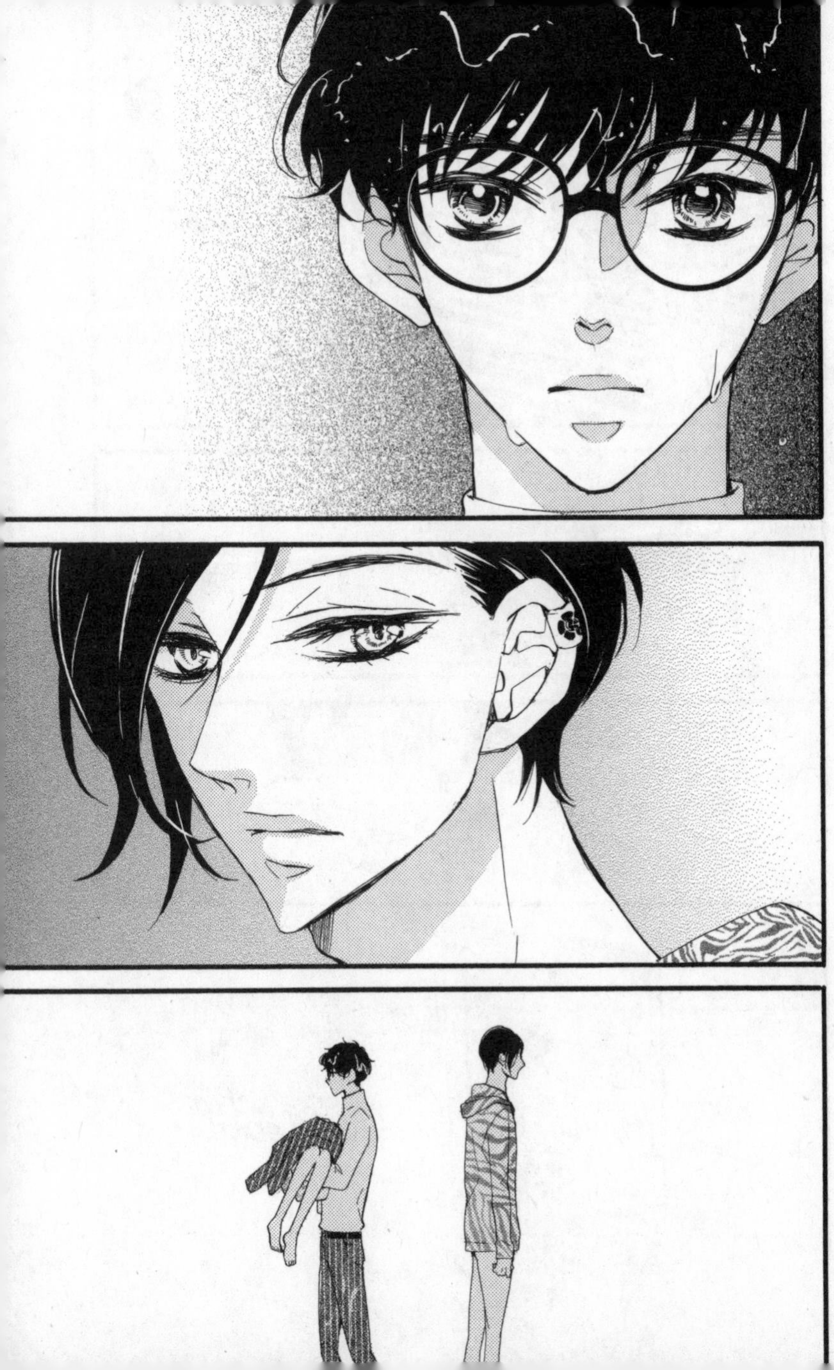

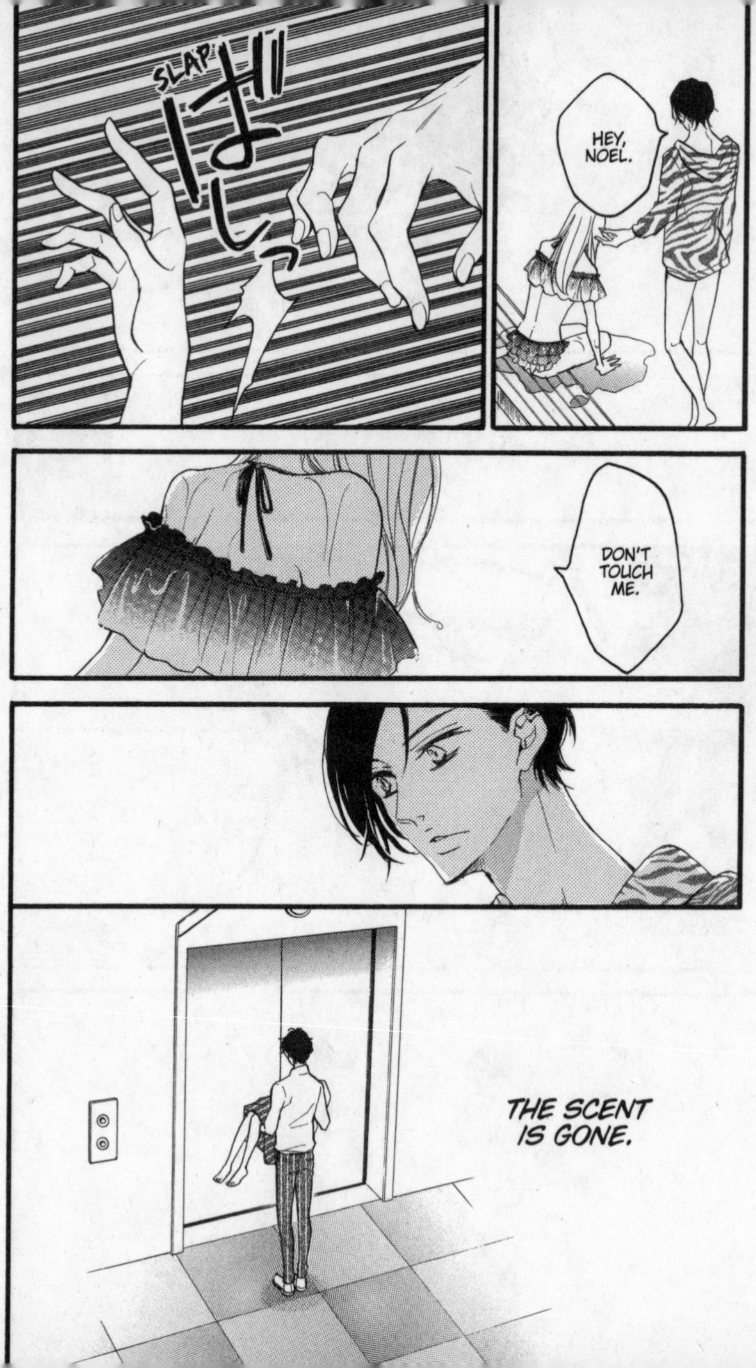
HEY, NOEL.
SLAP
ぱしっ
DON'T TOUCH ME.
THE SCENT IS GONE.

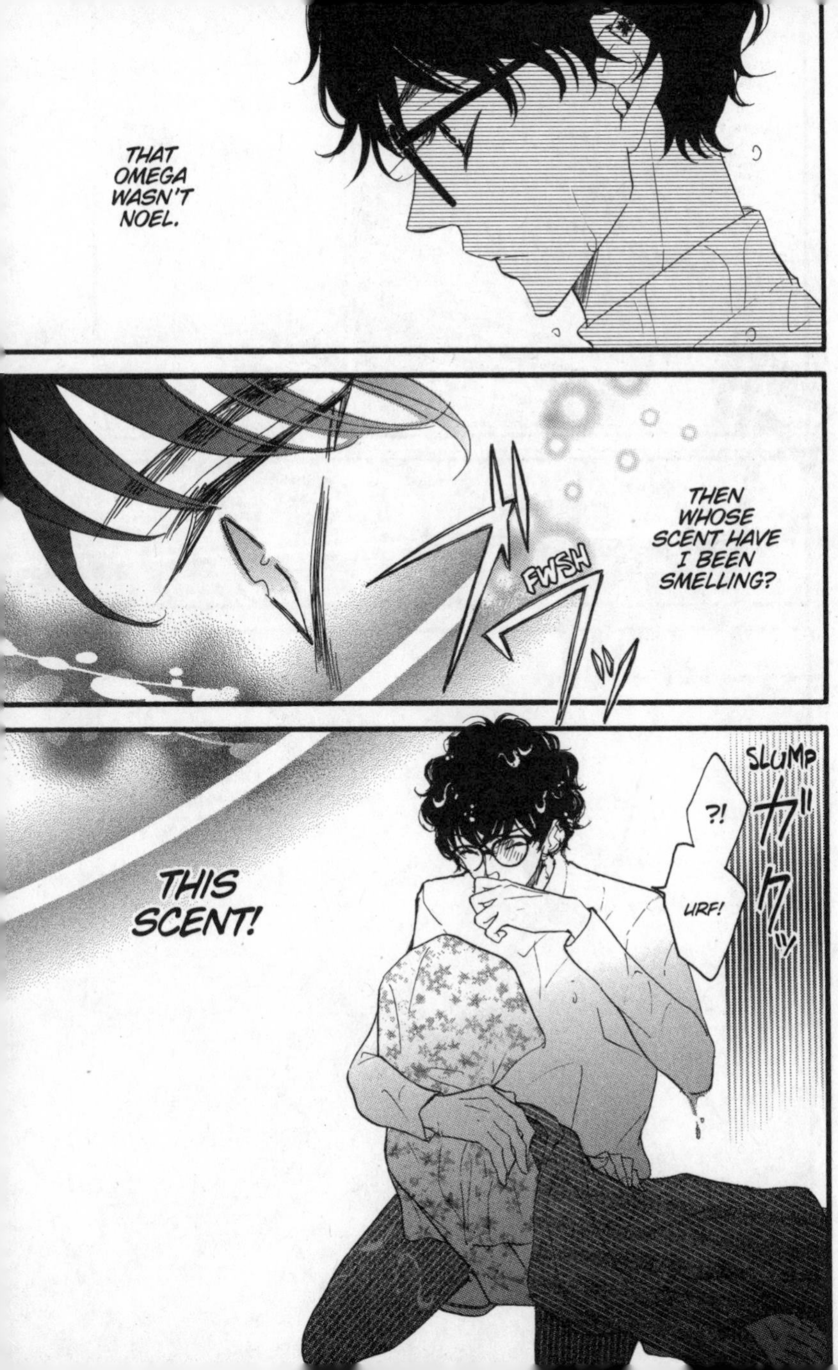
THAT OMEGA WASN'T NOEL.
THEN WHOSE SCENT HAVE I BEEN SMELLING?
FWSH
SLUMP
?!
URF!
THIS SCENT!

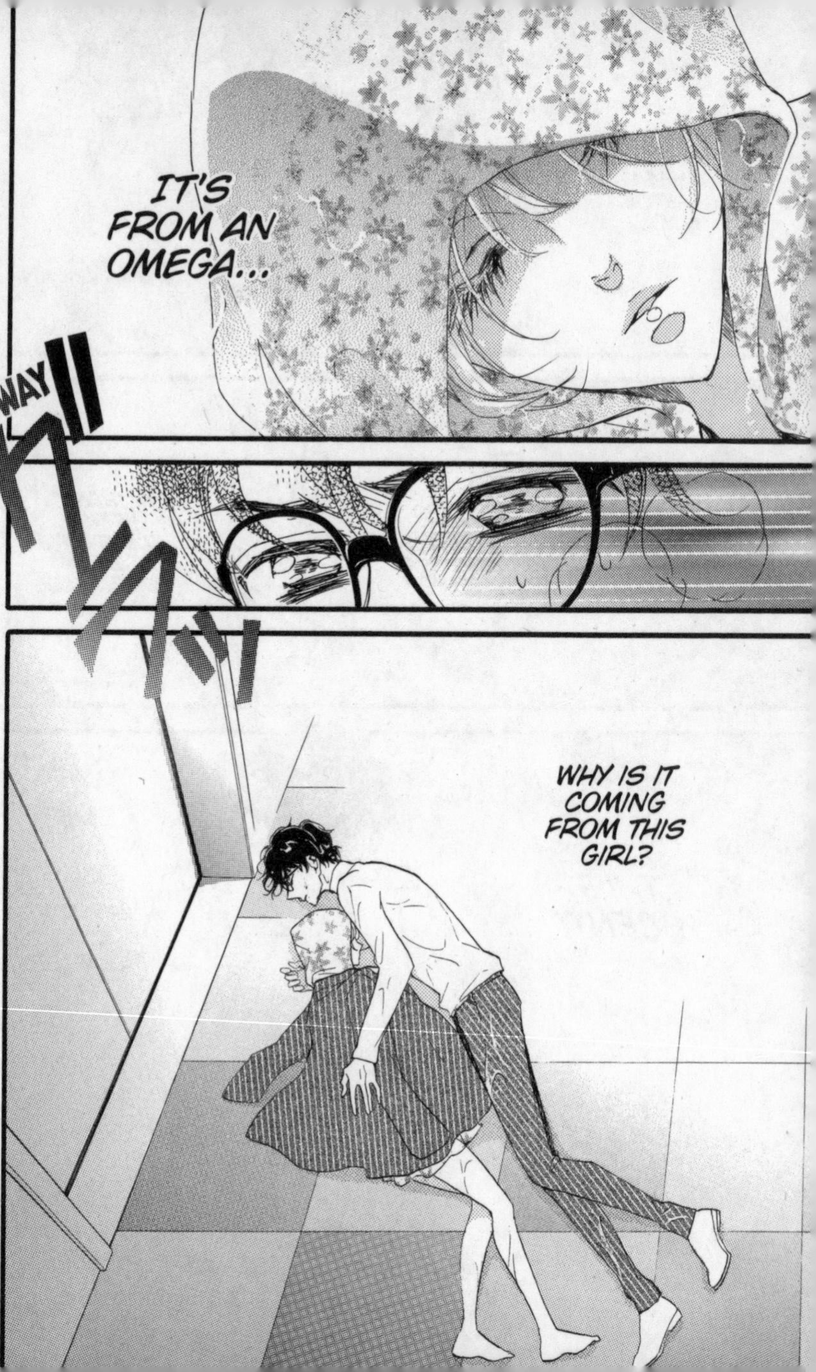
IT'S FROM AN OMEGA...
SWAY
WHY IS IT COMING FROM THIS GIRL?

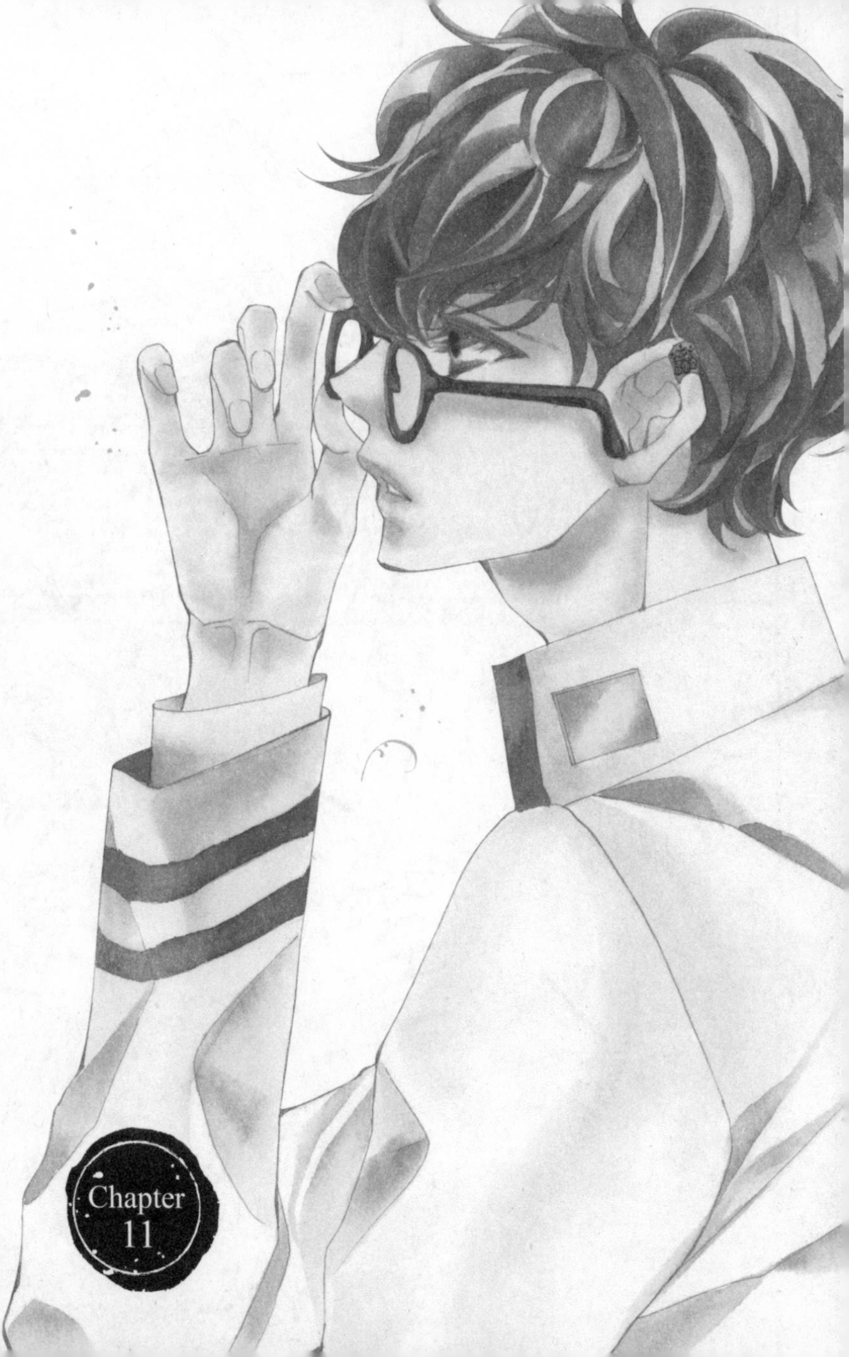
Chapter
11

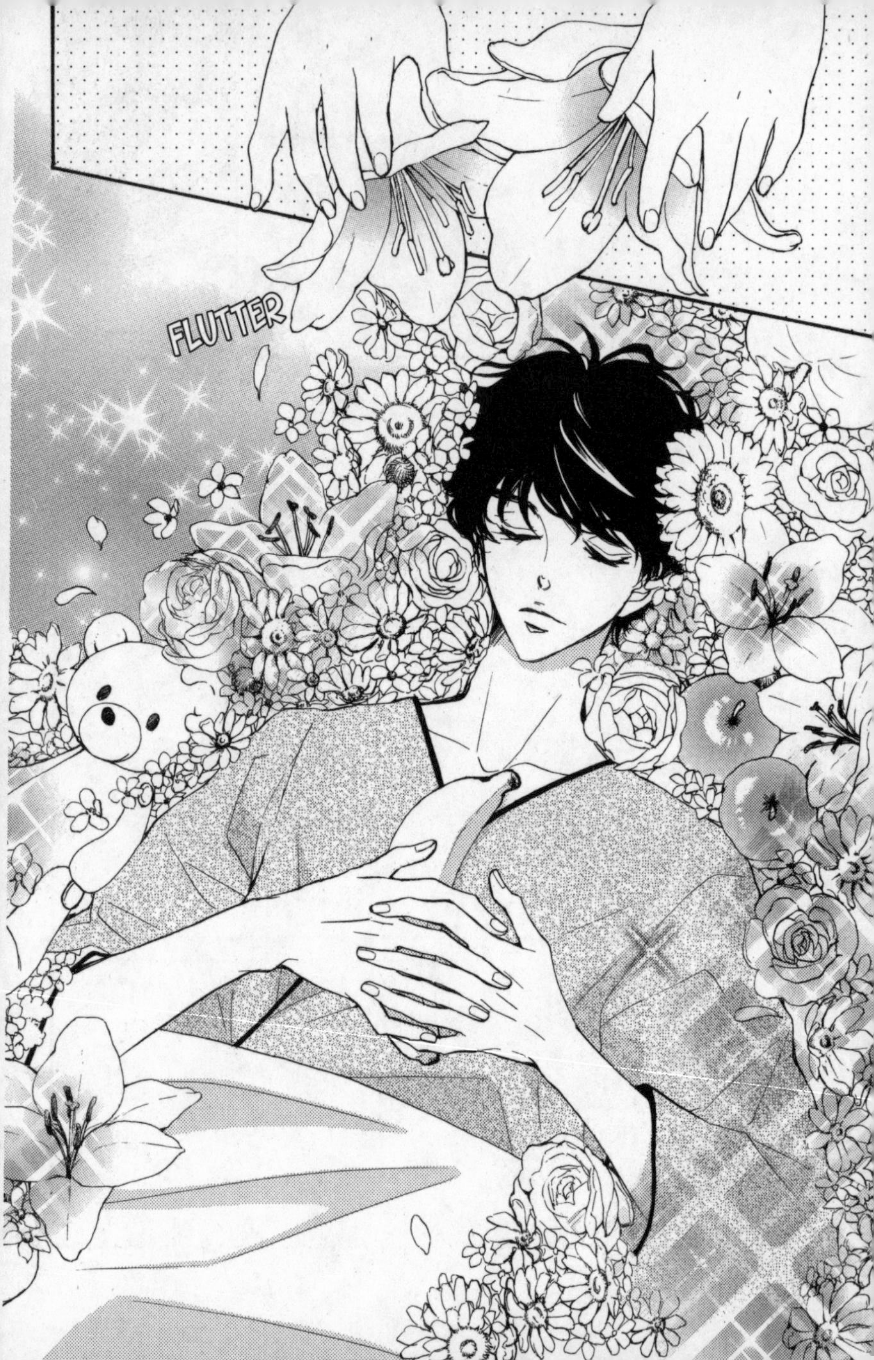
FLUTTER

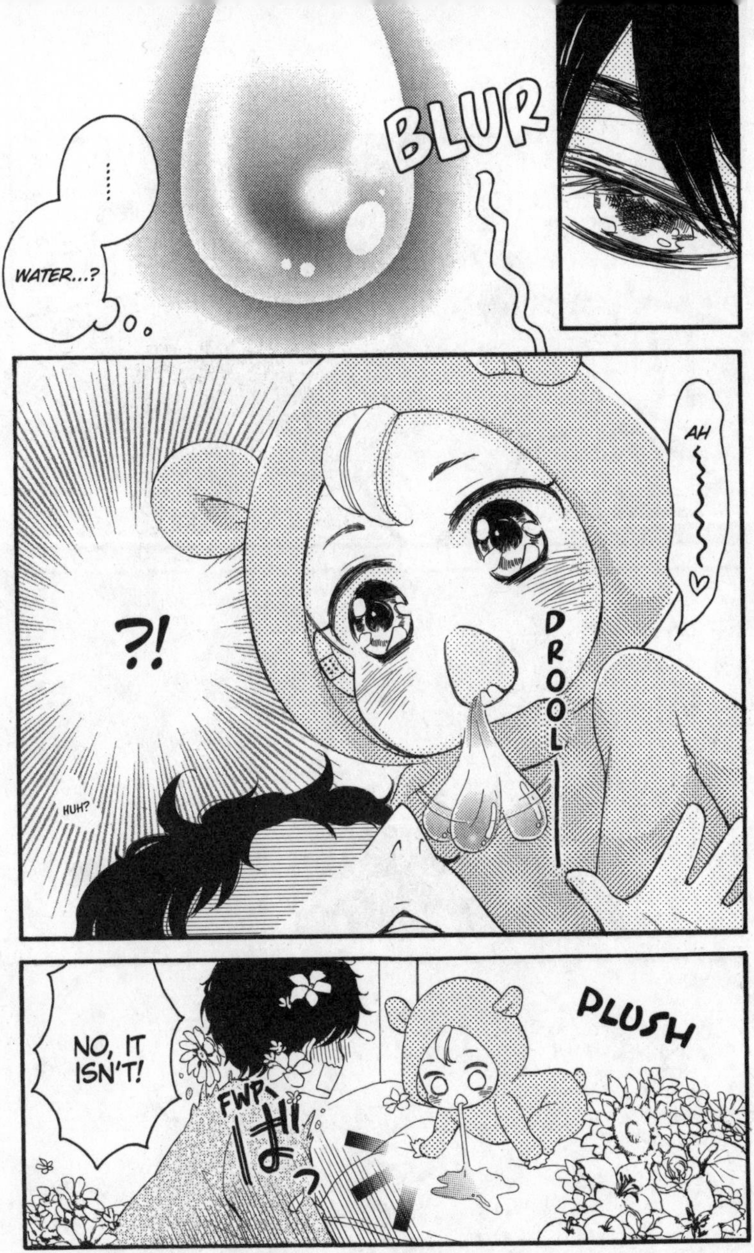
BLUR
......
WATER...?
AH~~~♥
DROOL
?!
HUH?
PLUSH
FWP
ぱっ
NO, IT ISN'T!

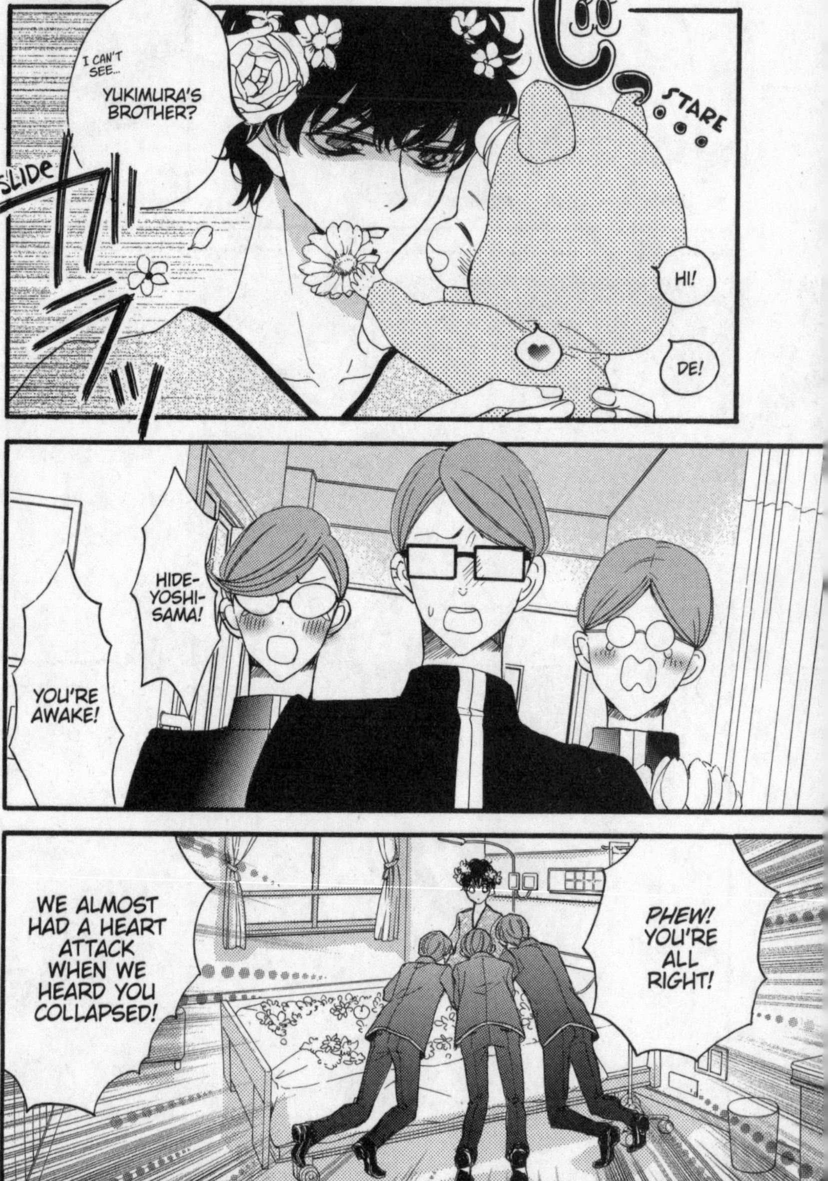
STARE
I CAN'T SEE... YUKIMURA'S BROTHER?
HI!
DE!
SLIDE
HIDE-YOSHI-SAMA!
YOU'RE AWAKE!
PHEW! YOU'RE ALL RIGHT!
WE ALMOST HAD A HEART ATTACK WHEN WE HEARD YOU COLLAPSED!

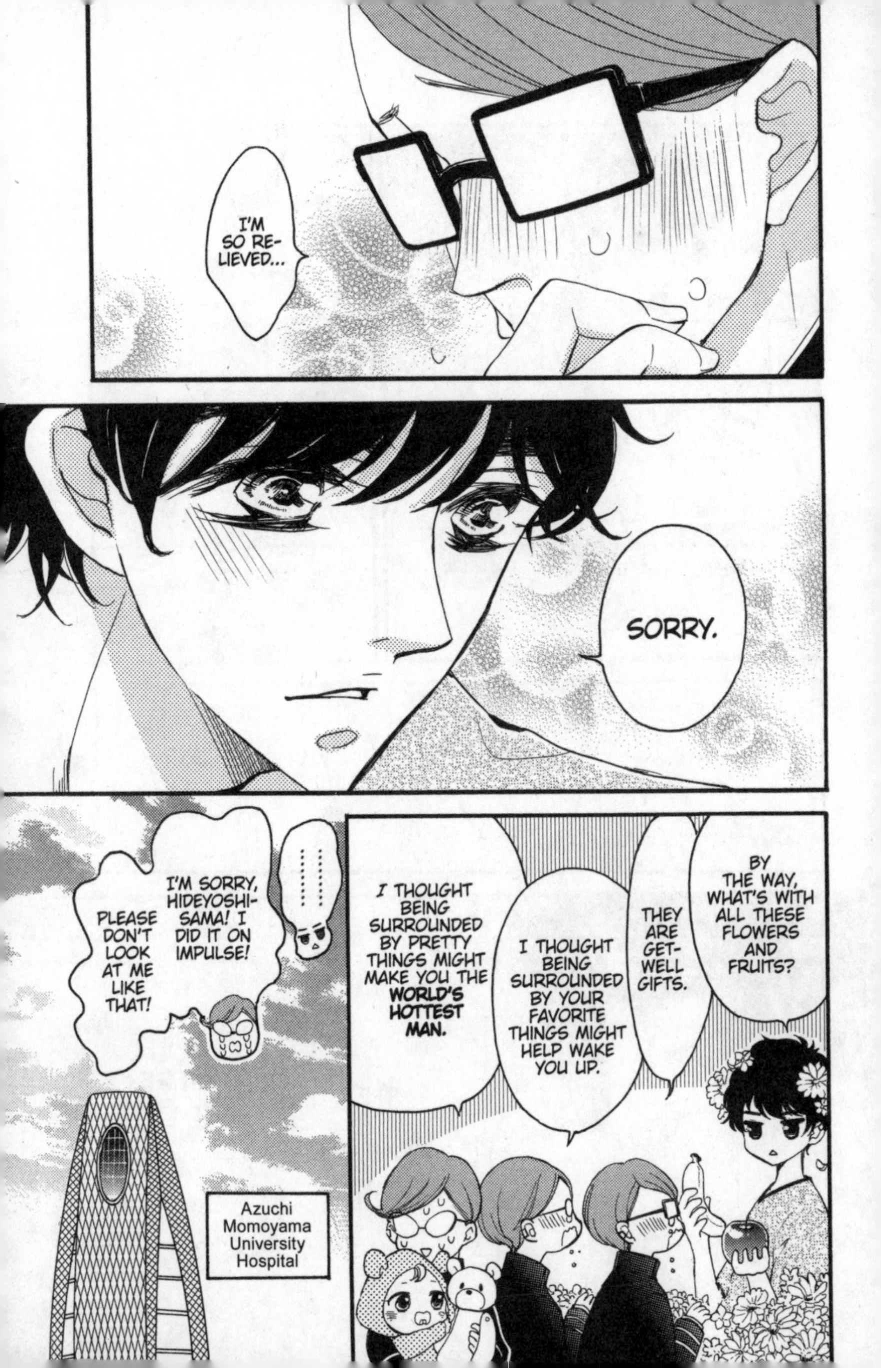
I'M SO RE-LIEVED...
SORRY.
BY THE WAY, WHAT'S WITH ALL THESE FLOWERS AND FRUITS?
THEY ARE GET-WELL GIFTS.
I THOUGHT BEING SURROUNDED BY YOUR FAVORITE THINGS MIGHT HELP WAKE YOU UP.
I THOUGHT BEING SURROUNDED BY PRETTY THINGS MIGHT MAKE YOU THE WORLD'S HOTTEST MAN.
......
I'M SORRY, HIDEYOSHI-SAMA! I DID IT ON IMPULSE!
PLEASE DON'T LOOK AT ME LIKE THAT!
Azuchi Momoyama University Hospital

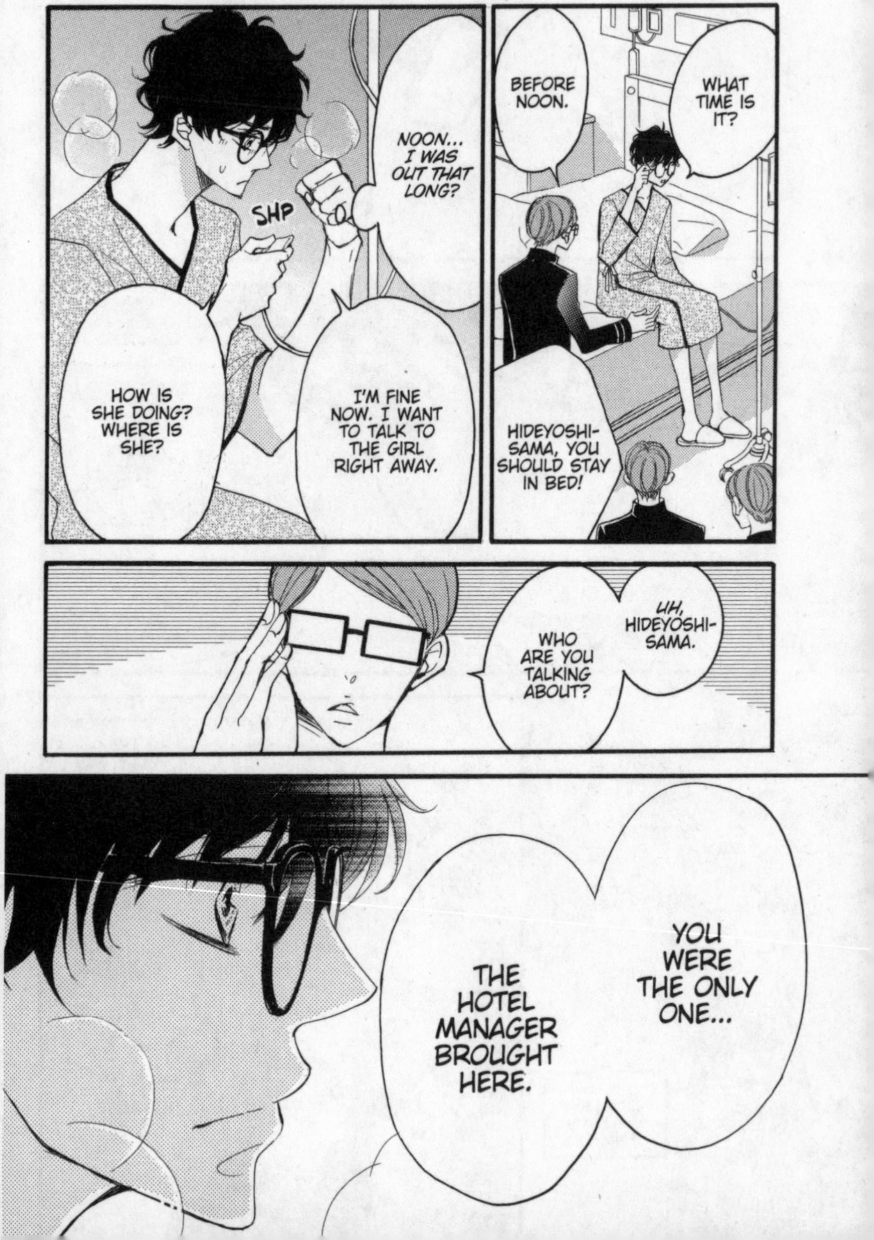
WHAT TIME IS IT?
BEFORE NOON.
HIDEYOSHI-SAMA, YOU SHOULD STAY IN BED!
NOON... I WAS OUT THAT LONG?
SHP
I'M FINE NOW. I WANT TO TALK TO THE GIRL RIGHT AWAY.
HOW IS SHE DOING? WHERE IS SHE?
UH, HIDEYOSHI-SAMA.
WHO ARE YOU TALKING ABOUT?
YOU WERE THE ONLY ONE...
THE HOTEL MANAGER BROUGHT HERE.

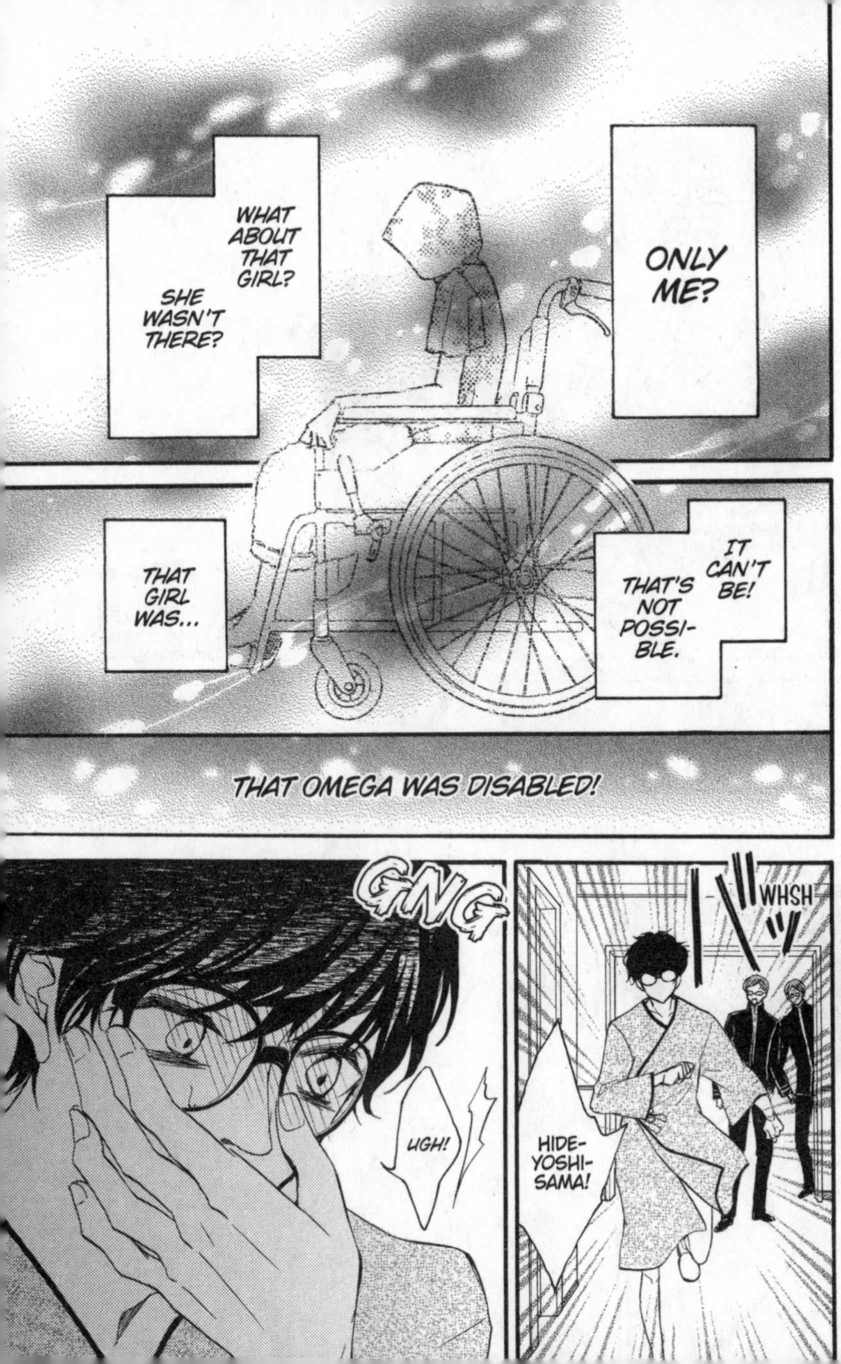
ONLY ME?
WHAT ABOUT THAT GIRL?
SHE WASN'T THERE?
IT CAN'T BE!
THAT'S NOT POSSI-BLE.
THAT GIRL WAS...
THAT OMEGA WAS DISABLED!
WHSH
HIDE-YOSHI-SAMA!
GNG
UGH!

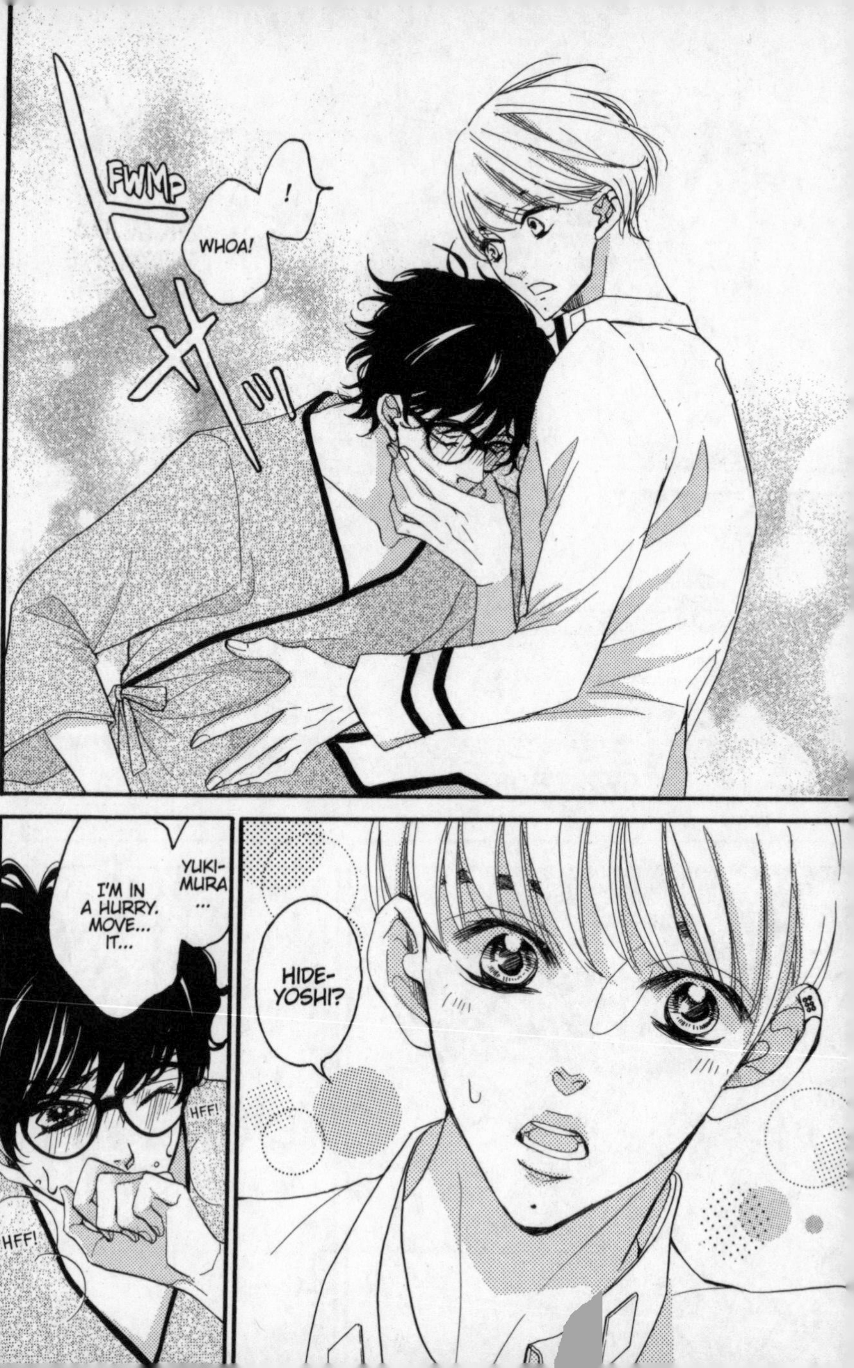
!
WHOA!
FWMP
HIDE-YOSHI?
YUKI-MURA ...
I'M IN A HURRY. MOVE... IT...
HFF!
HFF!

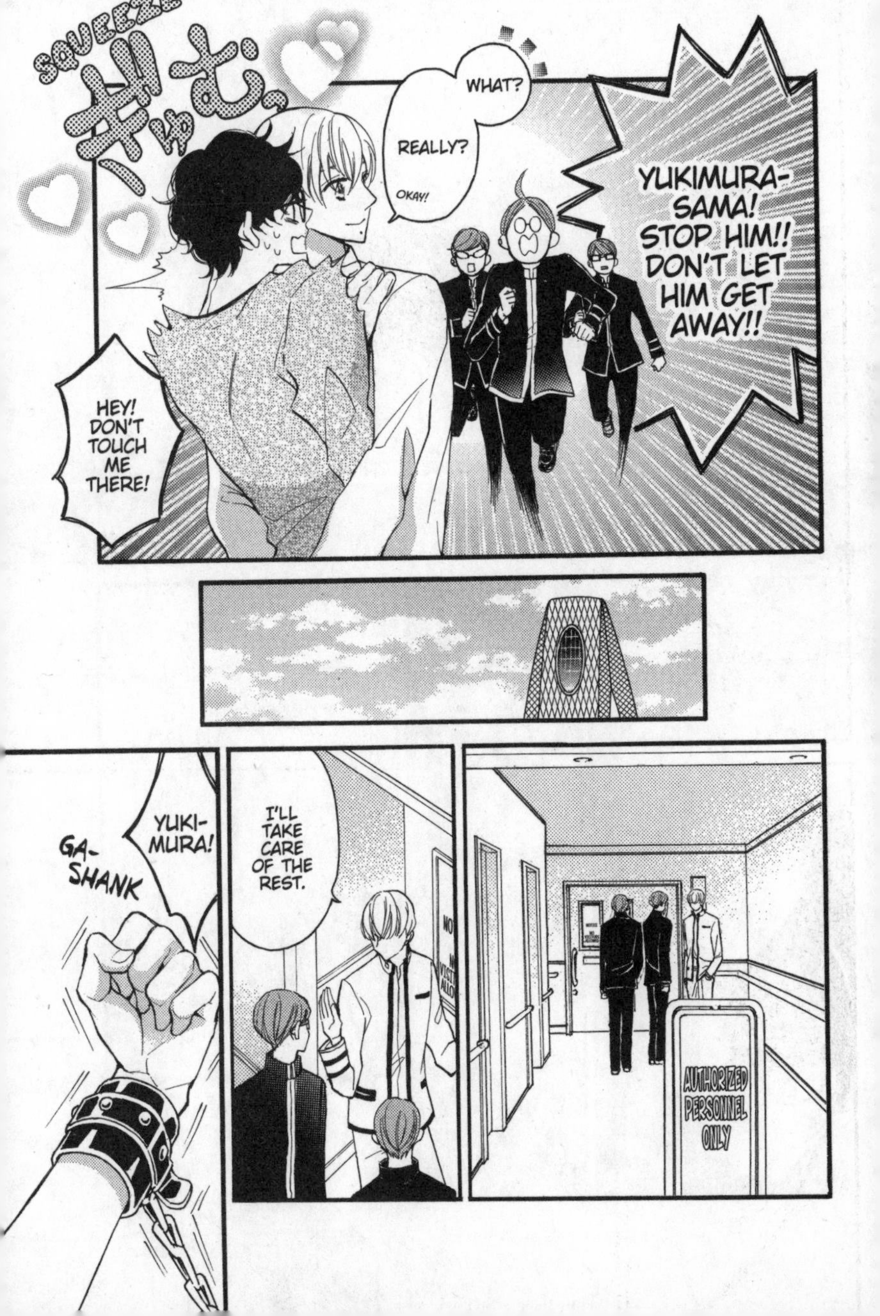
YUKIMURA-SAMA! STOP HIM!! DON'T LET HIM GET AWAY!!
WHAT?
REALLY?
OKAY!
HEY! DON'T TOUCH ME THERE!
SQUEEZE
AUTHORIZED PERSONNEL ONLY
I'LL TAKE CARE OF THE REST.
YUKI-MURA!
GA-SHANK

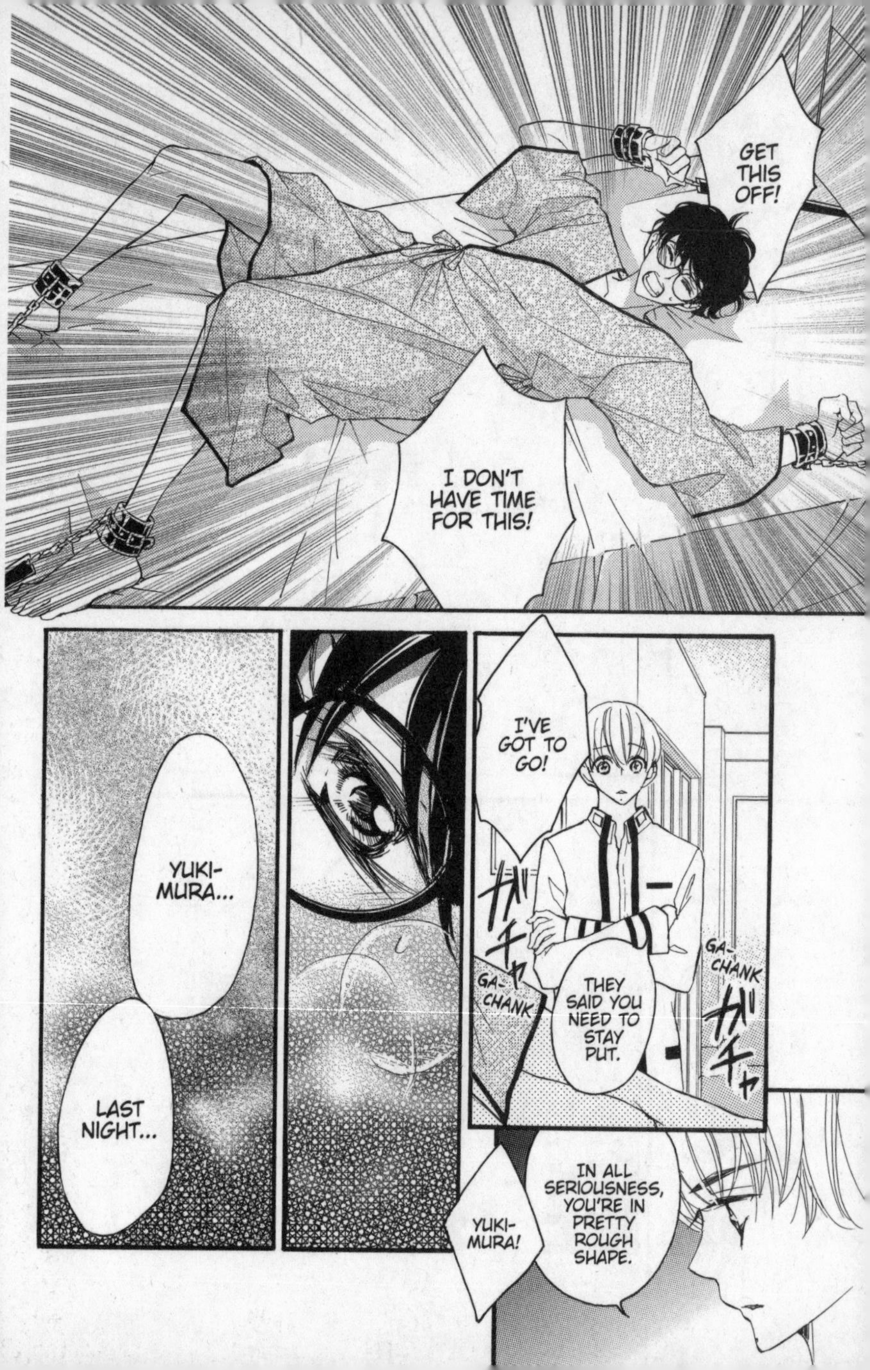
GET THIS OFF!
I DON'T HAVE TIME FOR THIS!
I'VE GOT TO GO!
GA-CHANK
THEY SAID YOU NEED TO STAY PUT.
GA-CHANK
IN ALL SERIOUSNESS, YOU'RE IN PRETTY ROUGH SHAPE.
YUKI-MURA!
YUKI-MURA...
LAST NIGHT...

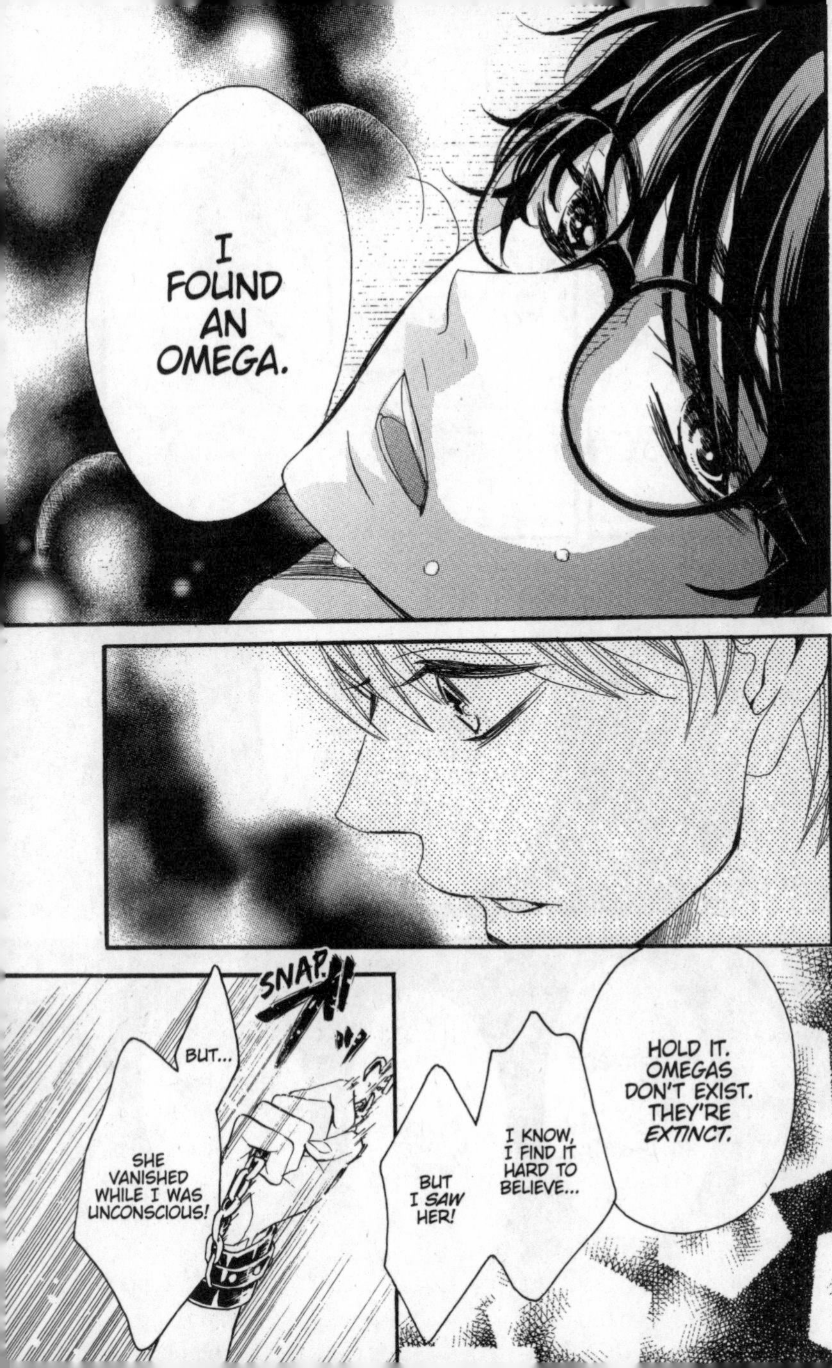
I FOUND AN OMEGA.
HOLD IT. OMEGAS DON'T EXIST. THEY'RE *EXTINCT*.
I KNOW, I FIND IT HARD TO BELIEVE...
BUT I *SAW* HER!
SNAP
BUT...
SHE VANISHED WHILE I WAS UNCONSCIOUS!

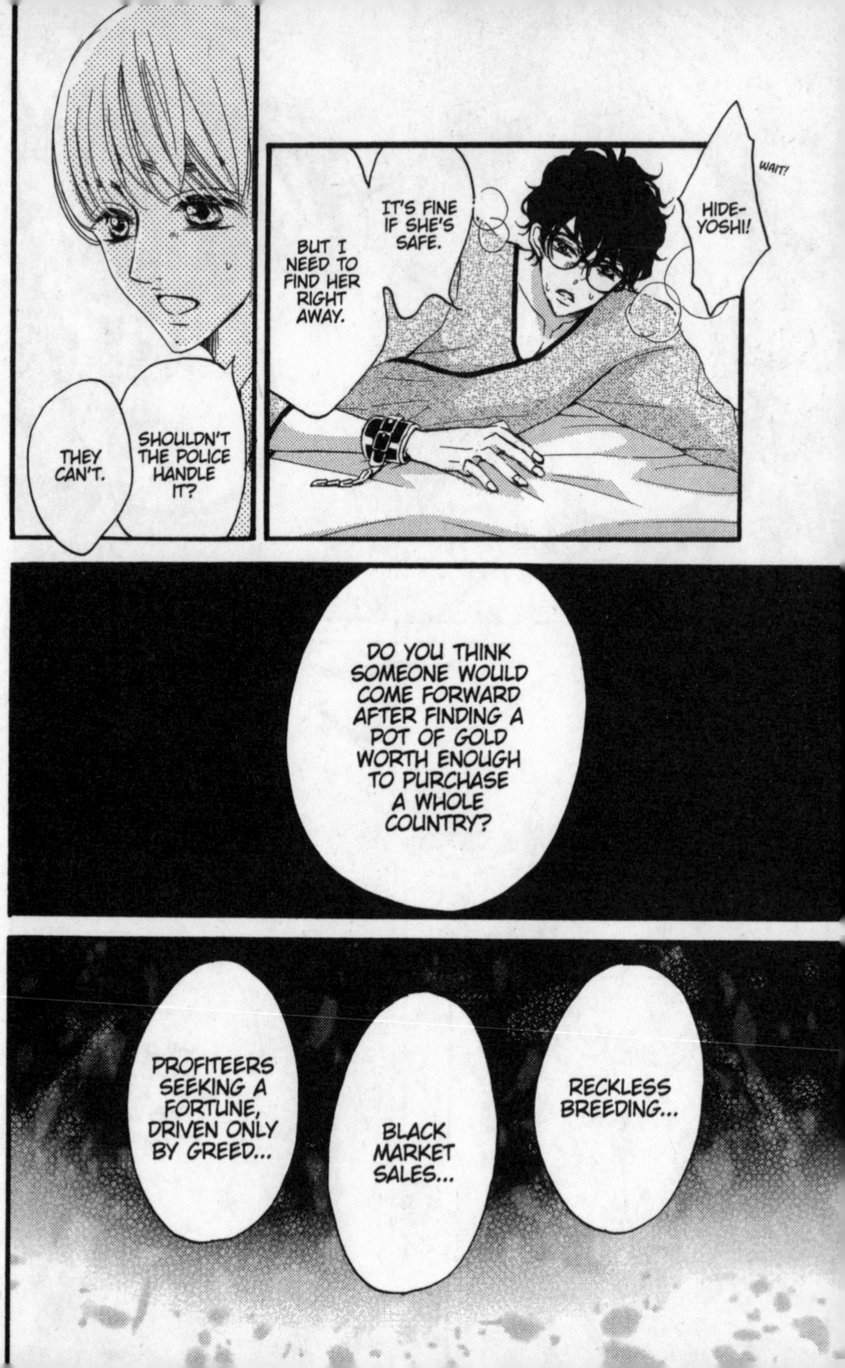
WAIT!
HIDE-YOSHI!
IT'S FINE IF SHE'S SAFE.
BUT I NEED TO FIND HER RIGHT AWAY.
SHOULDN'T THE POLICE HANDLE IT?
THEY CAN'T.
DO YOU THINK SOMEONE WOULD COME FORWARD AFTER FINDING A POT OF GOLD WORTH ENOUGH TO PURCHASE A WHOLE COUNTRY?
RECKLESS BREEDING...
BLACK MARKET SALES...
PROFITEERS SEEKING A FORTUNE, DRIVEN ONLY BY GREED...

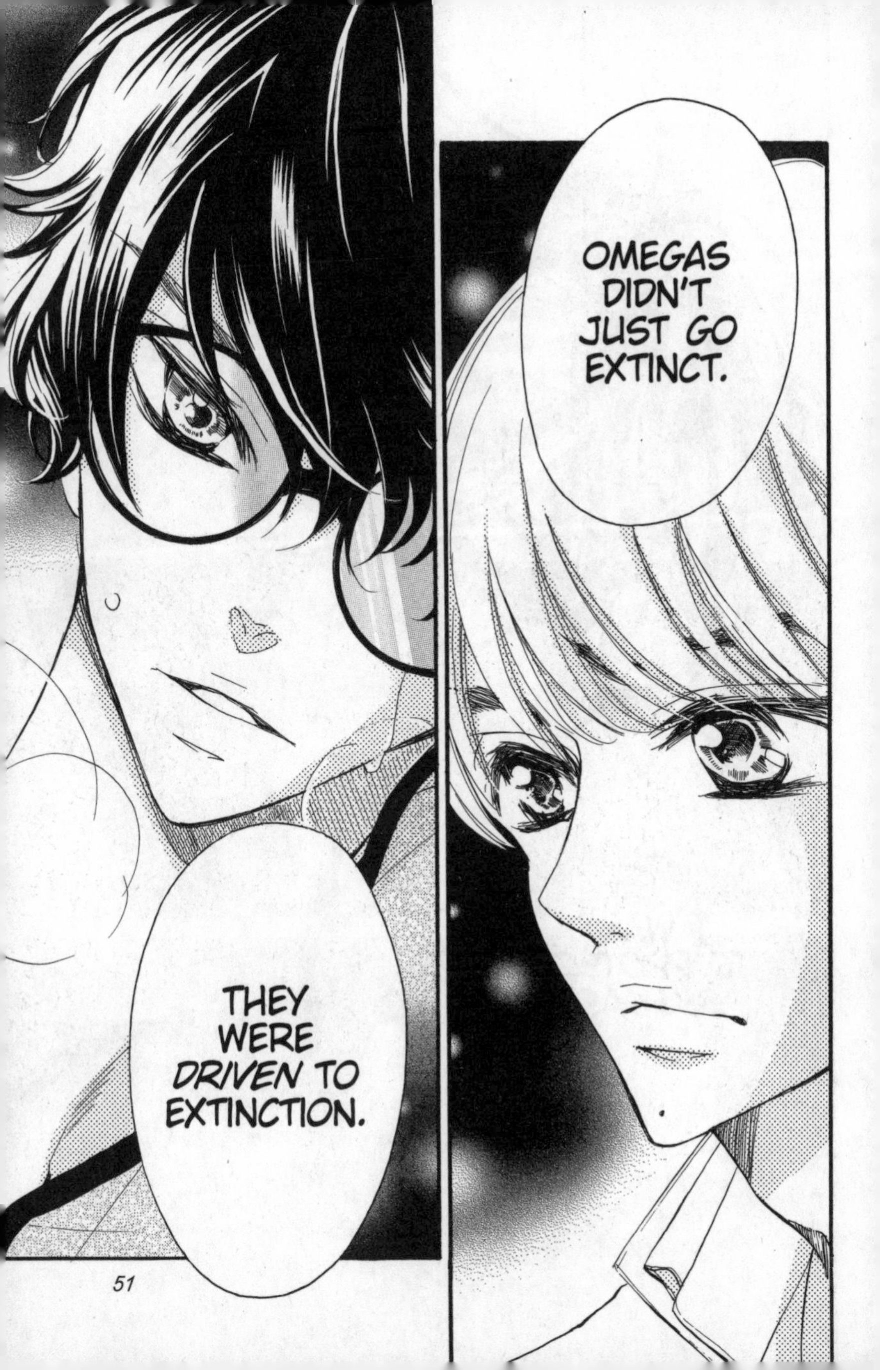
OMEGAS DIDN'T JUST GO EXTINCT.
THEY WERE *DRIVEN* TO EXTINCTION.

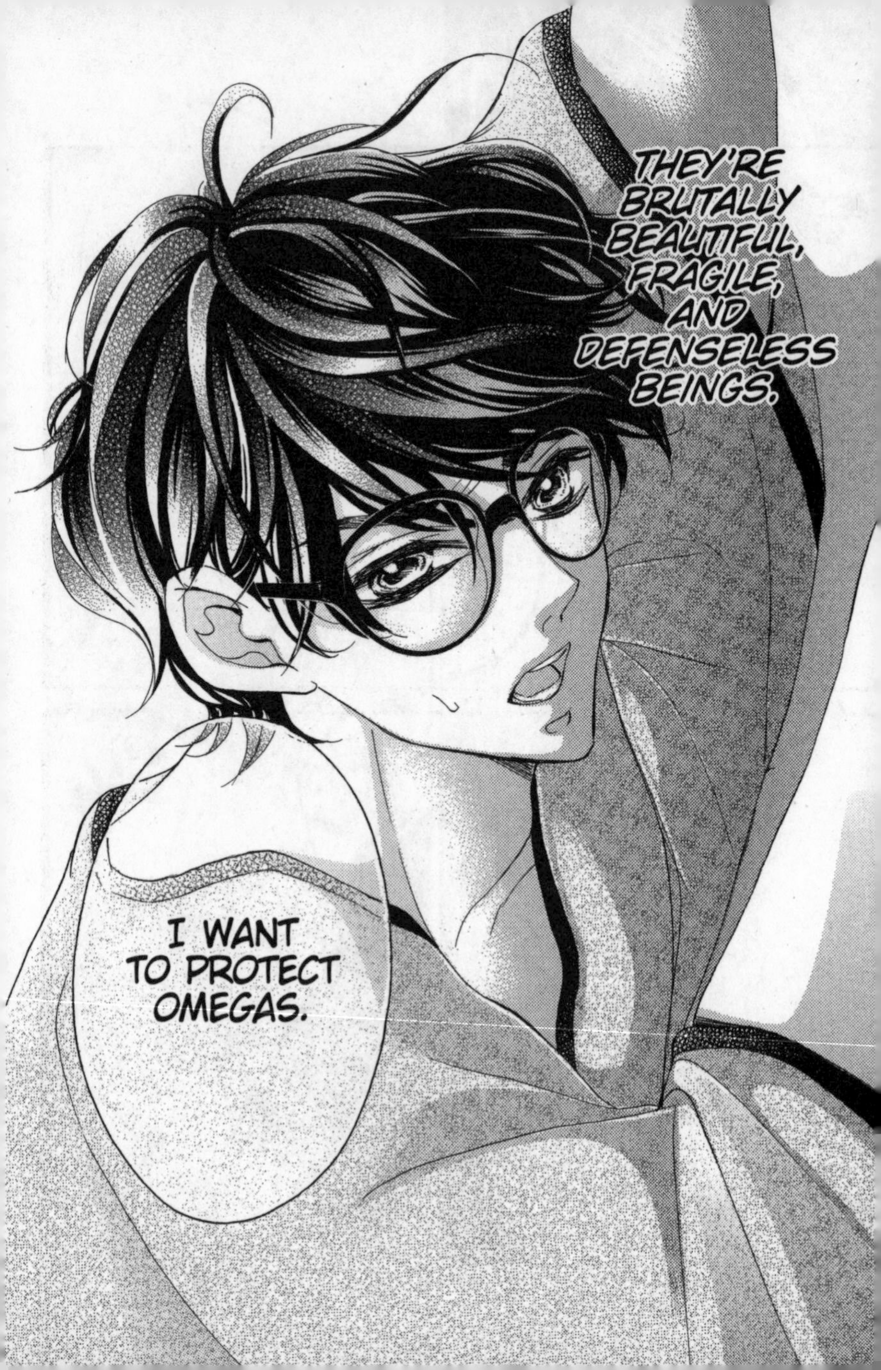
THEY'RE BRUTALLY BEAUTIFUL, FRAGILE, AND DEFENSELESS BEINGS.
I WANT TO PROTECT OMEGAS.

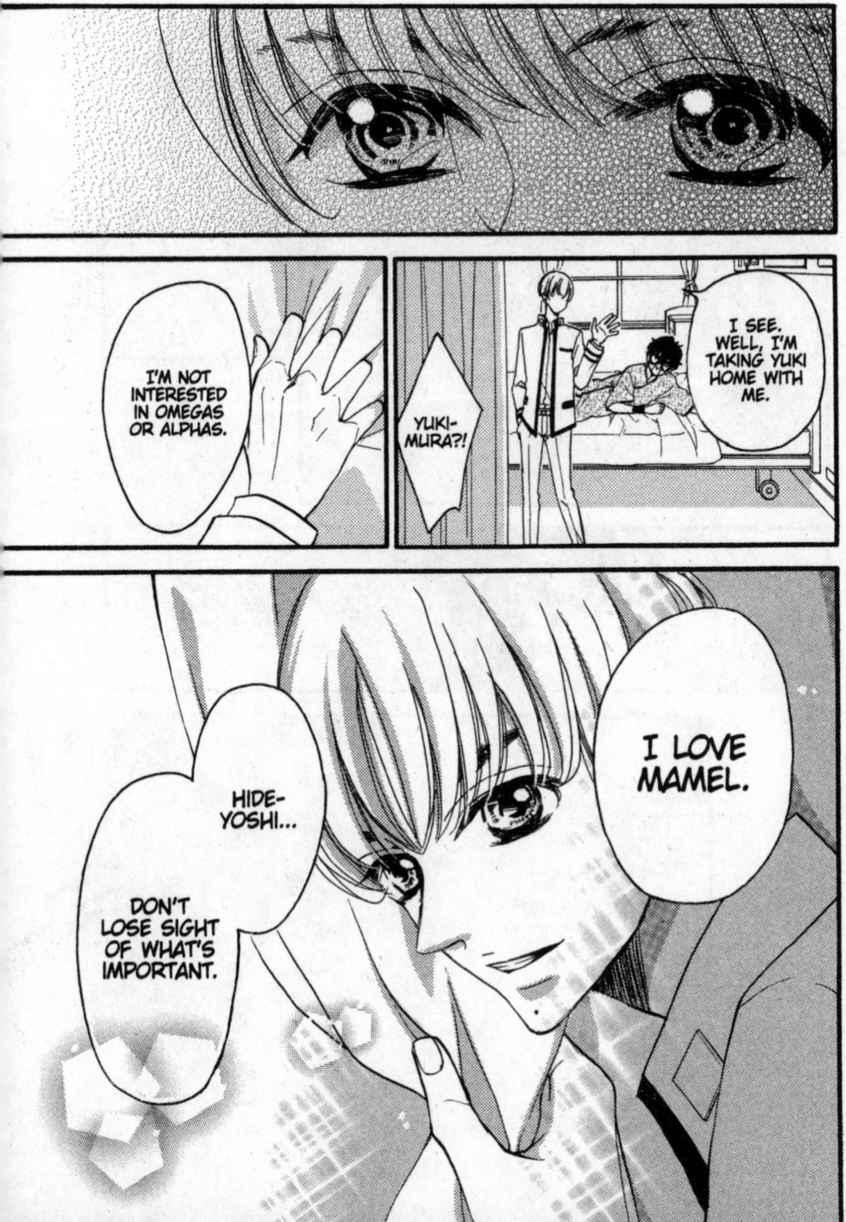
I SEE. WELL, I'M TAKING YUKI HOME WITH ME.
YUKI-MURA?!
I'M NOT INTERESTED IN OMEGAS OR ALPHAS.
I LOVE MAMEL.
HIDE-YOSHI...
DON'T LOSE SIGHT OF WHAT'S IMPORTANT.

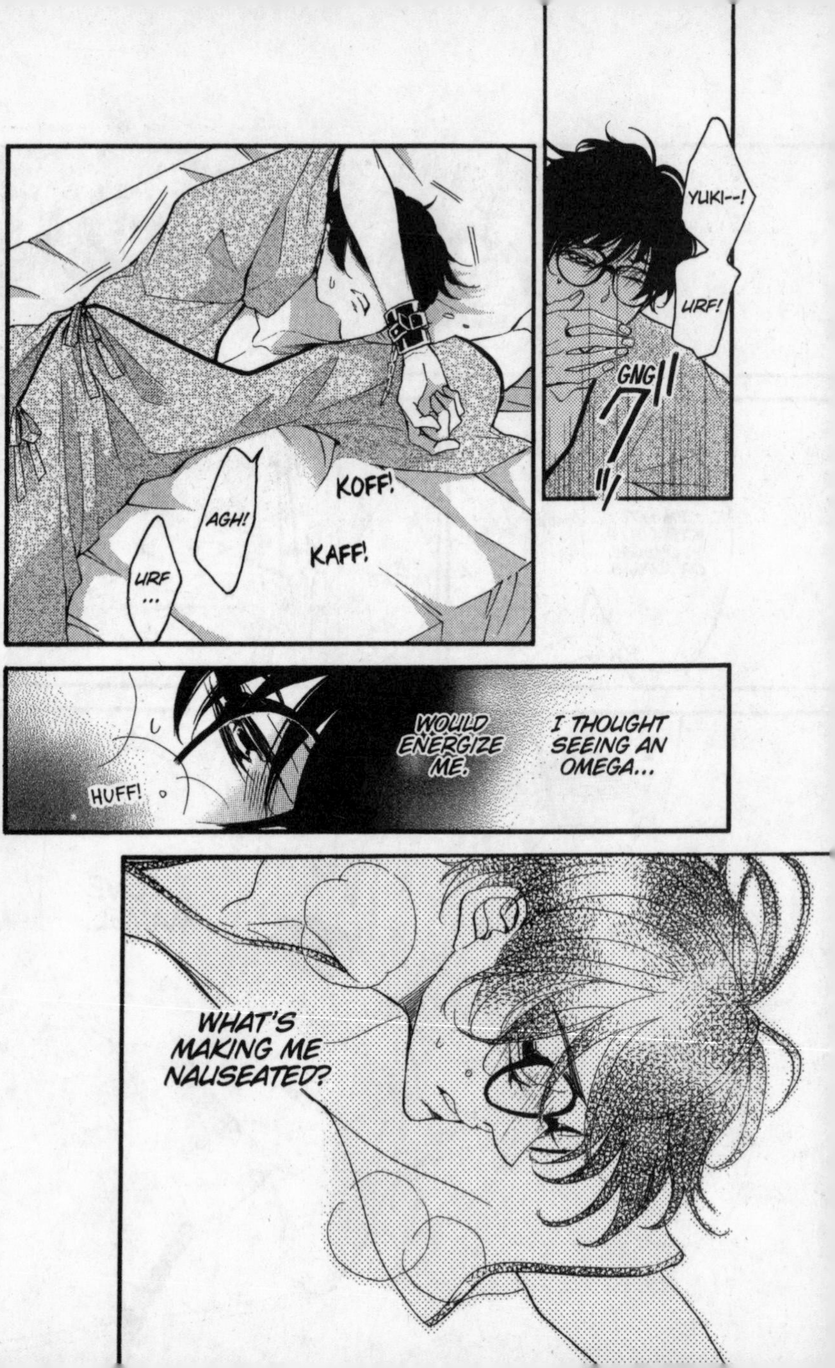
YUKI--!
URF!
GNG
KOFF!
AGH!
KAFF!
URF ...
I THOUGHT SEEING AN OMEGA...
WOULD ENERGIZE ME.
HUFF!
WHAT'S MAKING ME NAUSEATED?

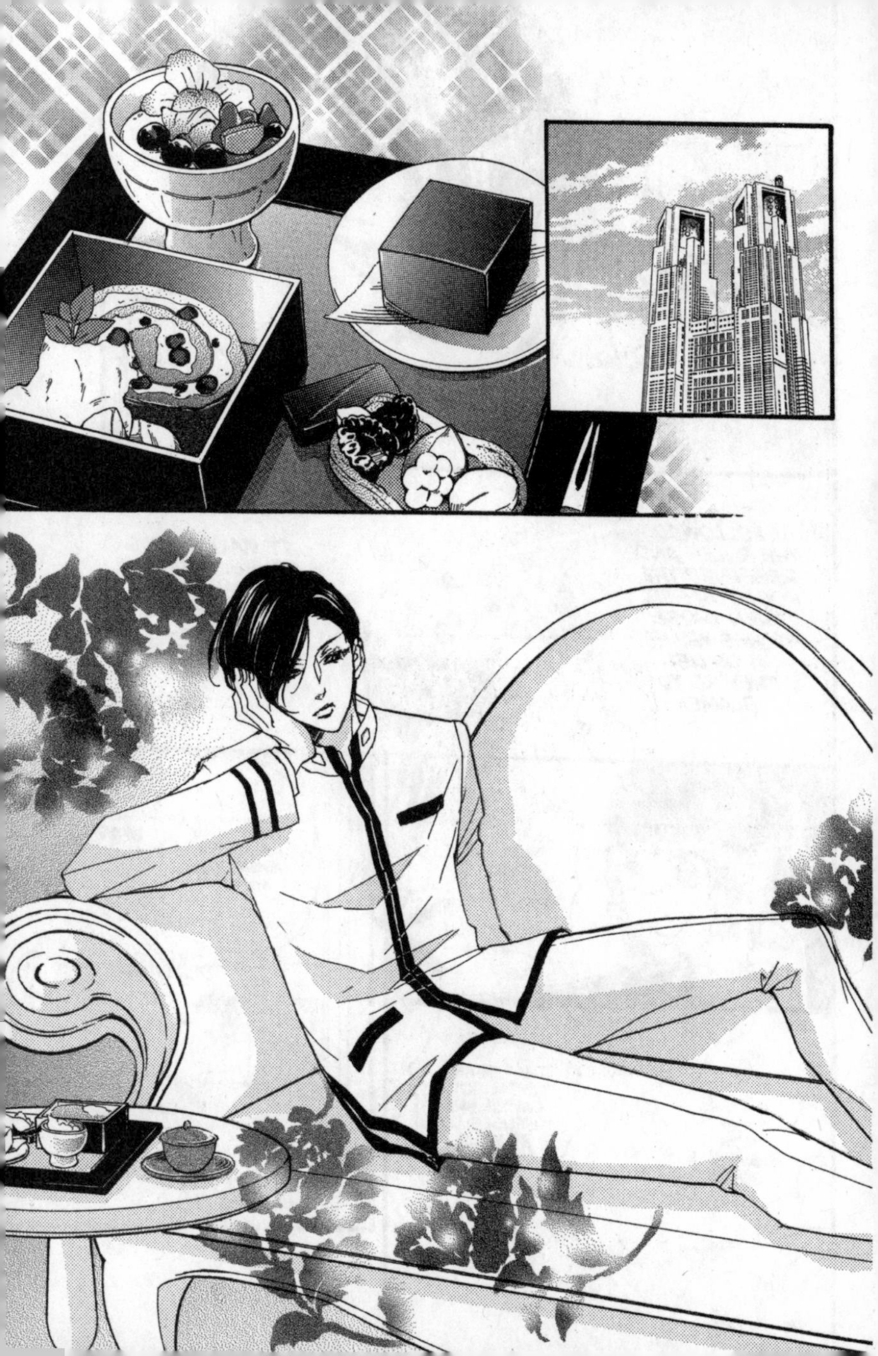

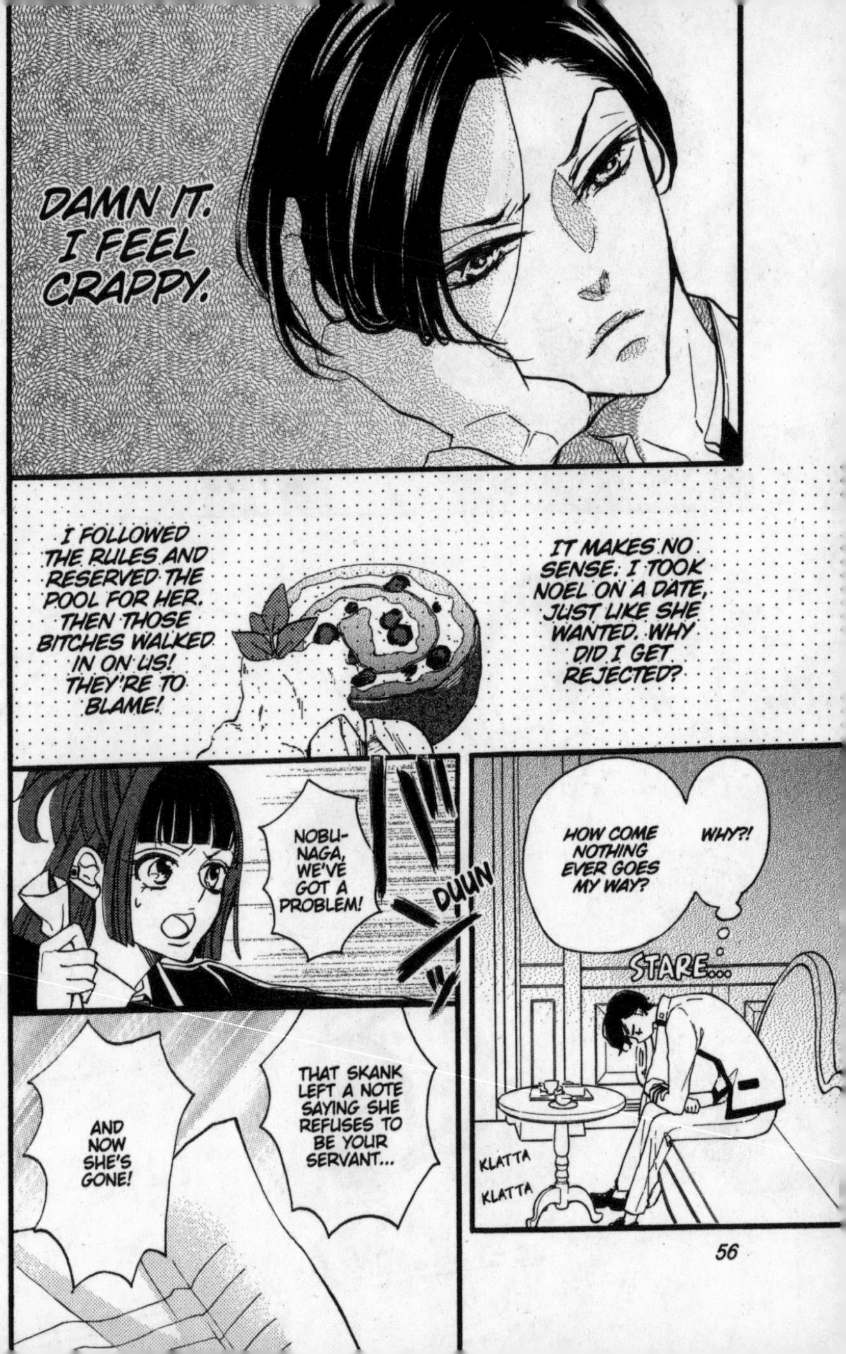

DAMN IT. I FEEL CRAPPY.
IT MAKES NO SENSE. I TOOK NOEL ON A DATE, JUST LIKE SHE WANTED. WHY DID I GET REJECTED?
I FOLLOWED THE RULES AND RESERVED THE POOL FOR HER. THEN THOSE BITCHES WALKED IN ON US! THEY'RE TO BLAME!
WHY?!
HOW COME NOTHING EVER GOES MY WAY?
STARE...
KLATTA
KLATTA
NOBU-NAGA, WE'VE GOT A PROBLEM!
DUUN
THAT SKANK LEFT A NOTE SAYING SHE REFUSES TO BE YOUR SERVANT...
AND NOW SHE'S GONE!

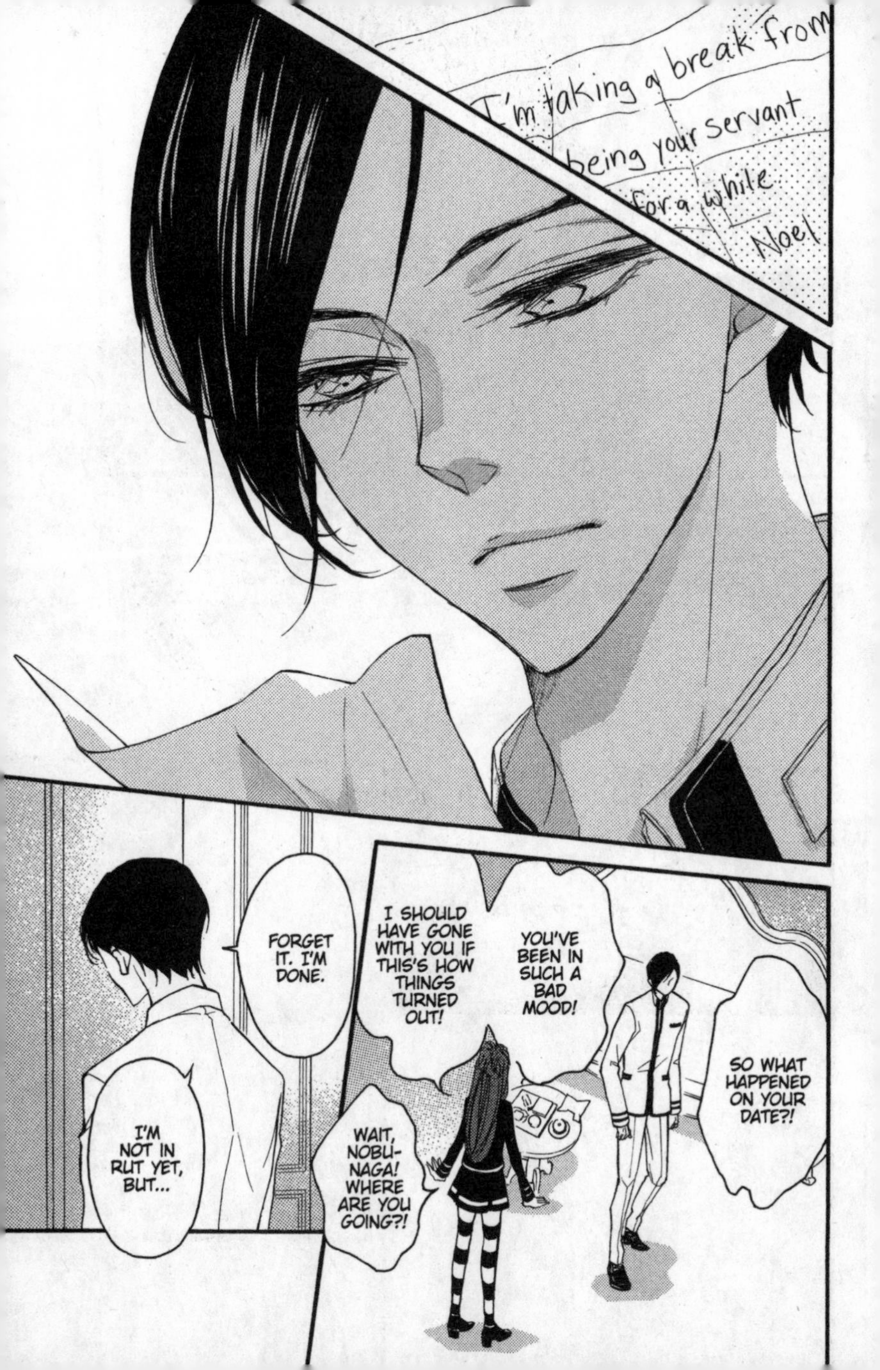
I'm taking a break from
being your servant
for a while
Noel
SO WHAT HAPPENED ON YOUR DATE?!
YOU'VE BEEN IN SUCH A BAD MOOD!
I SHOULD HAVE GONE WITH YOU IF THIS'S HOW THINGS TURNED OUT!
WAIT, NOBUNAGA! WHERE ARE YOU GOING?!
FORGET IT. I'M DONE.
I'M NOT IN RUT YET, BUT...

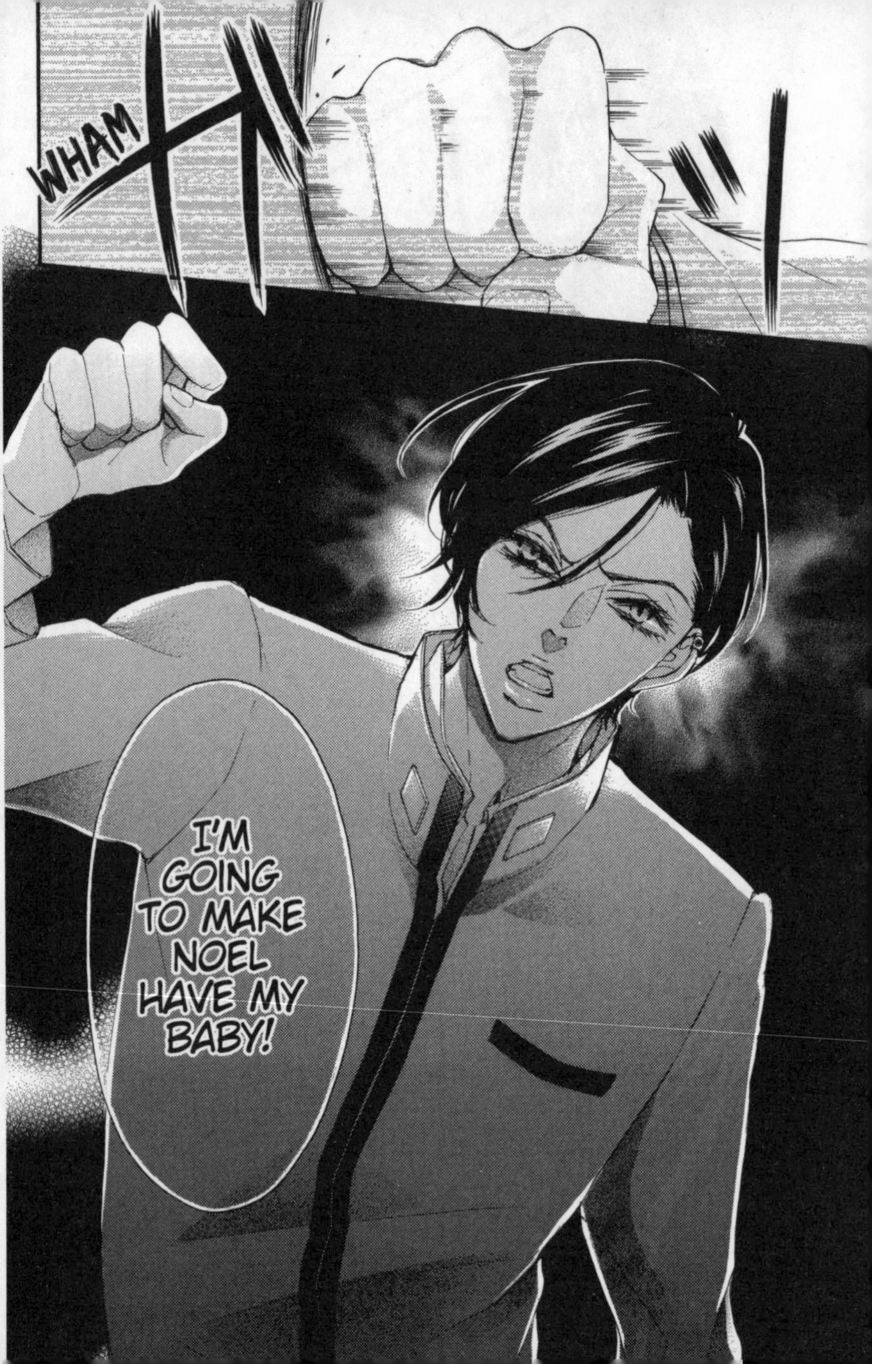
WHAM
I'M GOING TO MAKE NOEL HAVE MY BABY!

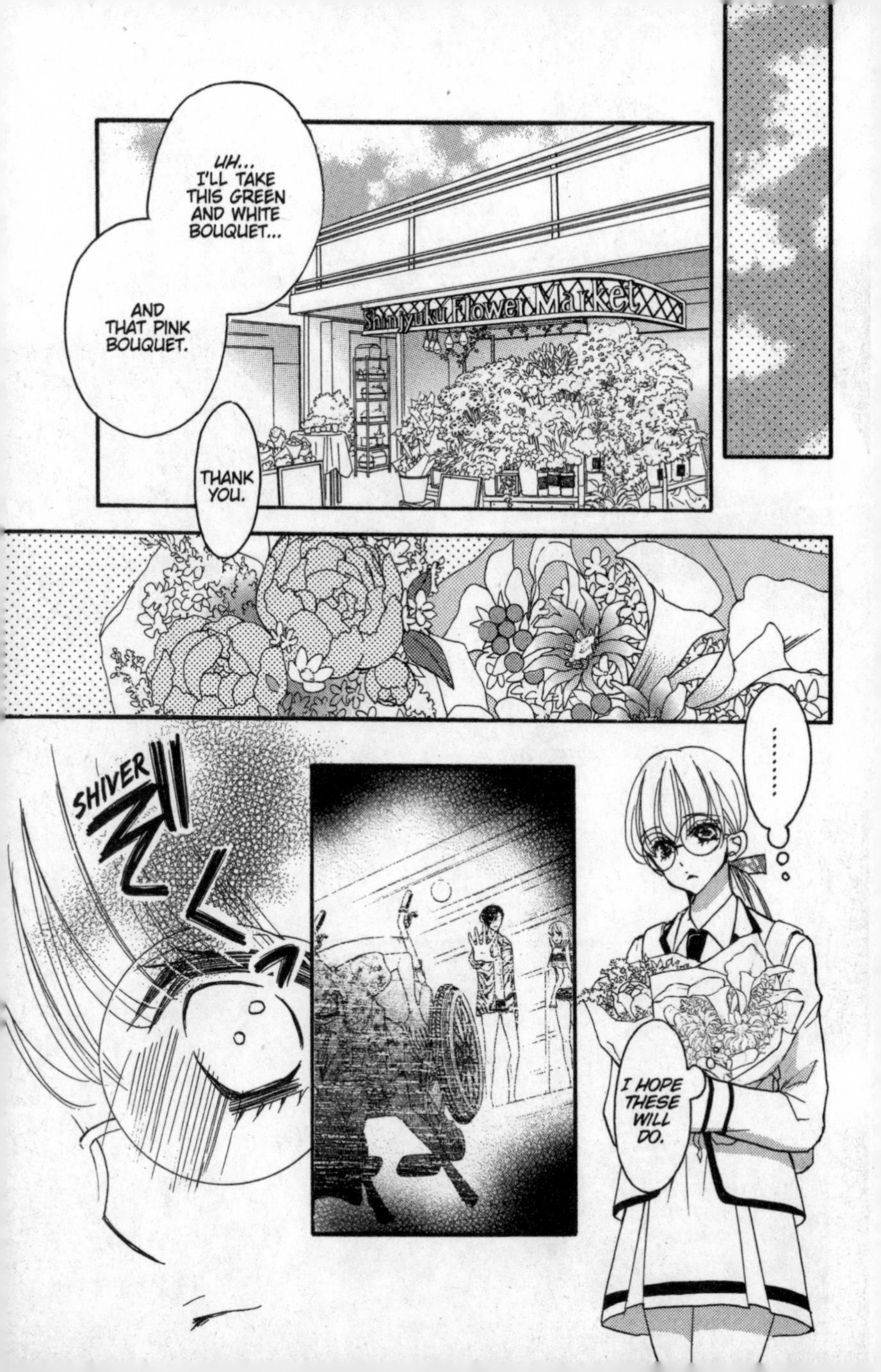
Shinjyuku Flower Market
UH... I'LL TAKE THIS GREEN AND WHITE BOUQUET...
AND THAT PINK BOUQUET.
THANK YOU.
......
I HOPE THESE WILL DO.
SHIVER

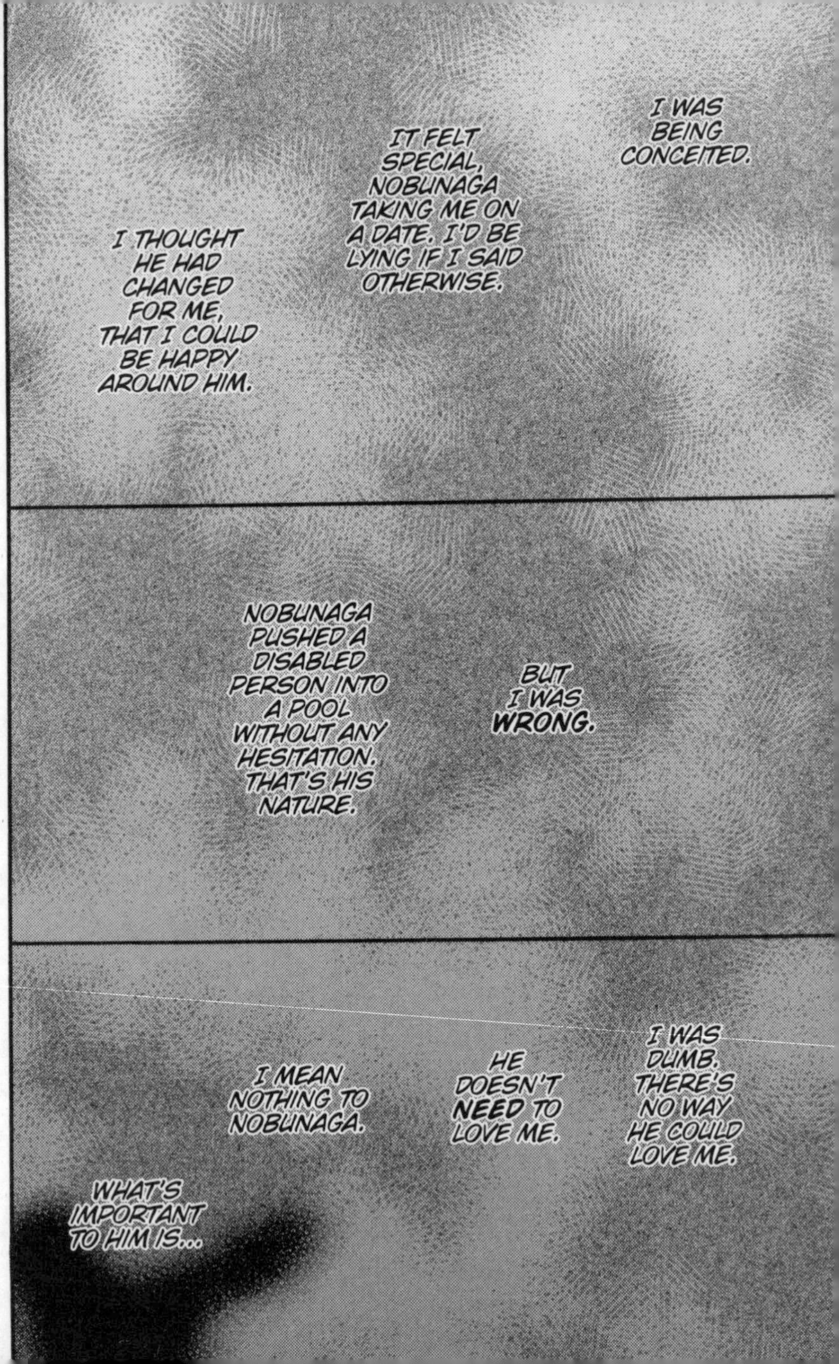
I WAS BEING CONCEITED.
IT FELT SPECIAL, NOBUNAGA TAKING ME ON A DATE. I'D BE LYING IF I SAID OTHERWISE.
I THOUGHT HE HAD CHANGED FOR ME, THAT I COULD BE HAPPY AROUND HIM.
BUT I WAS **WRONG.**
NOBUNAGA PUSHED A DISABLED PERSON INTO A POOL WITHOUT ANY HESITATION. THAT'S HIS NATURE.
I WAS DUMB. THERE'S NO WAY HE COULD LOVE ME.
HE DOESN'T **NEED** TO LOVE ME.
I MEAN NOTHING TO NOBUNAGA.
WHAT'S IMPORTANT TO HIM IS...

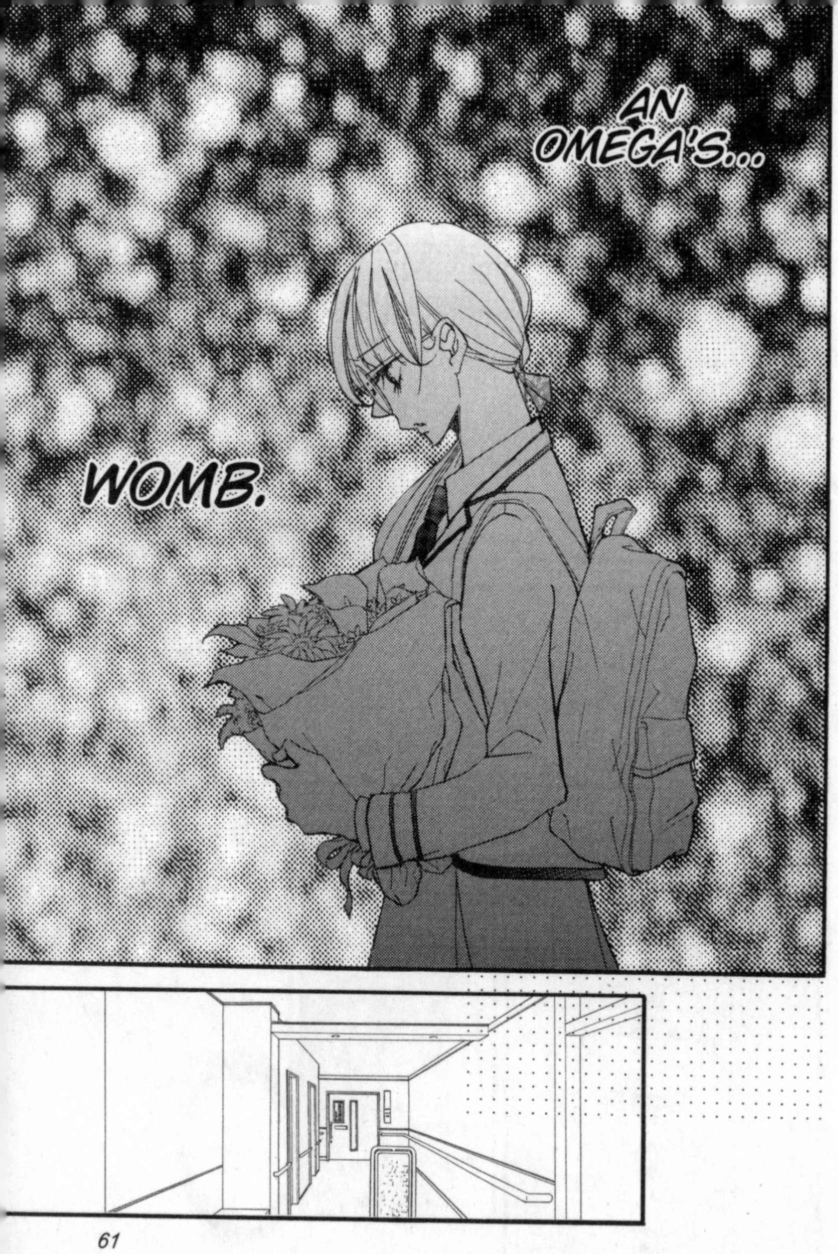
AN OMEGA'S...
WOMB.

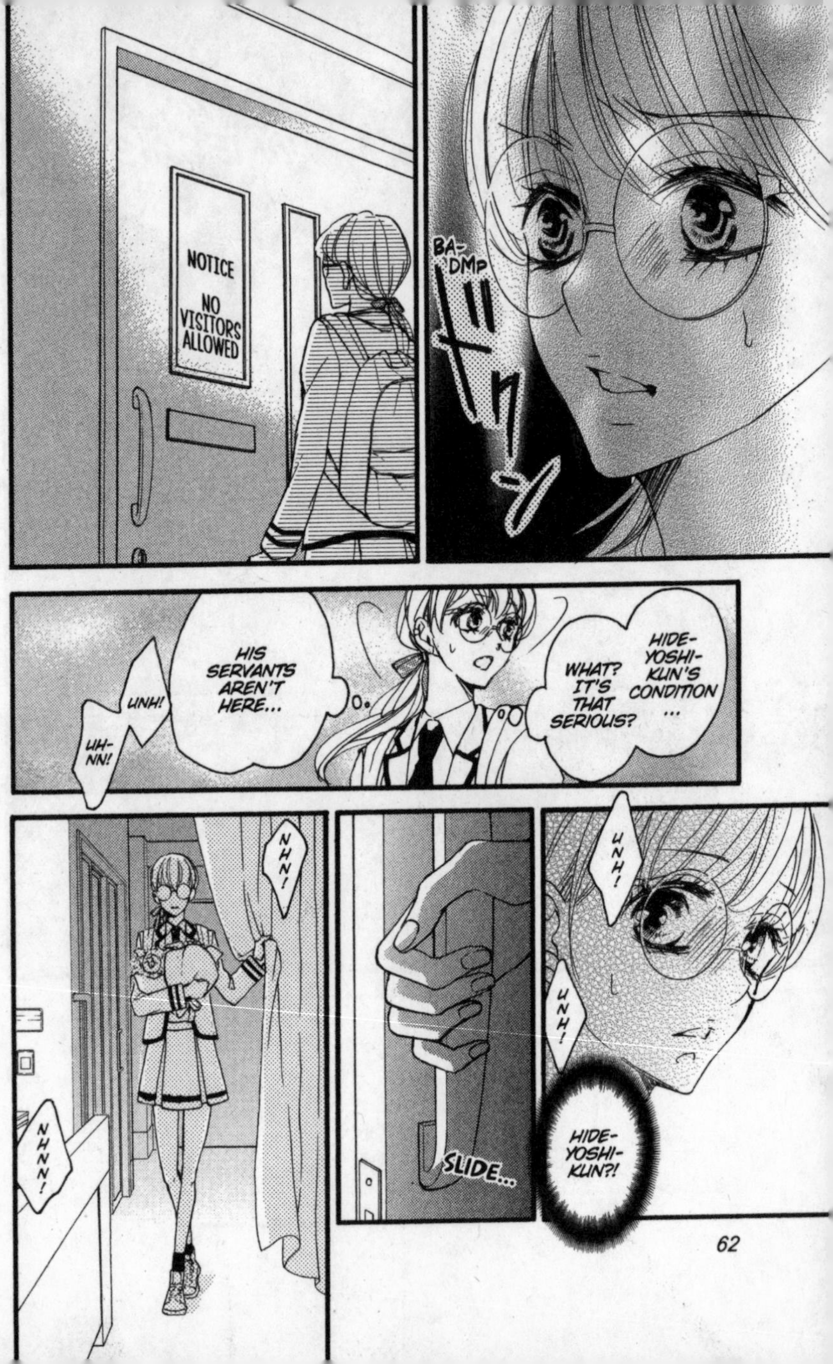
BA-DMP
NOTICE
NO VISITORS ALLOWED
HIDE-YOSHI-KUN'S CONDITION ...
WHAT? IT'S THAT SERIOUS?
HIS SERVANTS AREN'T HERE...
UNH!
UH-NN!
UNH!
UNH!
HIDE-YOSHI-KUN?!
SLIDE...
NHN!
NHNN!

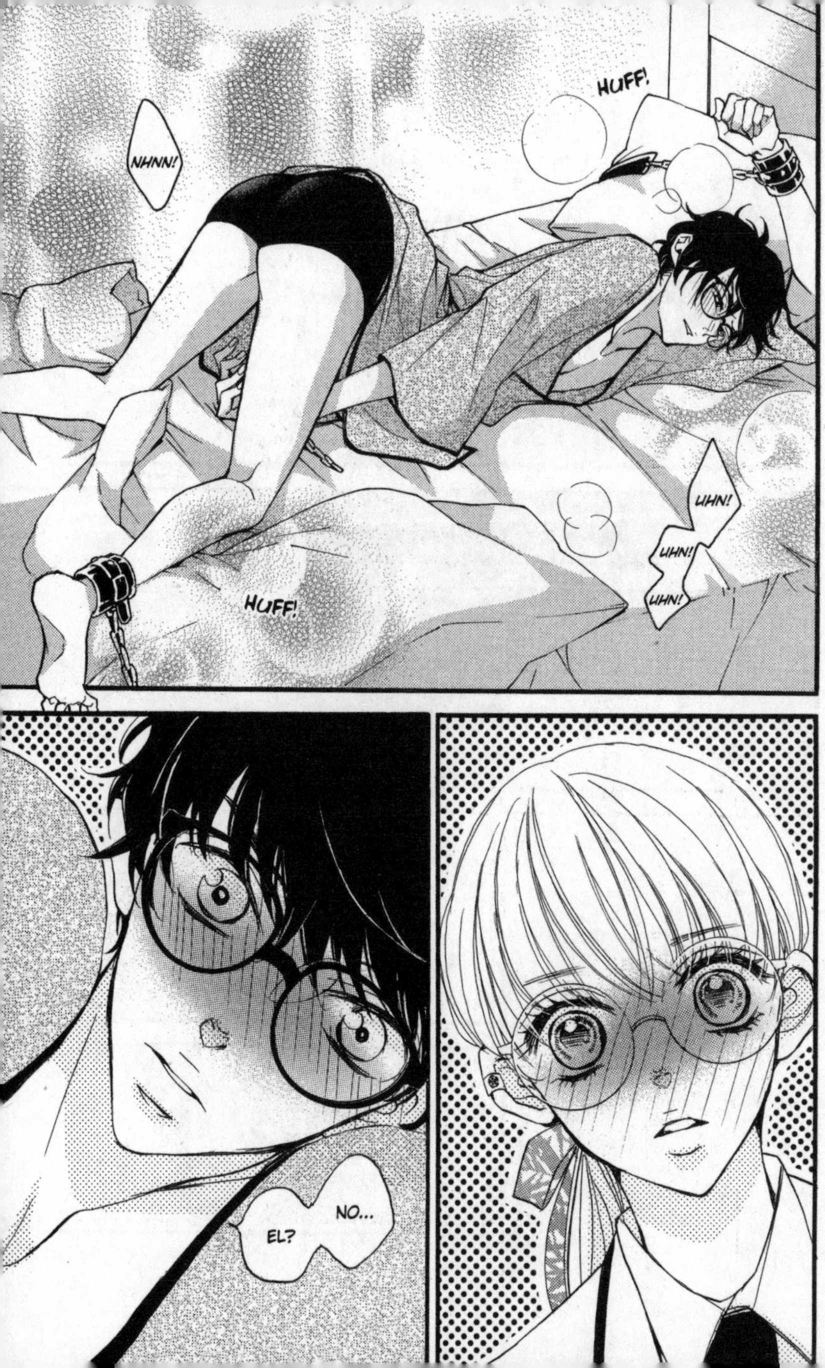
HUFF!
NHNN!
UHN!
UHN!
UHN!
HUFF!
NO...
EL?

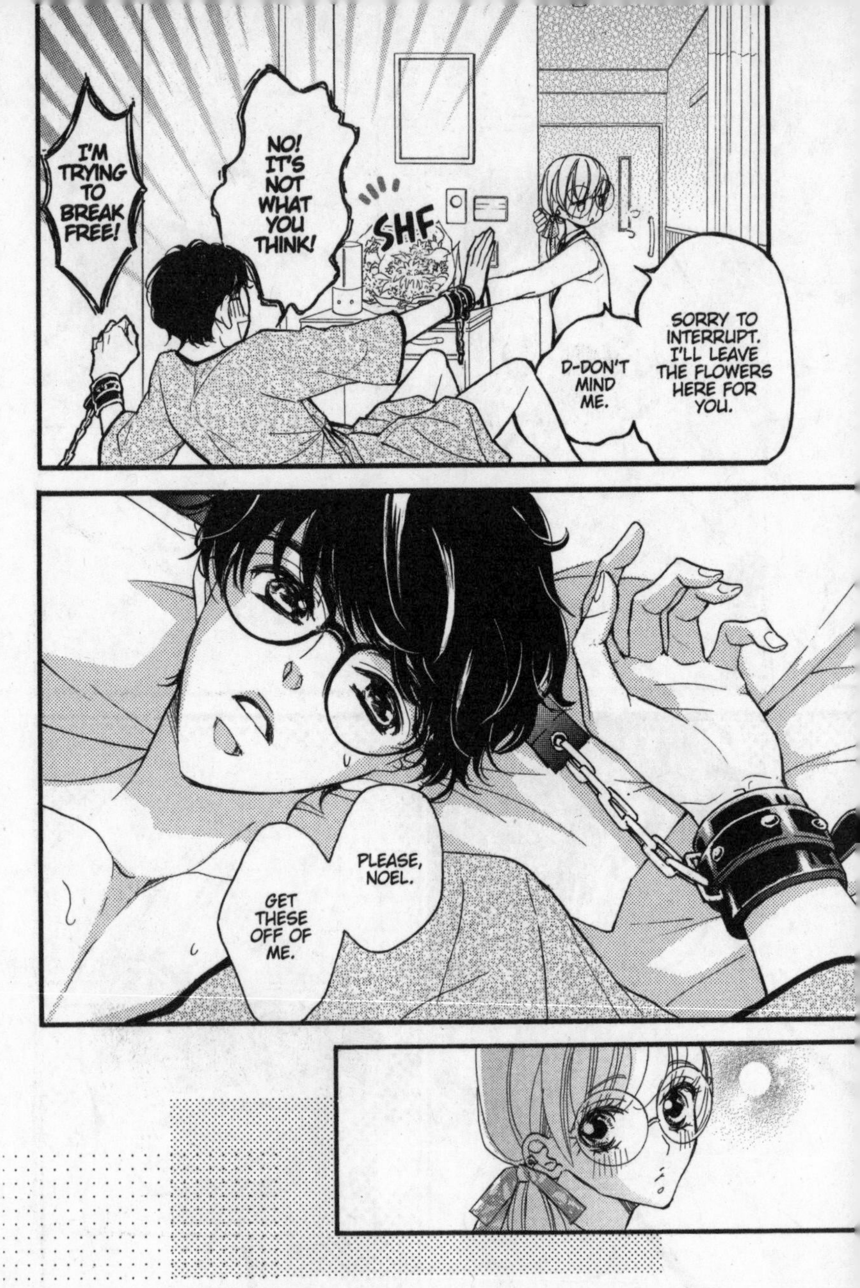
SORRY TO INTERRUPT. I'LL LEAVE THE FLOWERS HERE FOR YOU.
D-DON'T MIND ME.
SHF
NO! IT'S NOT WHAT YOU THINK!
I'M TRYING TO BREAK FREE!
PLEASE, NOEL.
GET THESE OFF OF ME.

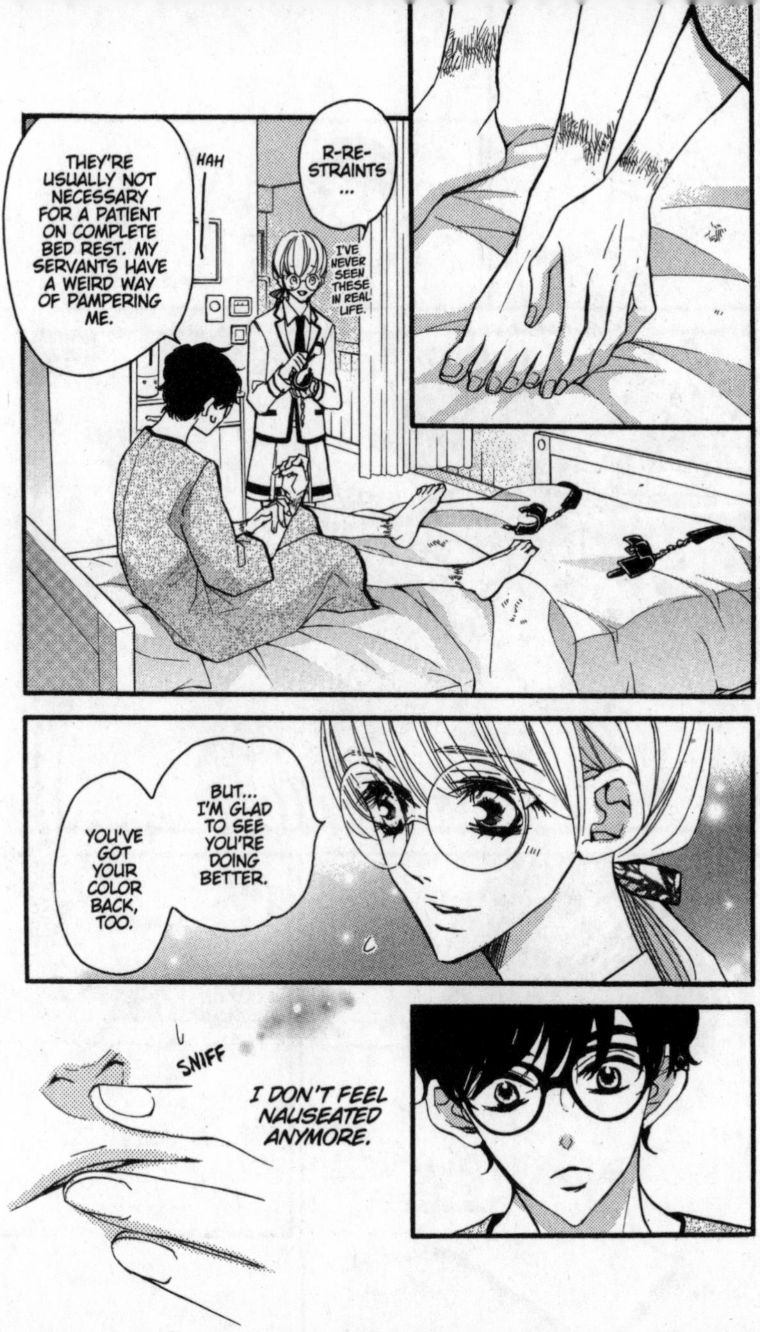
R-RE-STRAINTS...
I'VE NEVER SEEN THESE IN REAL LIFE.
HAH
THEY'RE USUALLY NOT NECESSARY FOR A PATIENT ON COMPLETE BED REST. MY SERVANTS HAVE A WEIRD WAY OF PAMPERING ME.
BUT... I'M GLAD TO SEE YOU'RE DOING BETTER.
YOU'VE GOT YOUR COLOR BACK, TOO.
I DON'T FEEL NAUSEATED ANYMORE.
SNIFF

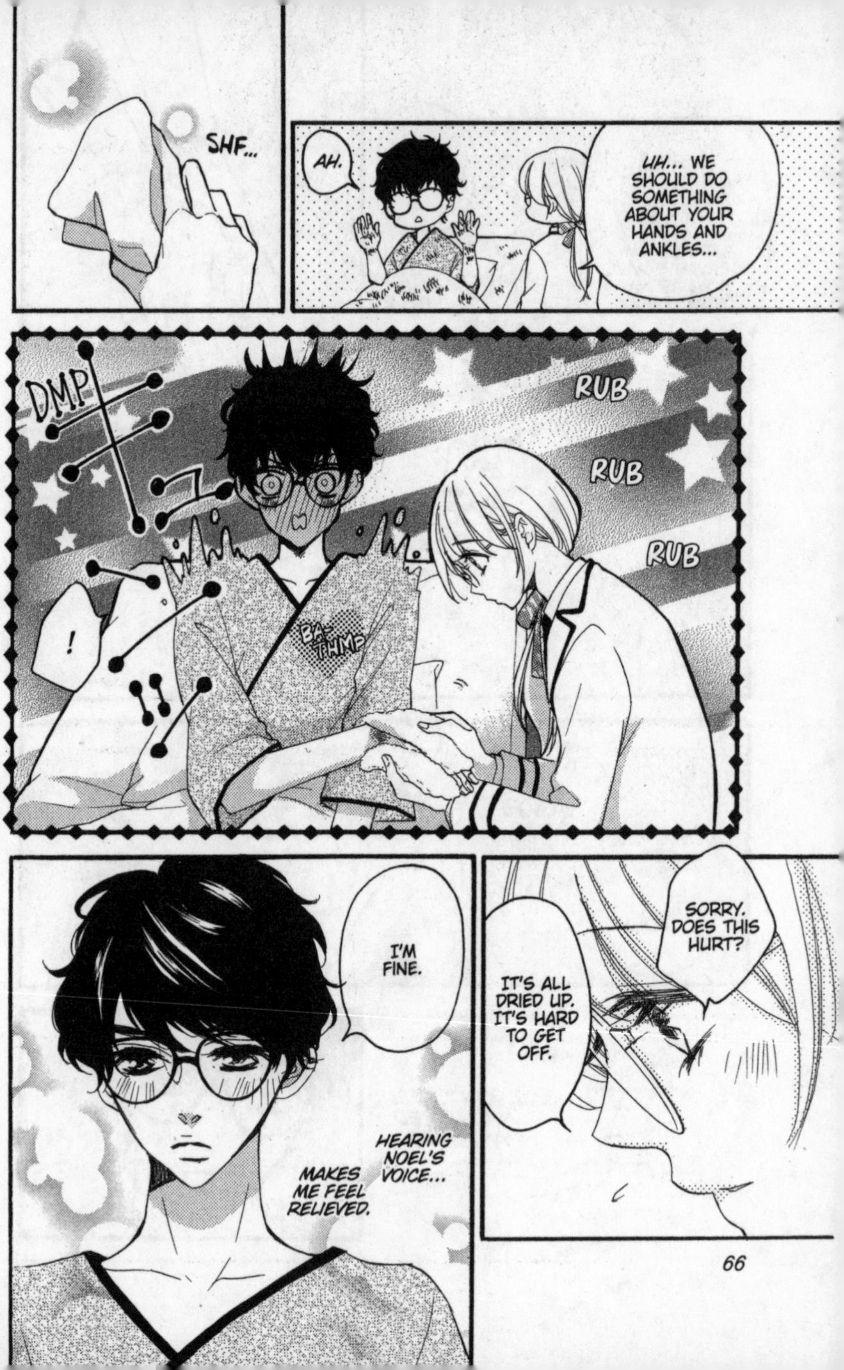
UH... WE SHOULD DO SOMETHING ABOUT YOUR HANDS AND ANKLES...
AH.
SHF...
RUB
RUB
RUB
DMP
BA-THMP
!
SORRY. DOES THIS HURT?
IT'S ALL DRIED UP. IT'S HARD TO GET OFF.
I'M FINE.
HEARING NOEL'S VOICE...
MAKES ME FEEL RELIEVED.

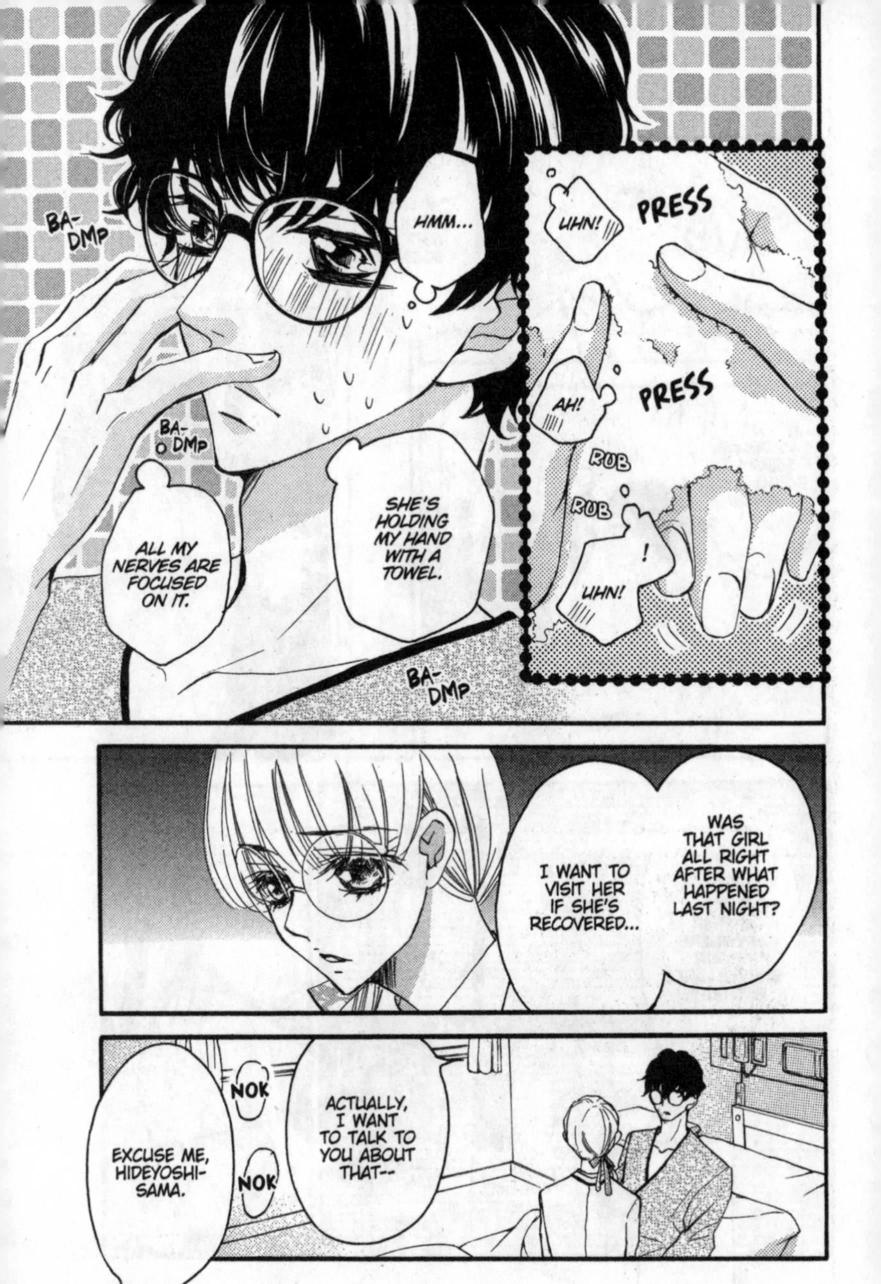
PRESS
UHN!
PRESS
AH!
RUB
RUB
!
UHN!
HMM...
BA-DMP
BA-DMP
SHE'S HOLDING MY HAND WITH A TOWEL.
ALL MY NERVES ARE FOCUSED ON IT.
BA-DMP
WAS THAT GIRL ALL RIGHT AFTER WHAT HAPPENED LAST NIGHT?
I WANT TO VISIT HER IF SHE'S RECOVERED...
ACTUALLY, I WANT TO TALK TO YOU ABOUT THAT--
NOK
NOK
EXCUSE ME, HIDEYOSHI-SAMA.

OH.

FROM THE HOTEL?

I'M SORRY I COULDN'T VISIT YOU SOONER.

NO PROBLEM. SORRY TO BOTHER YOU AGAIN.

SHE DIDN'T APPEAR ANYWHERE IN OUR SURVEILLANCE FOOTAGE.

WHAT?

IT'S ABOUT THE DISABLED GIRL.

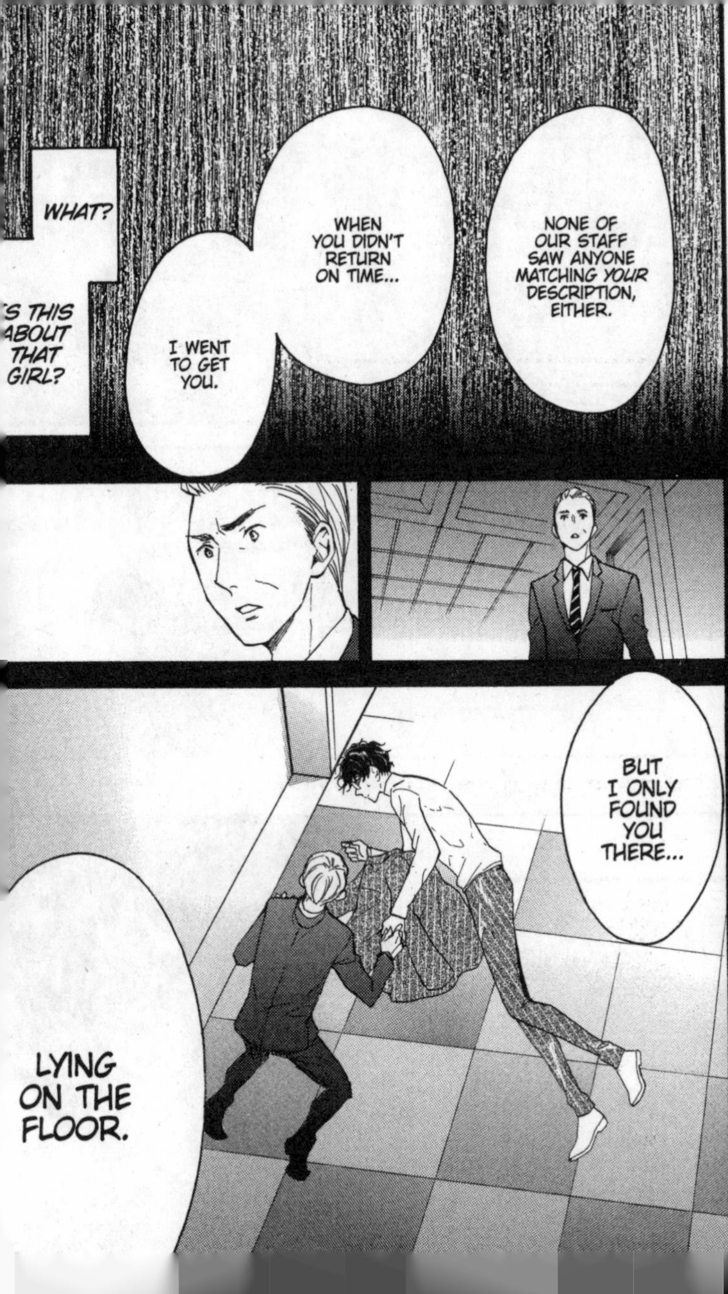
NONE OF OUR STAFF SAW ANYONE MATCHING *YOUR* DESCRIPTION, EITHER.
WHEN YOU DIDN'T RETURN ON TIME...
I WENT TO GET YOU.
WHAT?
S THIS ABOUT THAT GIRL?
BUT I ONLY FOUND YOU THERE...
LYING ON THE FLOOR.

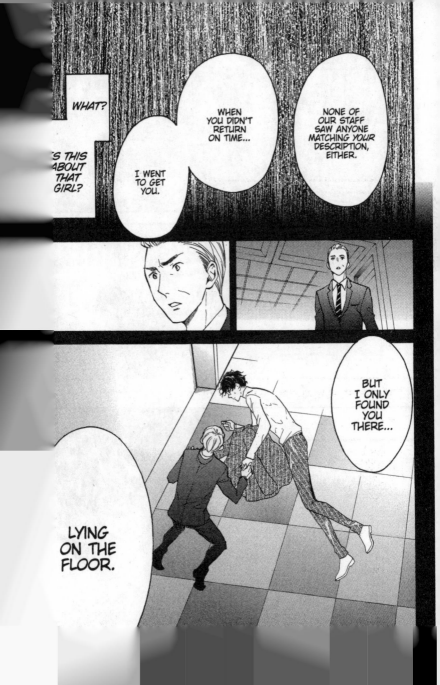

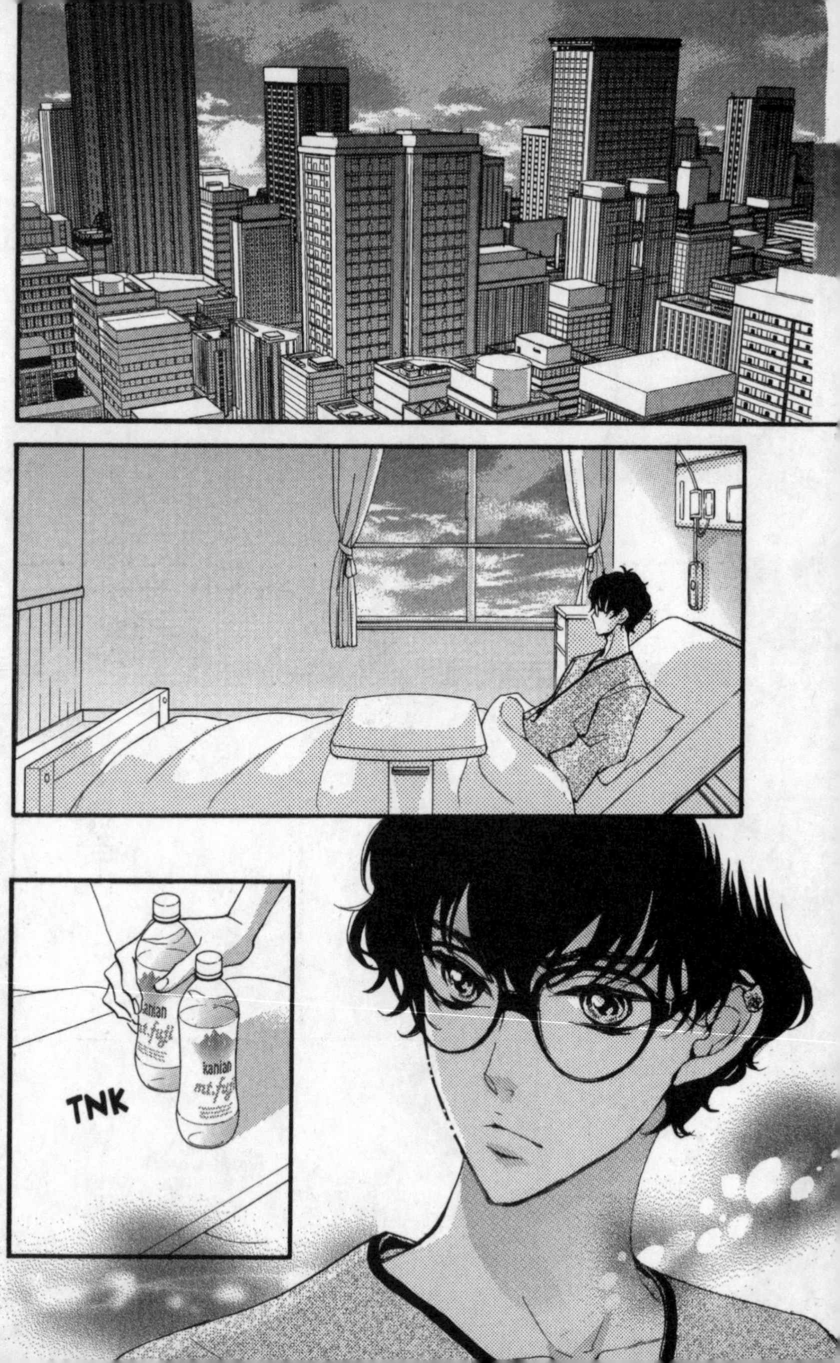
kanian
mt.fuji
TNK

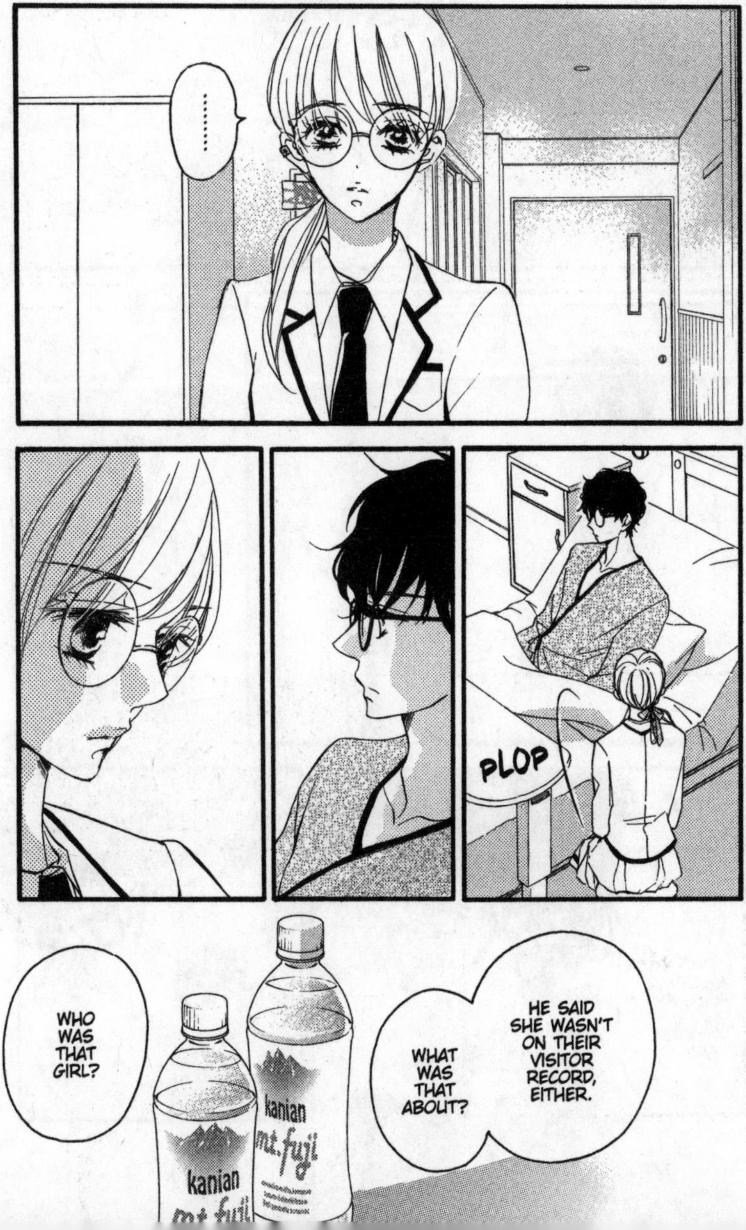
……
PLOP
HE SAID SHE WASN'T ON THEIR VISITOR RECORD, EITHER.
WHAT WAS THAT ABOUT?
WHO WAS THAT GIRL?
kanian
mt. fuji
kanian

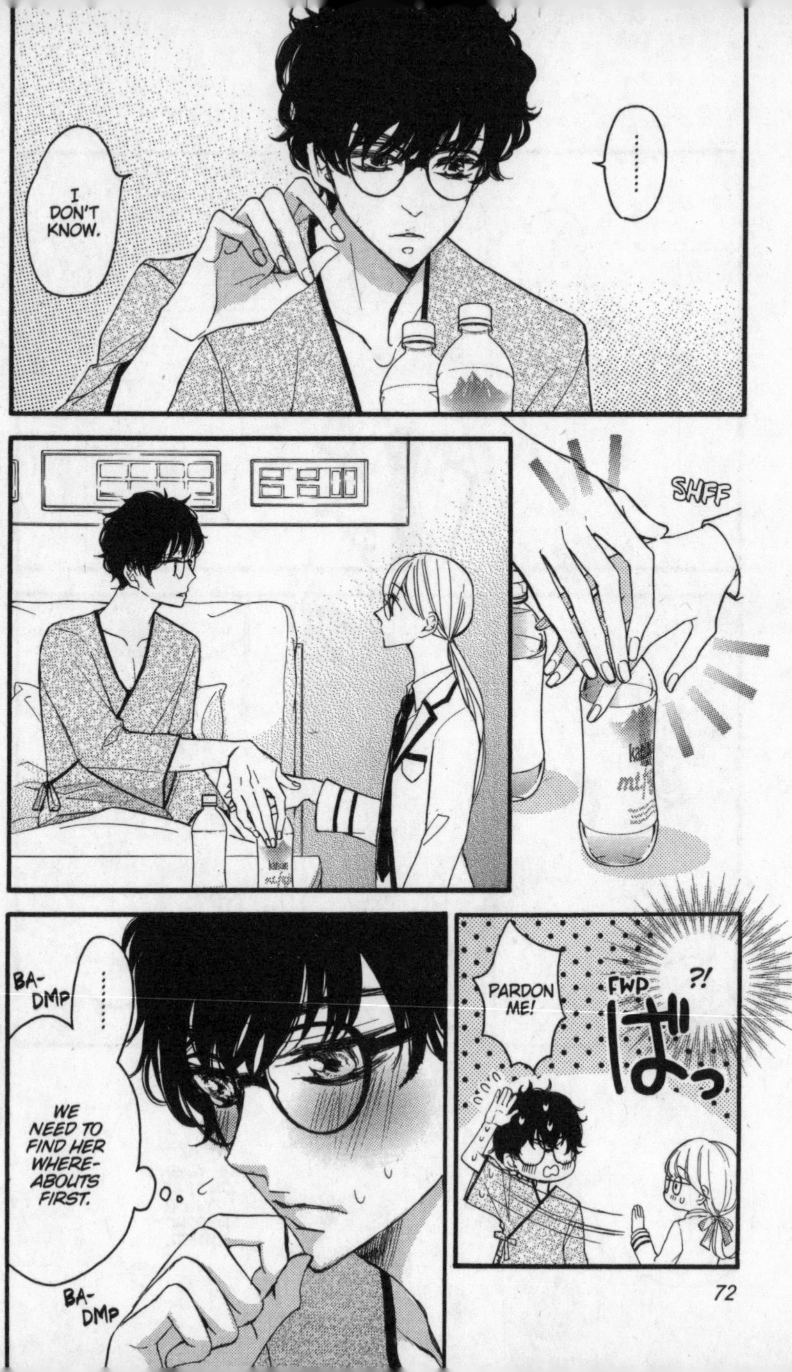
......
I DON'T KNOW.
SHFF
?!
FWP
ばっ
PARDON ME!
BA-DMP
......
WE NEED TO FIND HER WHERE-ABOUTS FIRST.
BA-DMP

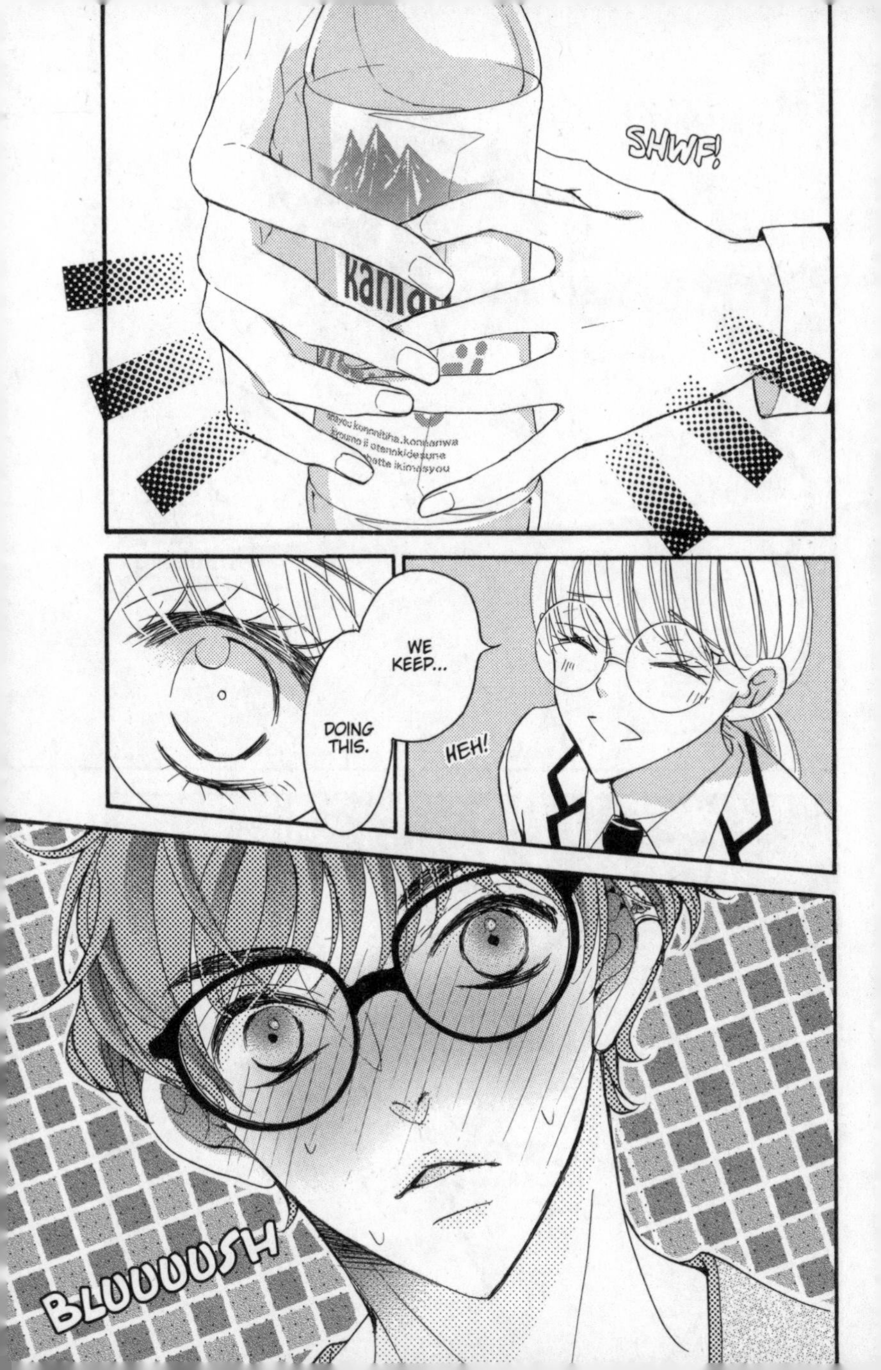
SHWF!
WE KEEP...
DOING THIS.
HEH!
BLUUUUSH

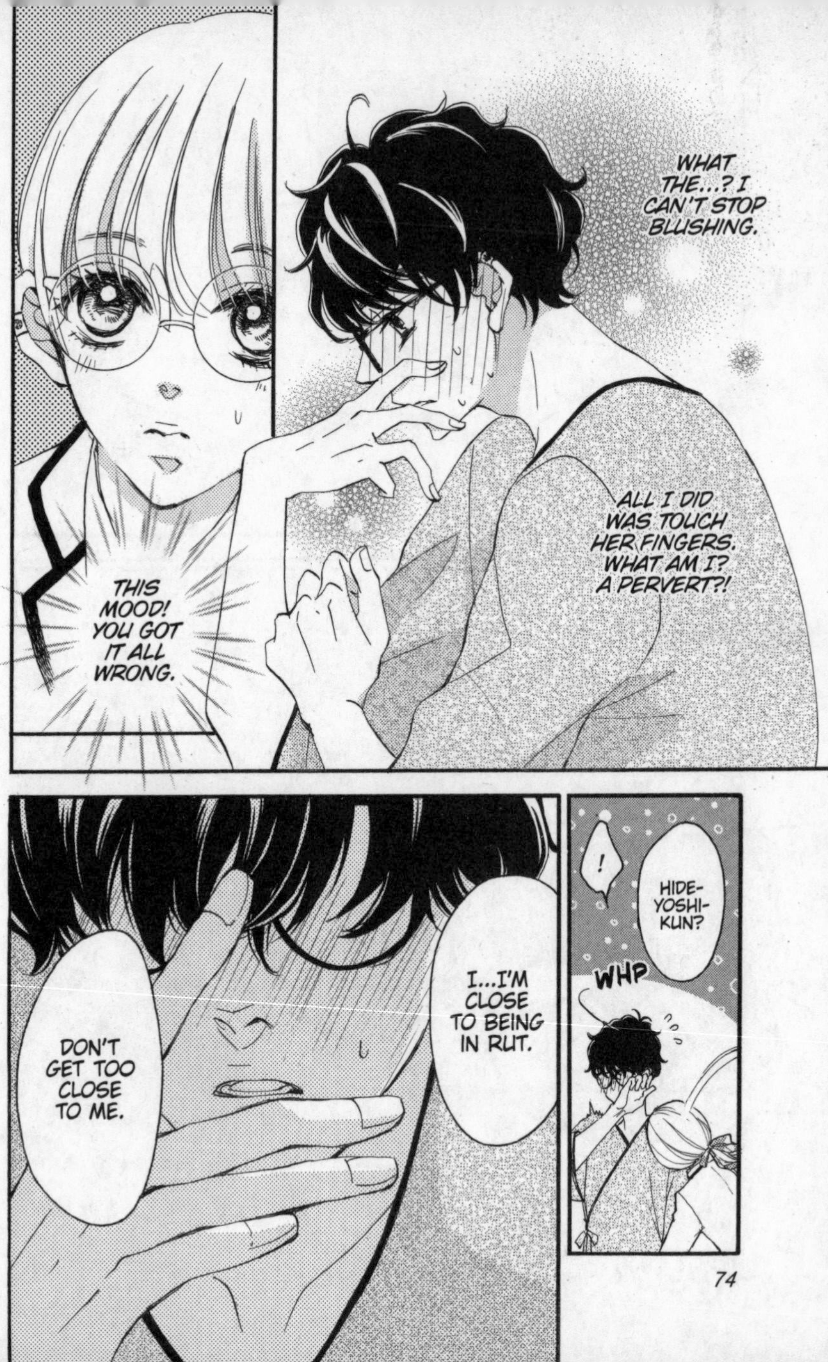
WHAT THE...? I CAN'T STOP BLUSHING.
ALL I DID WAS TOUCH HER FINGERS. WHAT AM I? A PERVERT?!
THIS MOOD! YOU GOT IT ALL WRONG.
HIDE-YOSHI-KUN?
!
WHP
I...I'M CLOSE TO BEING IN RUT.
DON'T GET TOO CLOSE TO ME.

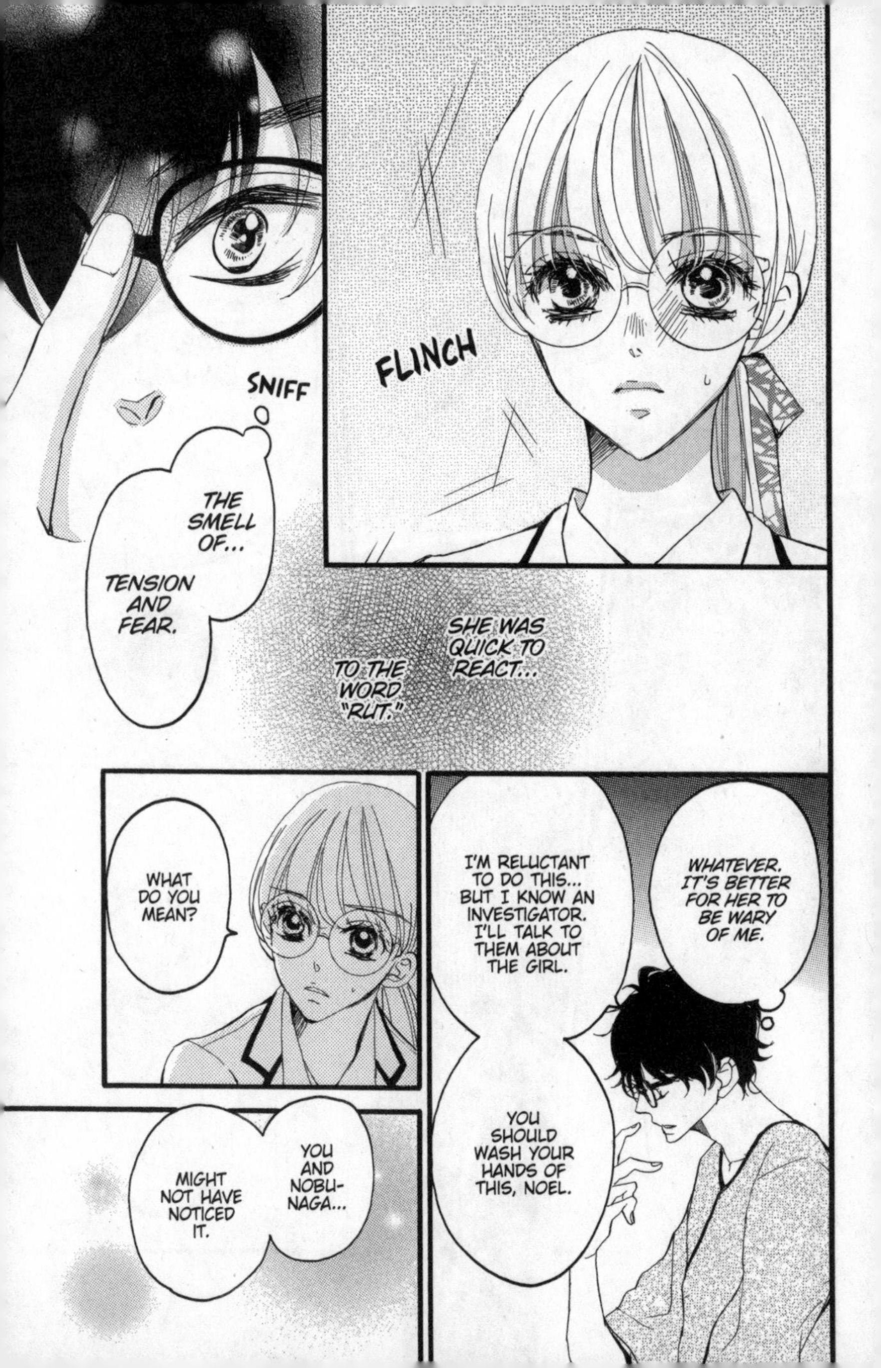
FLINCH
SNIFF
THE SMELL OF...
TENSION AND FEAR.
SHE WAS QUICK TO REACT...
TO THE WORD "RUT."
WHATEVER. IT'S BETTER FOR HER TO BE WARY OF ME.
I'M RELUCTANT TO DO THIS... BUT I KNOW AN INVESTIGATOR. I'LL TALK TO THEM ABOUT THE GIRL.
YOU SHOULD WASH YOUR HANDS OF THIS, NOEL.
WHAT DO YOU MEAN?
YOU AND NOBU-NAGA...
MIGHT NOT HAVE NOTICED IT.

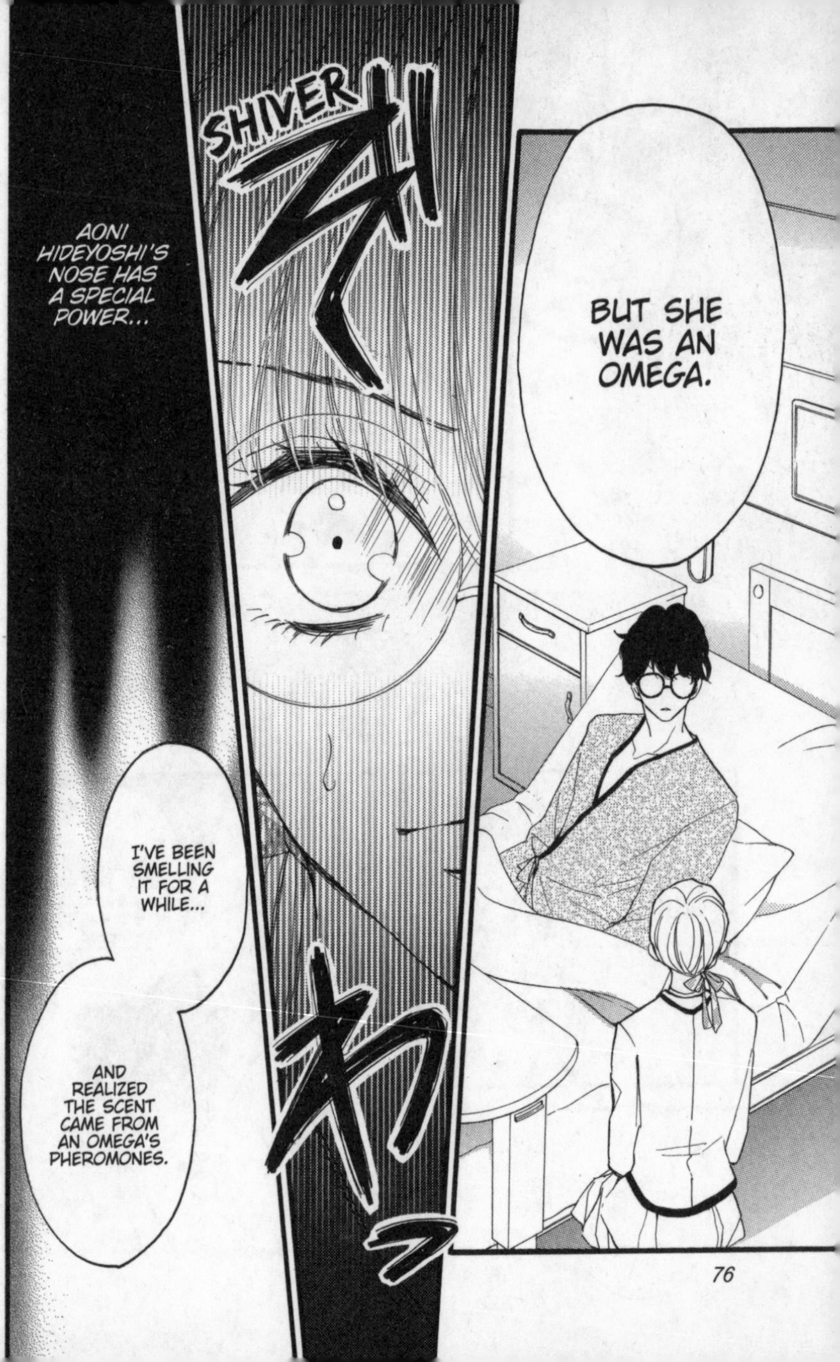
BUT SHE WAS AN OMEGA.
SHIVER
AONI HIDEYOSHI'S NOSE HAS A SPECIAL POWER...
I'VE BEEN SMELLING IT FOR A WHILE...
AND REALIZED THE SCENT CAME FROM AN OMEGA'S PHEROMONES.

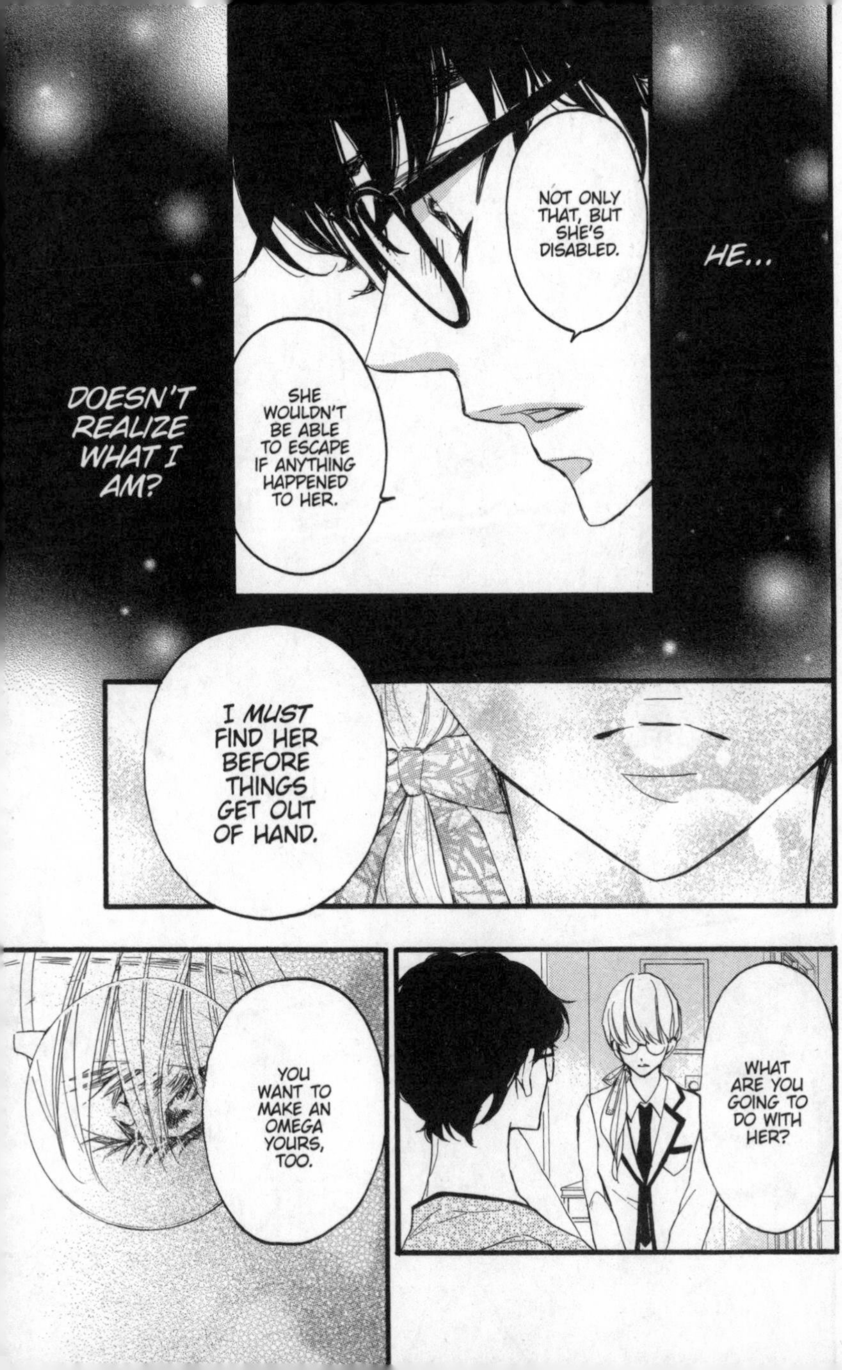
HE...
NOT ONLY THAT, BUT SHE'S DISABLED.
SHE WOULDN'T BE ABLE TO ESCAPE IF ANYTHING HAPPENED TO HER.
DOESN'T REALIZE WHAT I AM?
I *MUST* FIND HER BEFORE THINGS GET OUT OF HAND.
WHAT ARE YOU GOING TO DO WITH HER?
YOU WANT TO MAKE AN OMEGA YOURS, TOO.

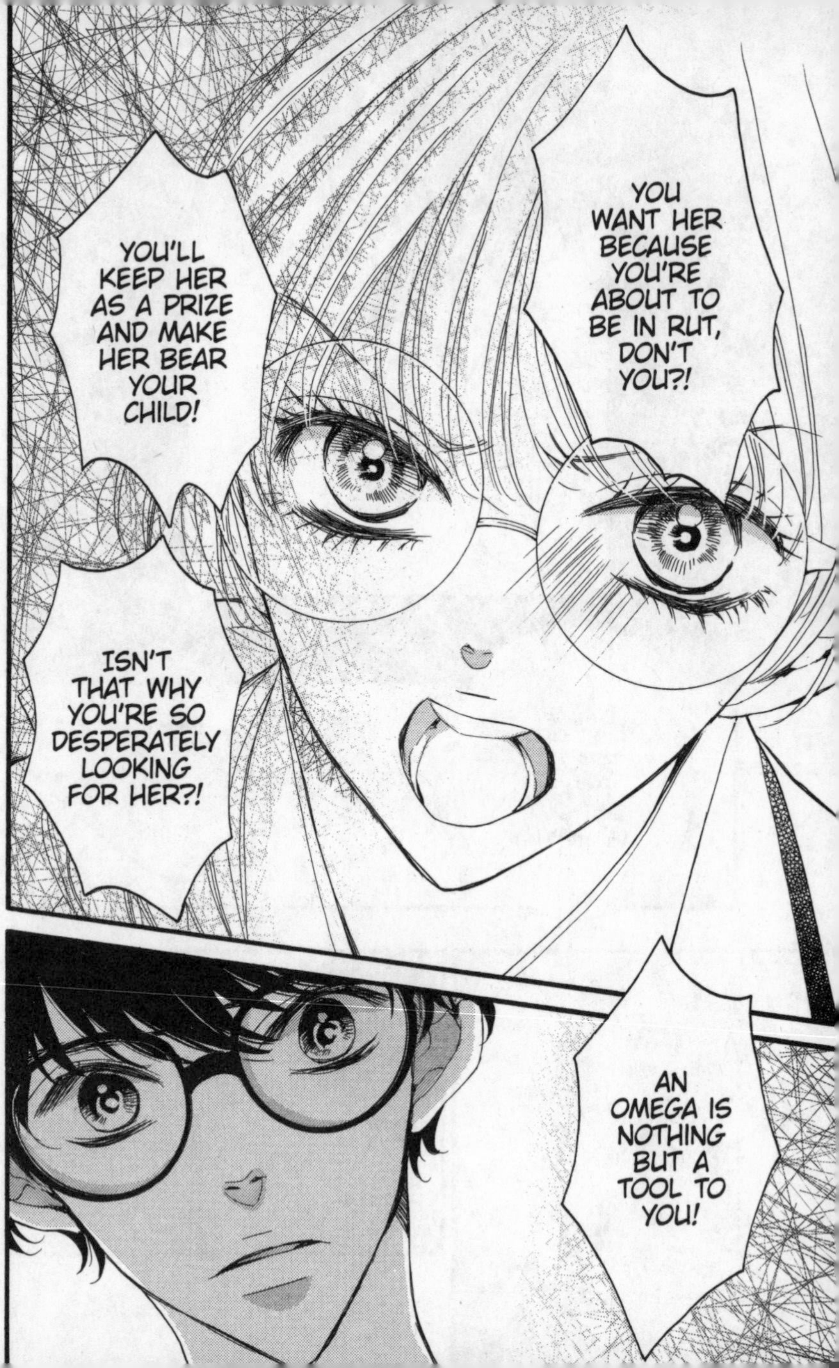
YOU WANT HER BECAUSE YOU'RE ABOUT TO BE IN RUT, DON'T YOU?!
YOU'LL KEEP HER AS A PRIZE AND MAKE HER BEAR YOUR CHILD!
ISN'T THAT WHY YOU'RE SO DESPERATELY LOOKING FOR HER?!
AN OMEGA IS NOTHING BUT A TOOL TO YOU!

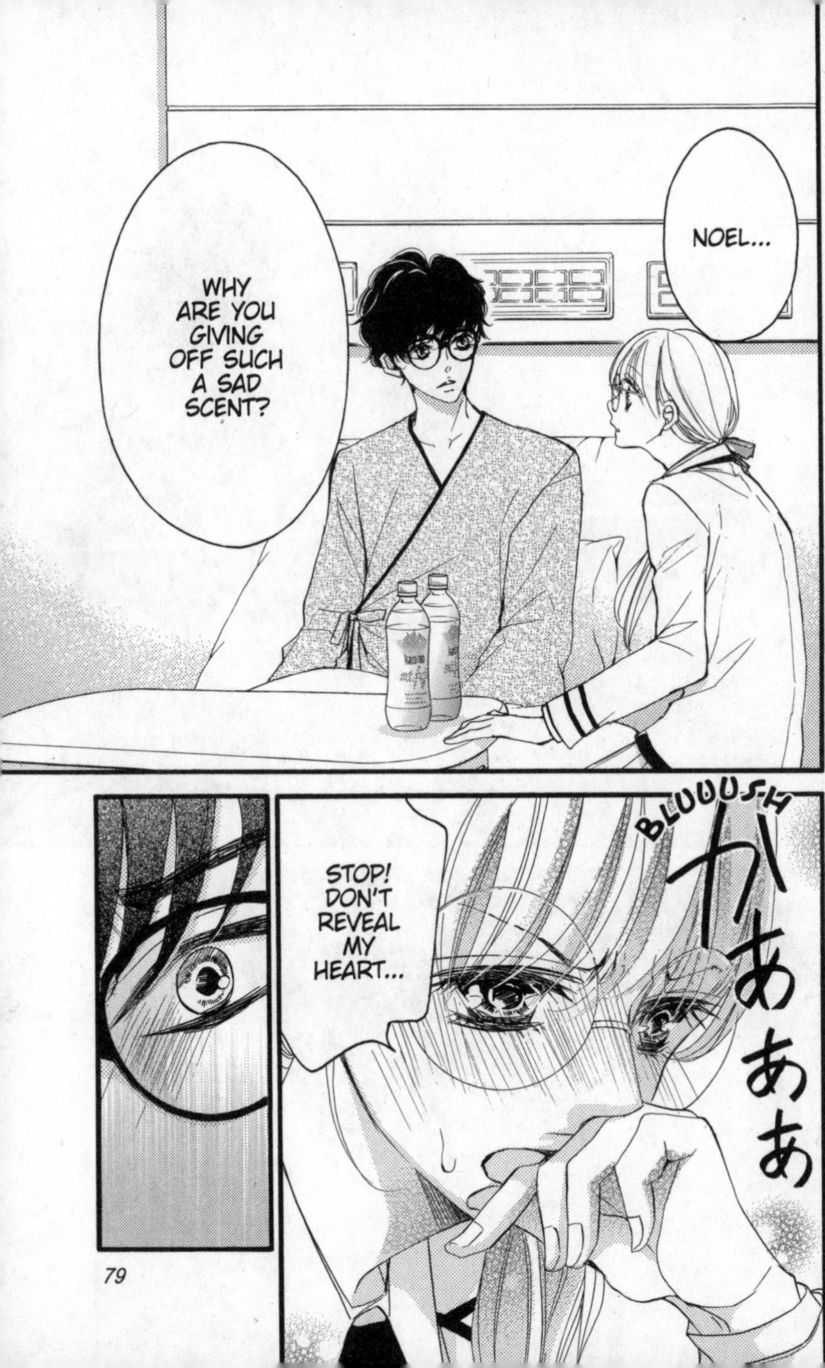
NOEL...
WHY ARE YOU GIVING OFF SUCH A SAD SCENT?
BLUUUSH
かあああ
STOP! DON'T REVEAL MY HEART...

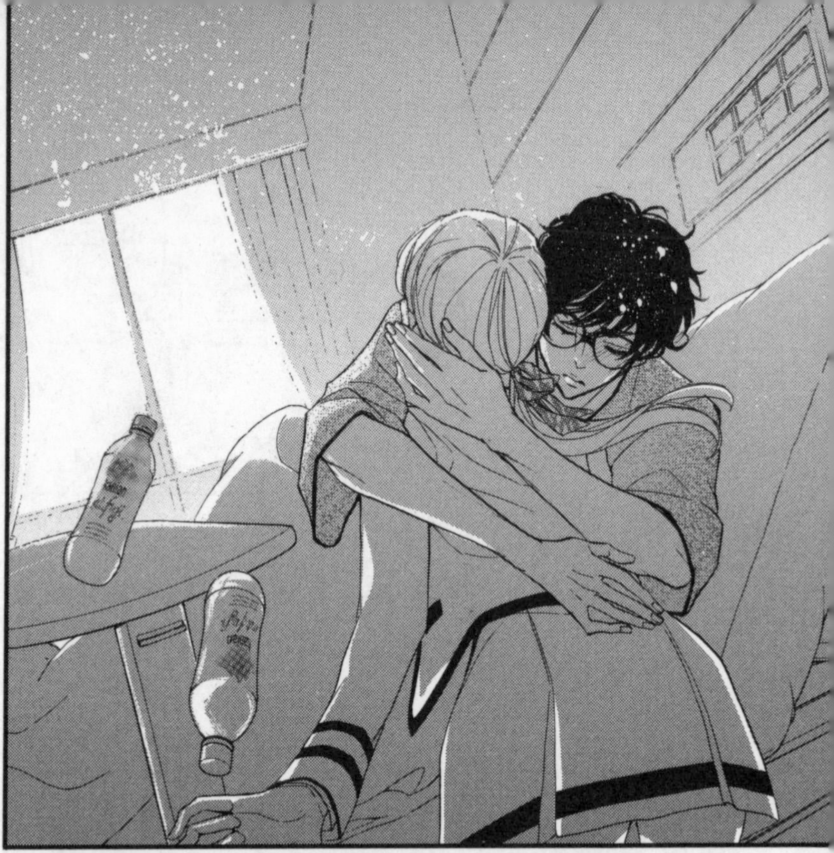

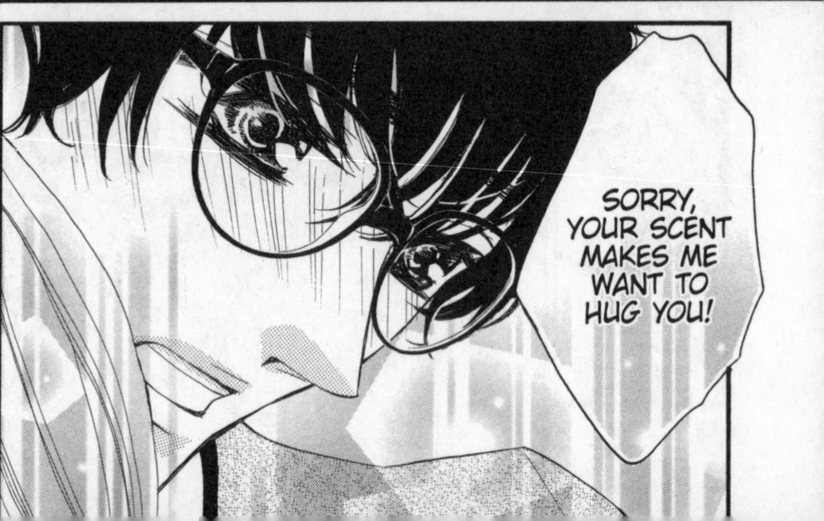
SORRY, YOUR SCENT MAKES ME WANT TO HUG YOU!

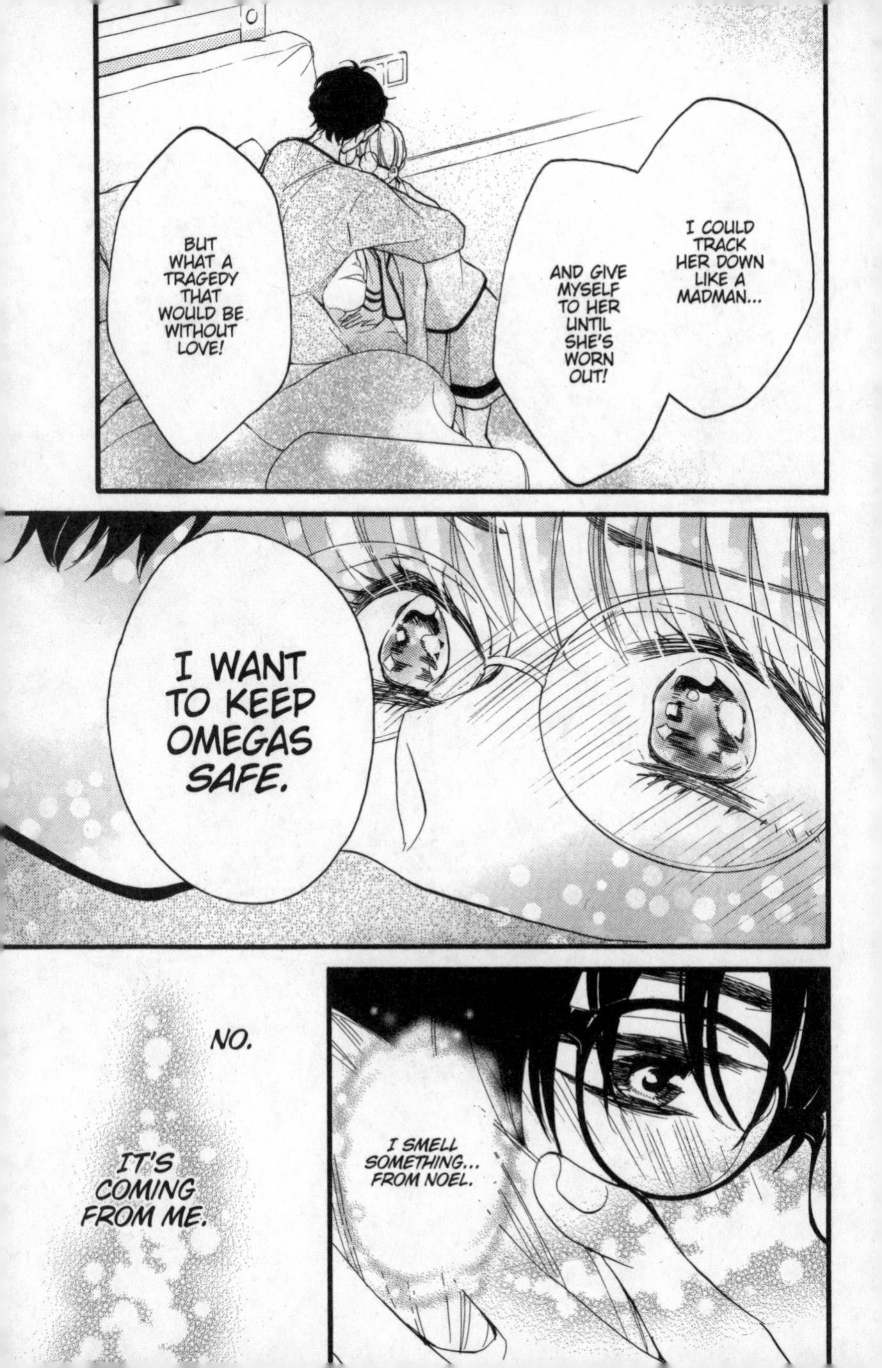
I COULD TRACK HER DOWN LIKE A MADMAN...
AND GIVE MYSELF TO HER UNTIL SHE'S WORN OUT!
BUT WHAT A TRAGEDY THAT WOULD BE WITHOUT LOVE!
I WANT TO KEEP OMEGAS SAFE.
I SMELL SOMETHING... FROM NOEL.
NO.
IT'S COMING FROM ME.

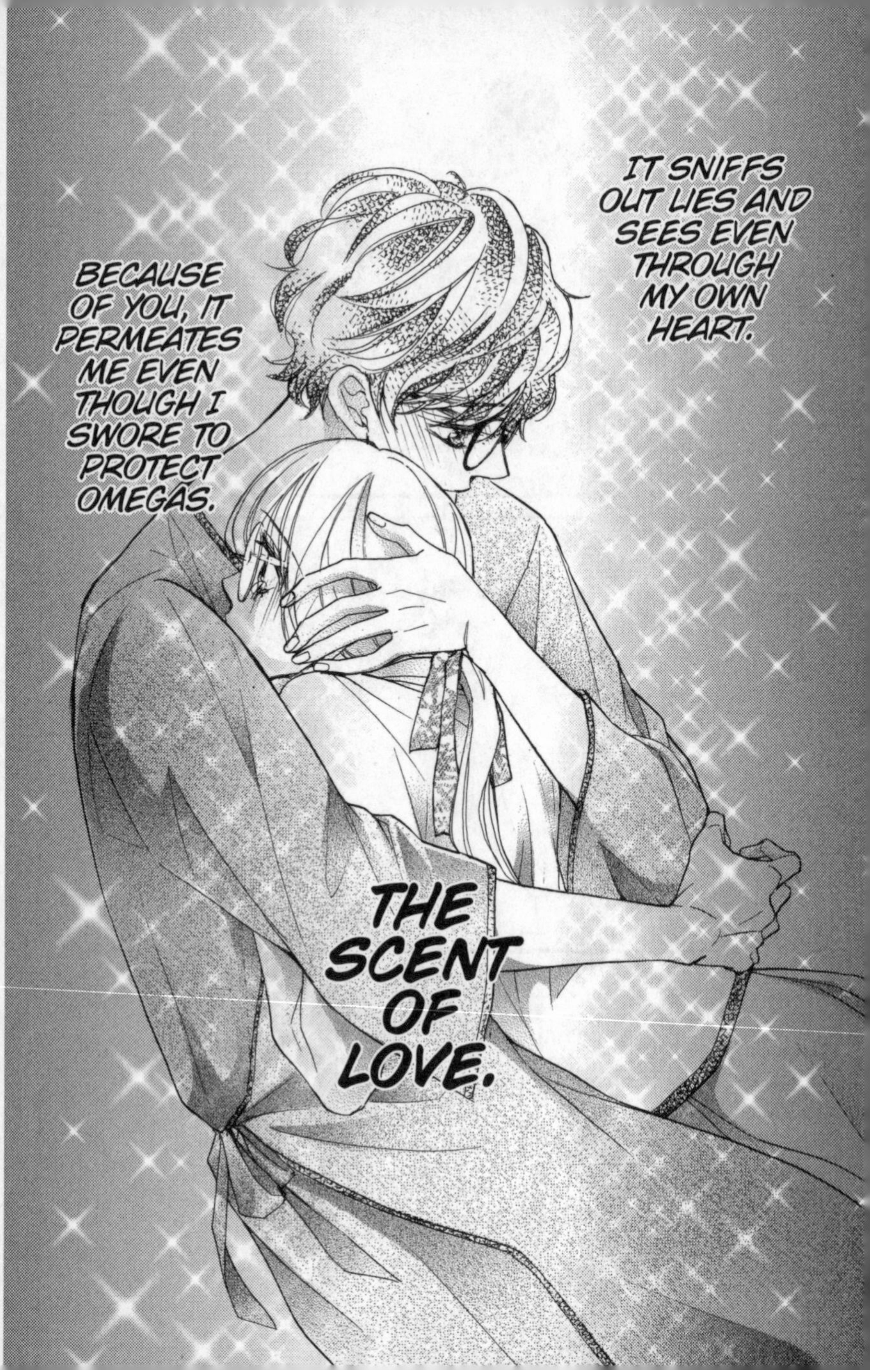
IT SNIFFS OUT LIES AND SEES EVEN THROUGH MY OWN HEART.
BECAUSE OF YOU, IT PERMEATES ME EVEN THOUGH I SWORE TO PROTECT OMEGAS.
THE SCENT OF LOVE.

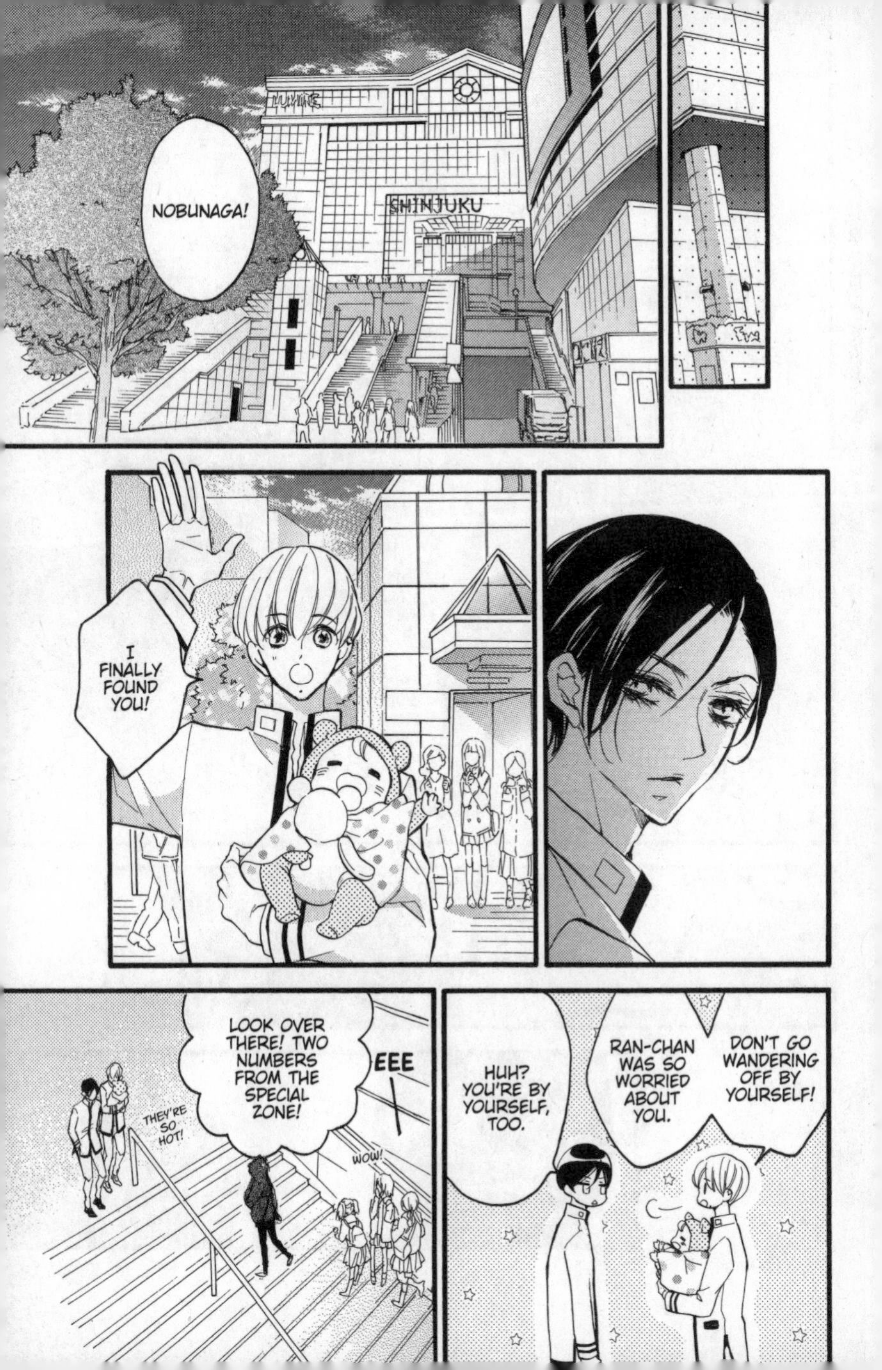
SHINJUKU
NOBUNAGA!
I FINALLY FOUND YOU!
DON'T GO WANDERING OFF BY YOURSELF!
RAN-CHAN WAS SO WORRIED ABOUT YOU.
HUH? YOU'RE BY YOURSELF, TOO.
EEE
LOOK OVER THERE! TWO NUMBERS FROM THE SPECIAL ZONE!
THEY'RE SO HOT!
WOW!

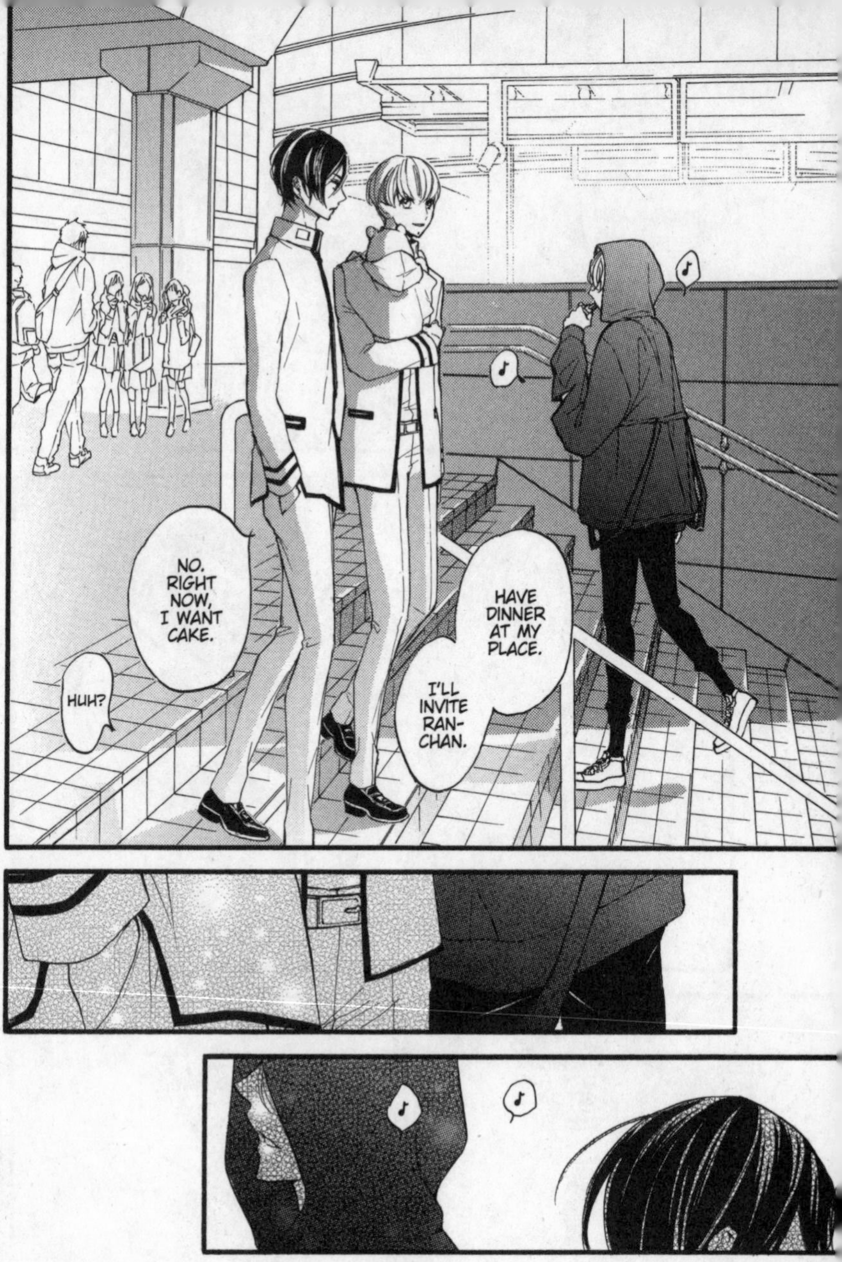
HAVE DINNER AT MY PLACE.
I'LL INVITE RAN-CHAN.
NO. RIGHT NOW, I WANT CAKE.
HUH?

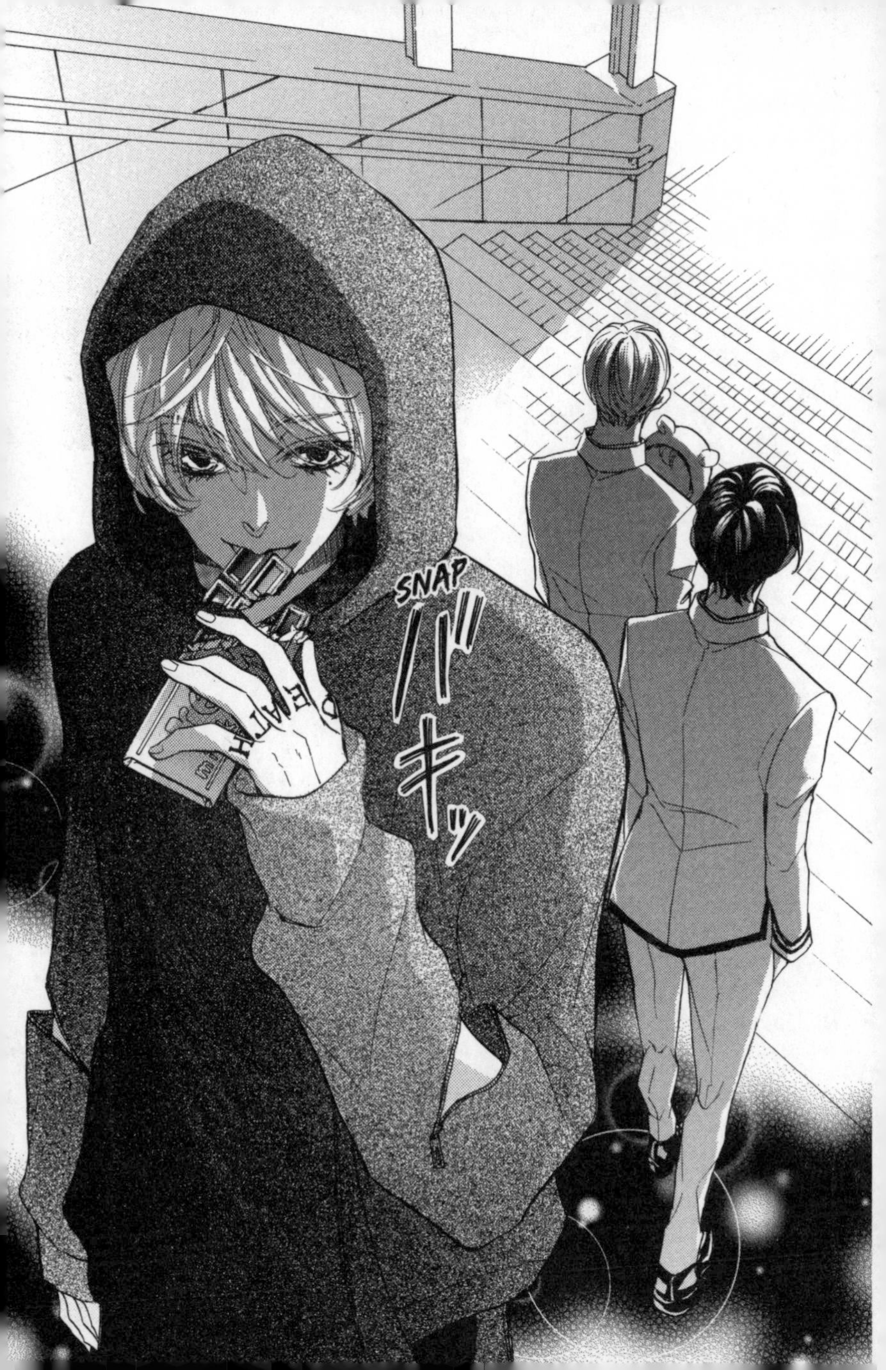
SNAP
バキッ

Bite Maker

—The King's Omega—

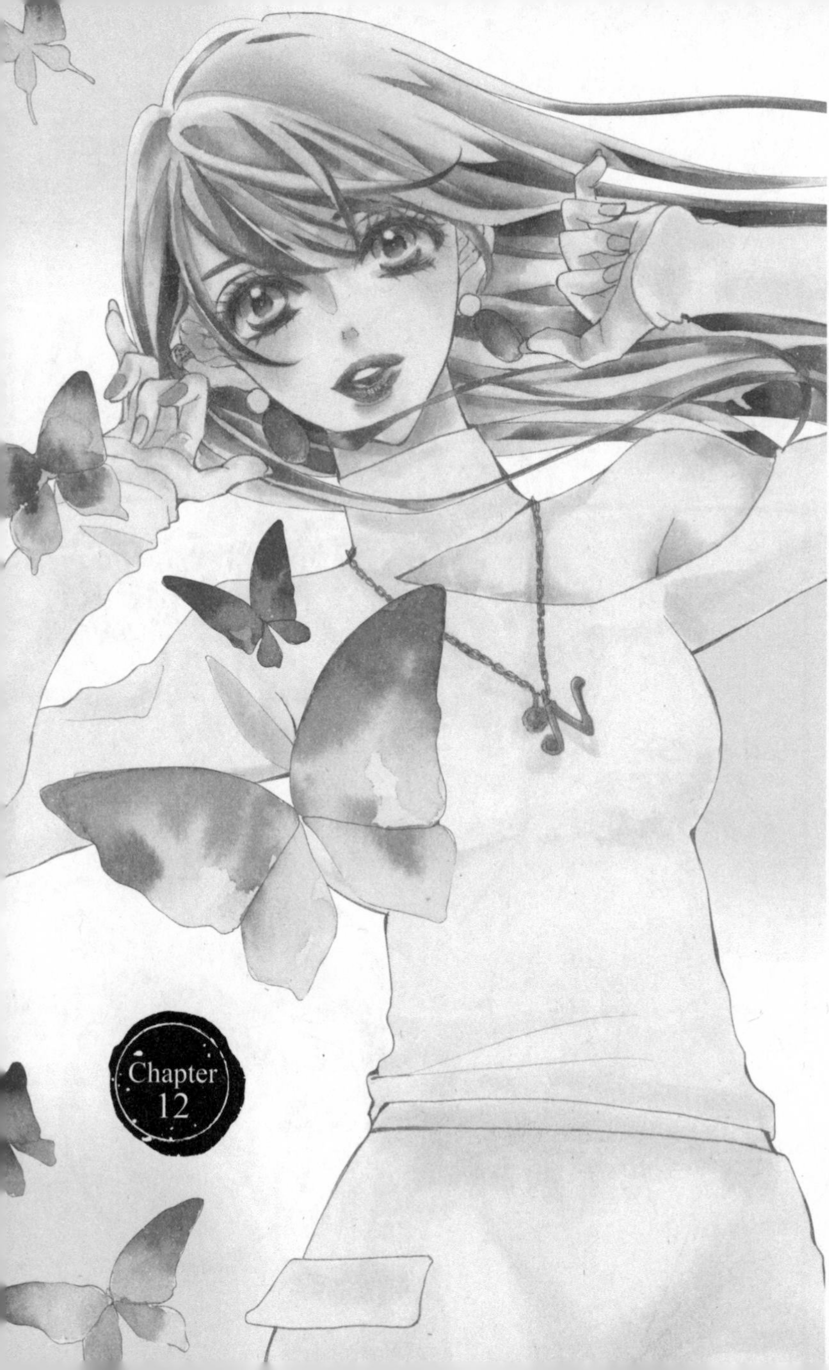
Chapter
12

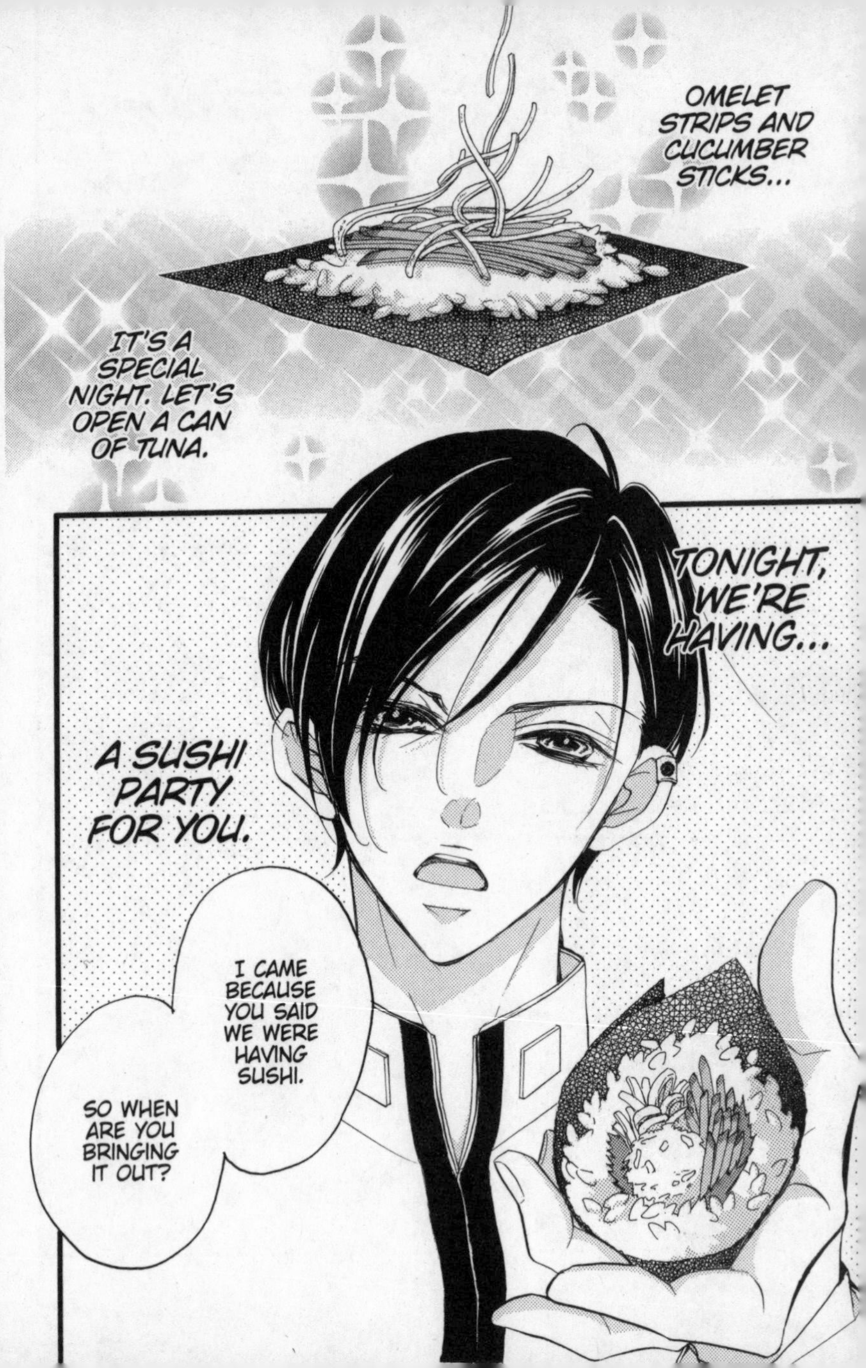
OMELET STRIPS AND CUCUMBER STICKS...
IT'S A SPECIAL NIGHT. LET'S OPEN A CAN OF TUNA.
TONIGHT, WE'RE HAVING...
A SUSHI PARTY FOR YOU.
I CAME BECAUSE YOU SAID WE WERE HAVING SUSHI.
SO WHEN ARE YOU BRINGING IT OUT?

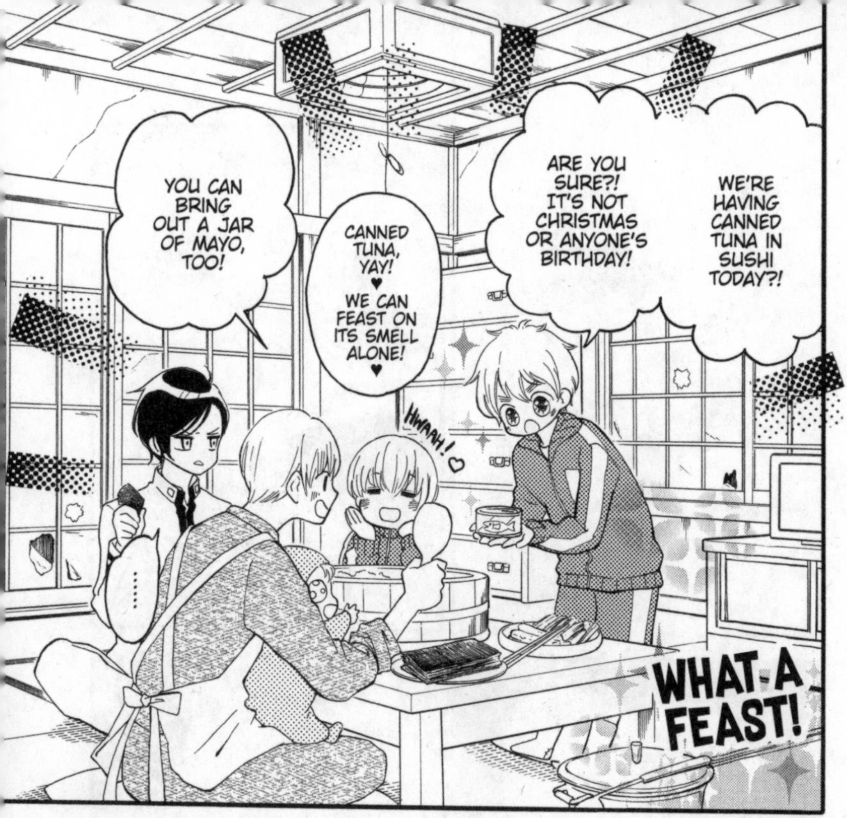
WE'RE HAVING CANNED TUNA IN SUSHI TODAY?!
ARE YOU SURE?! IT'S NOT CHRISTMAS OR ANYONE'S BIRTHDAY!
CANNED TUNA, YAY! ♥ WE CAN FEAST ON ITS SMELL ALONE! ♥
YOU CAN BRING OUT A JAR OF MAYO, TOO!
HWAAH! ♥
WHAT A FEAST!

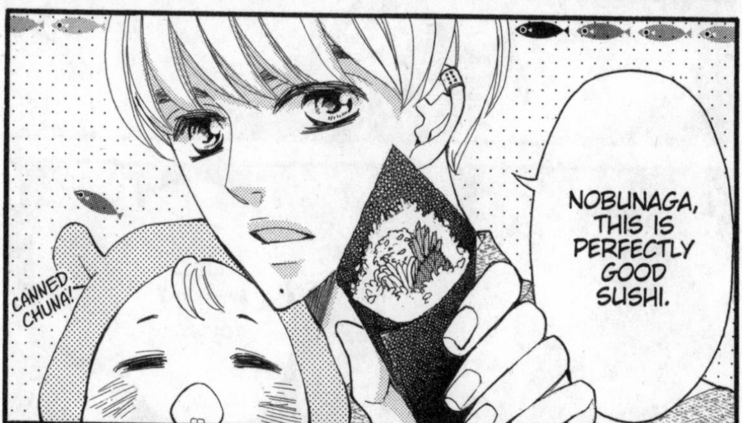
NOBUNAGA, THIS IS PERFECTLY GOOD SUSHI.
CANNED CHUNA!

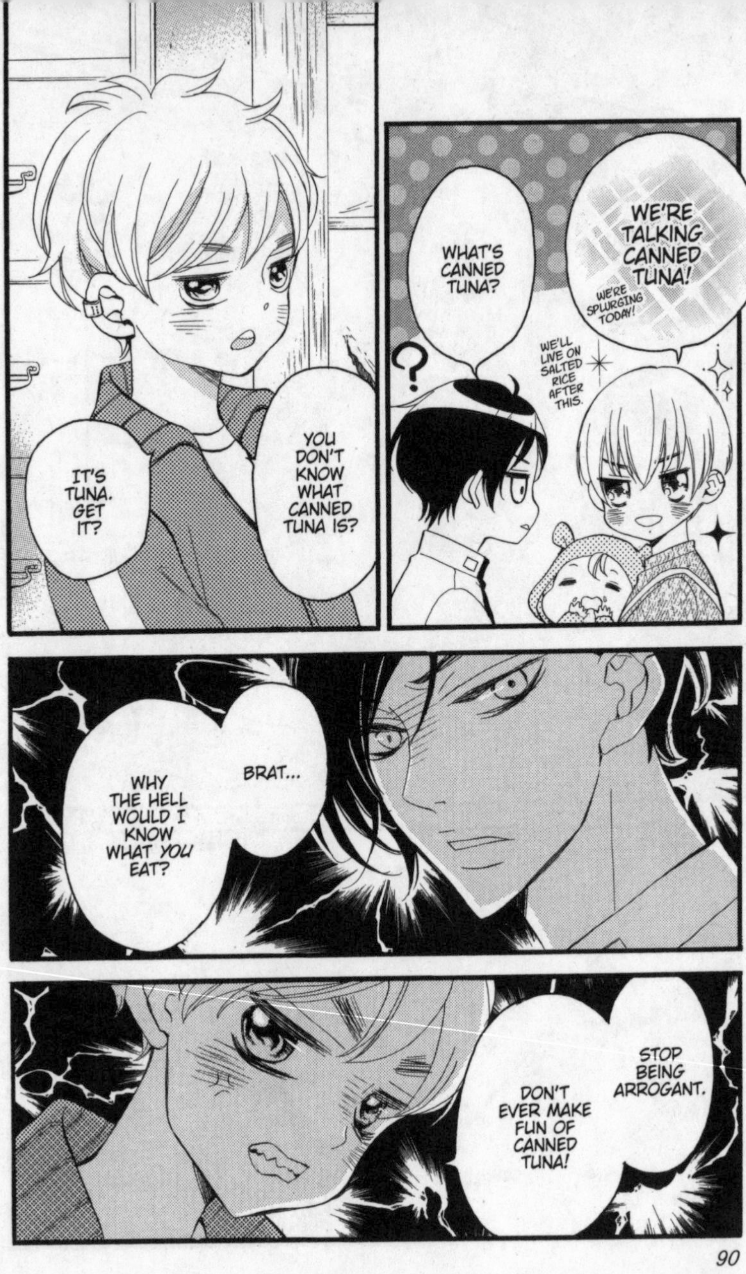
WE'RE TALKING CANNED TUNA!
WE'RE SPLURGING TODAY!
WE'LL LIVE ON SALTED RICE AFTER THIS.
WHAT'S CANNED TUNA?
YOU DON'T KNOW WHAT CANNED TUNA IS?
IT'S TUNA. GET IT?
BRAT...
WHY THE HELL WOULD I KNOW WHAT *YOU* EAT?
STOP BEING ARROGANT.
DON'T EVER MAKE FUN OF CANNED TUNA!

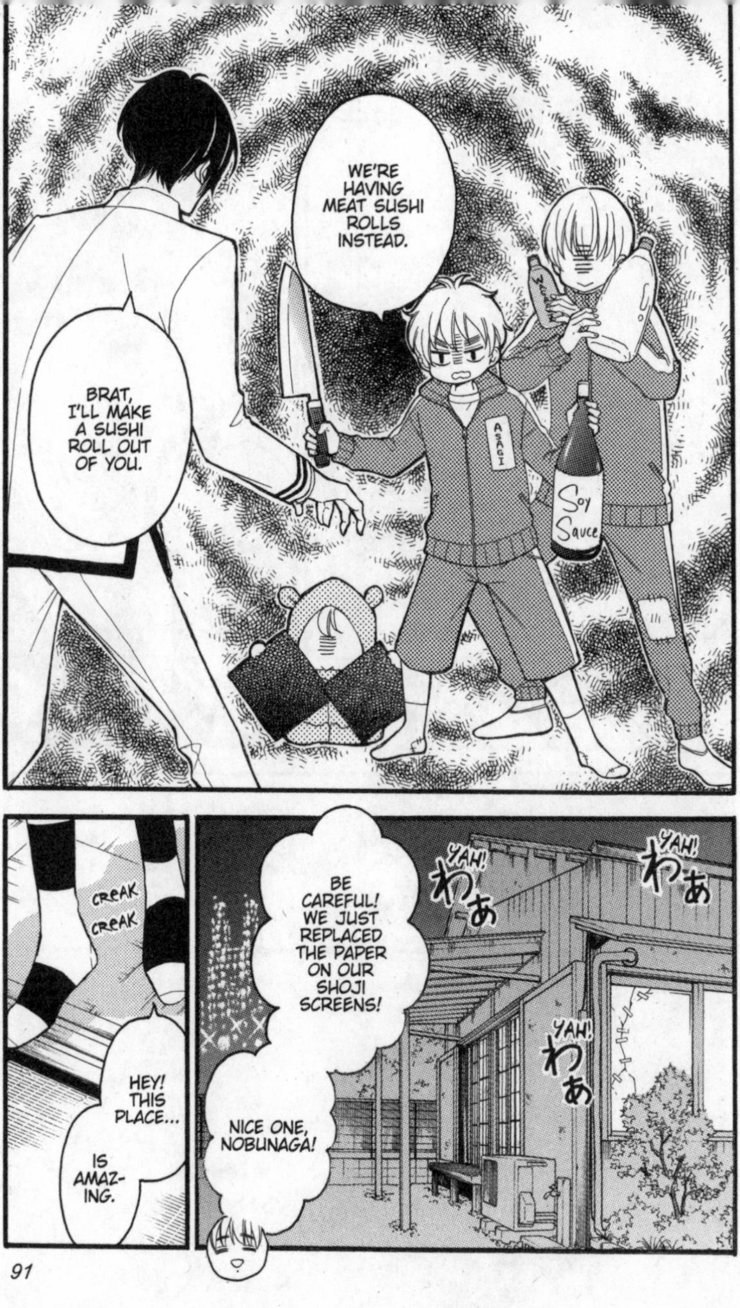
WE'RE HAVING MEAT SUSHI ROLLS INSTEAD.
ASAGI
Soy Sauce
BRAT, I'LL MAKE A SUSHI ROLL OUT OF YOU.
YAH! わあ
YAH! わあ
YAH! わあ
BE CAREFUL! WE JUST REPLACED THE PAPER ON OUR SHOJI SCREENS!
NICE ONE, NOBUNAGA!
CREAK
CREAK
HEY! THIS PLACE...
IS AMAZ-ING.

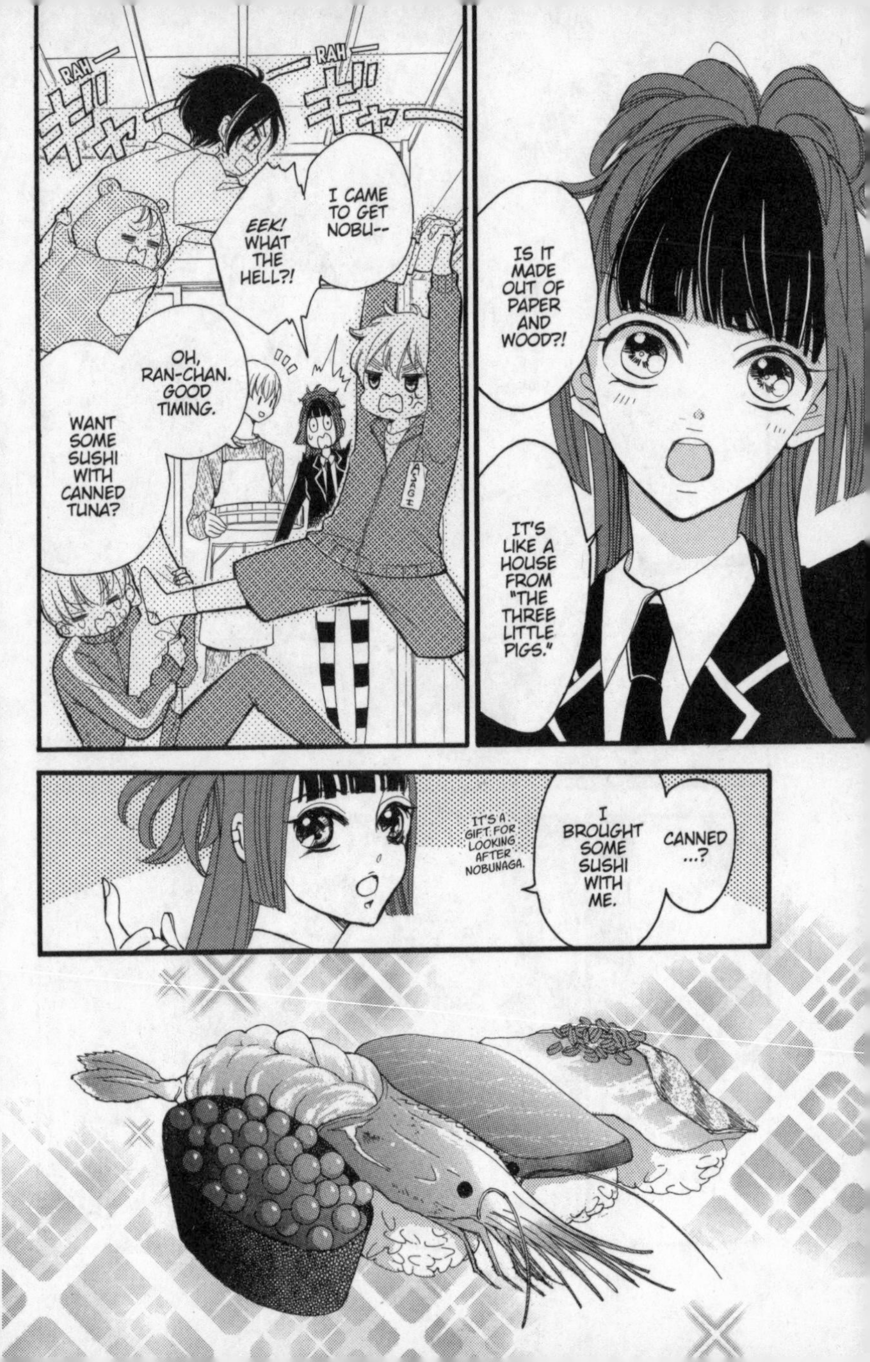
IS IT MADE OUT OF PAPER AND WOOD?!
IT'S LIKE A HOUSE FROM "THE THREE LITTLE PIGS."
ギャー
RAH—
ギャー
RAH—
I CAME TO GET NOBU--
EEK! WHAT THE HELL?!
OH, RAN-CHAN. GOOD TIMING.
WANT SOME SUSHI WITH CANNED TUNA?
ASAGI
CANNED ...?
I BROUGHT SOME SUSHI WITH ME.
IT'S A GIFT FOR LOOKING AFTER NOBUNAGA.

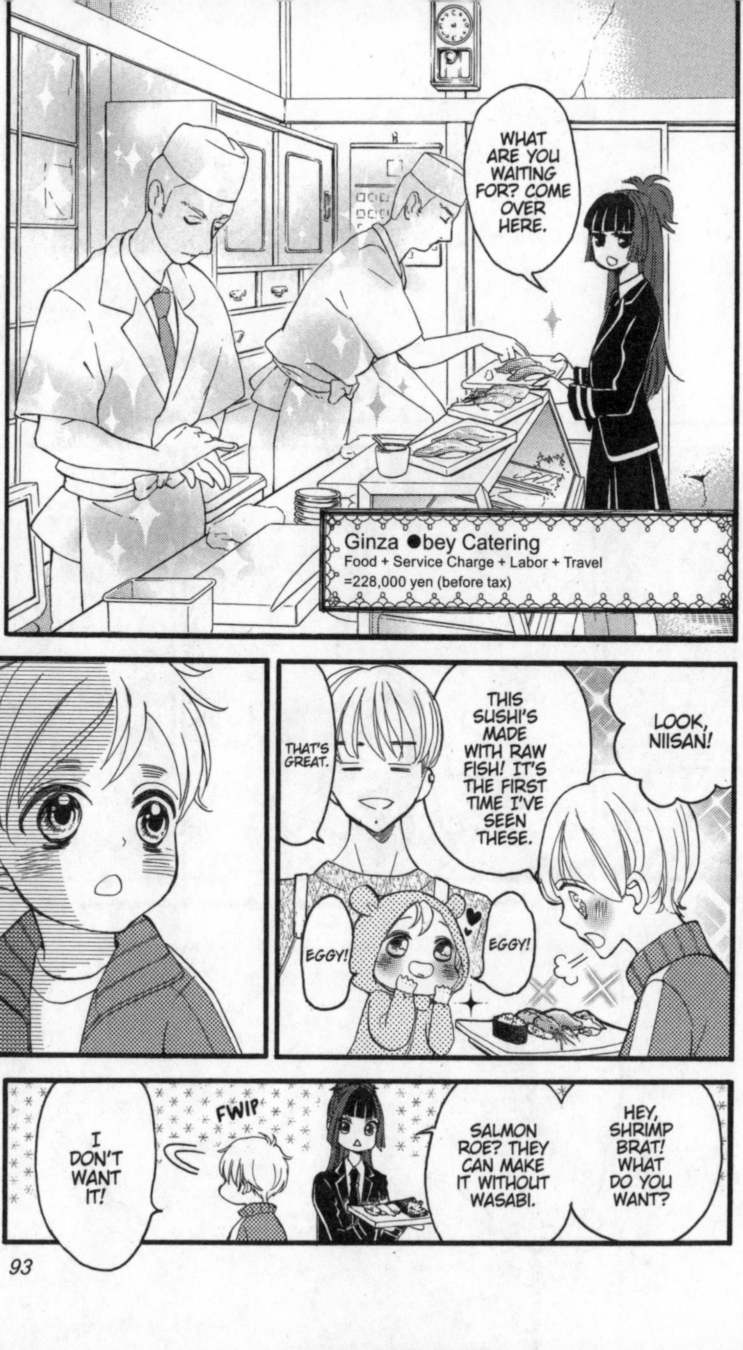
WHAT ARE YOU WAITING FOR? COME OVER HERE.
Ginza ●bey Catering
Food + Service Charge + Labor + Travel
=228,000 yen (before tax)
LOOK, NIISAN!
THIS SUSHI'S MADE WITH RAW FISH! IT'S THE FIRST TIME I'VE SEEN THESE.
THAT'S GREAT.
EGGY!
EGGY!
HEY, SHRIMP BRAT! WHAT DO YOU WANT?
SALMON ROE? THEY CAN MAKE IT WITHOUT WASABI.
FWIP
I DON'T WANT IT!

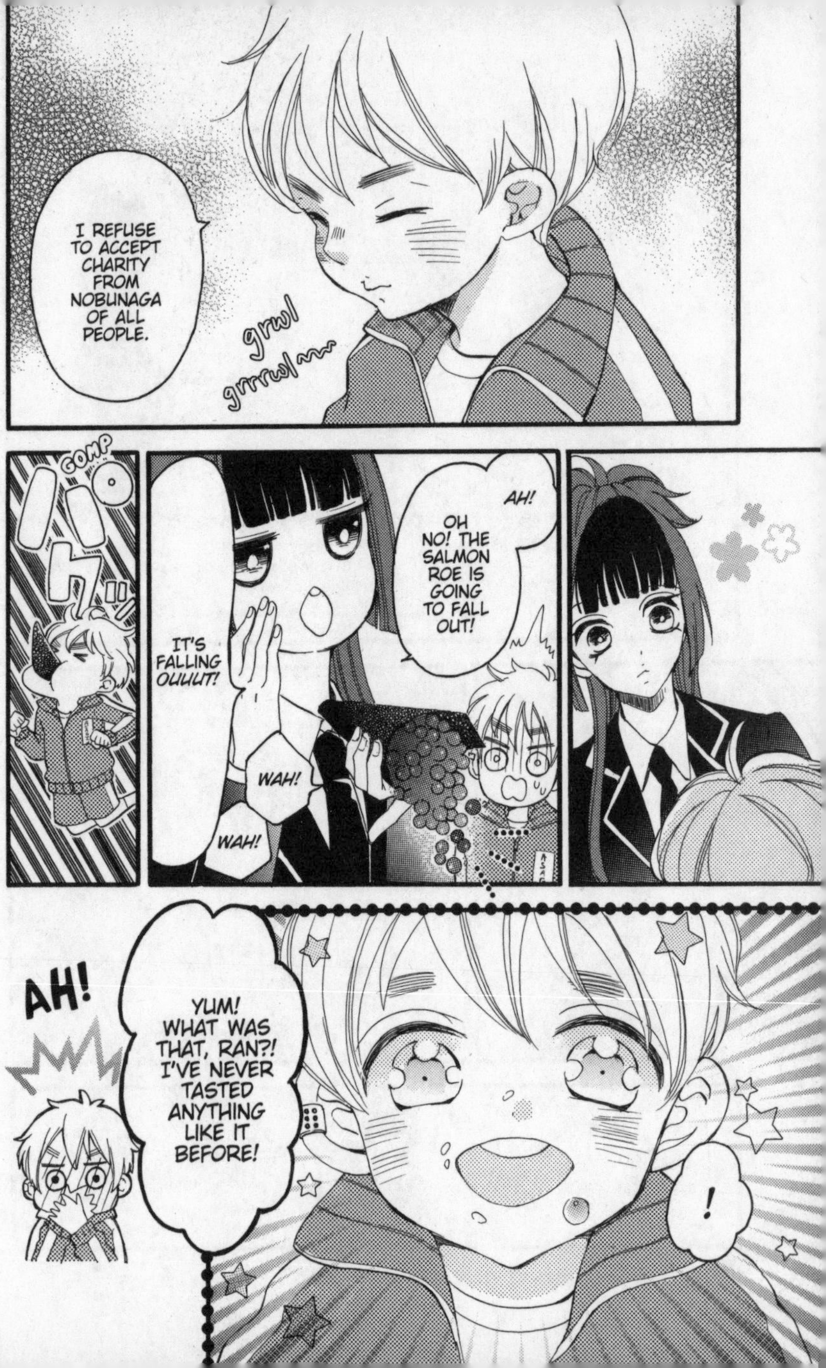
I REFUSE TO ACCEPT CHARITY FROM NOBUNAGA OF ALL PEOPLE.
grwl
grrrwl~~
AH!
OH NO! THE SALMON ROE IS GOING TO FALL OUT!
IT'S FALLING OUUUT!
WAH!
WAH!
GOMP
YUM! WHAT WAS THAT, RAN?! I'VE NEVER TASTED ANYTHING LIKE IT BEFORE!
!
AH!

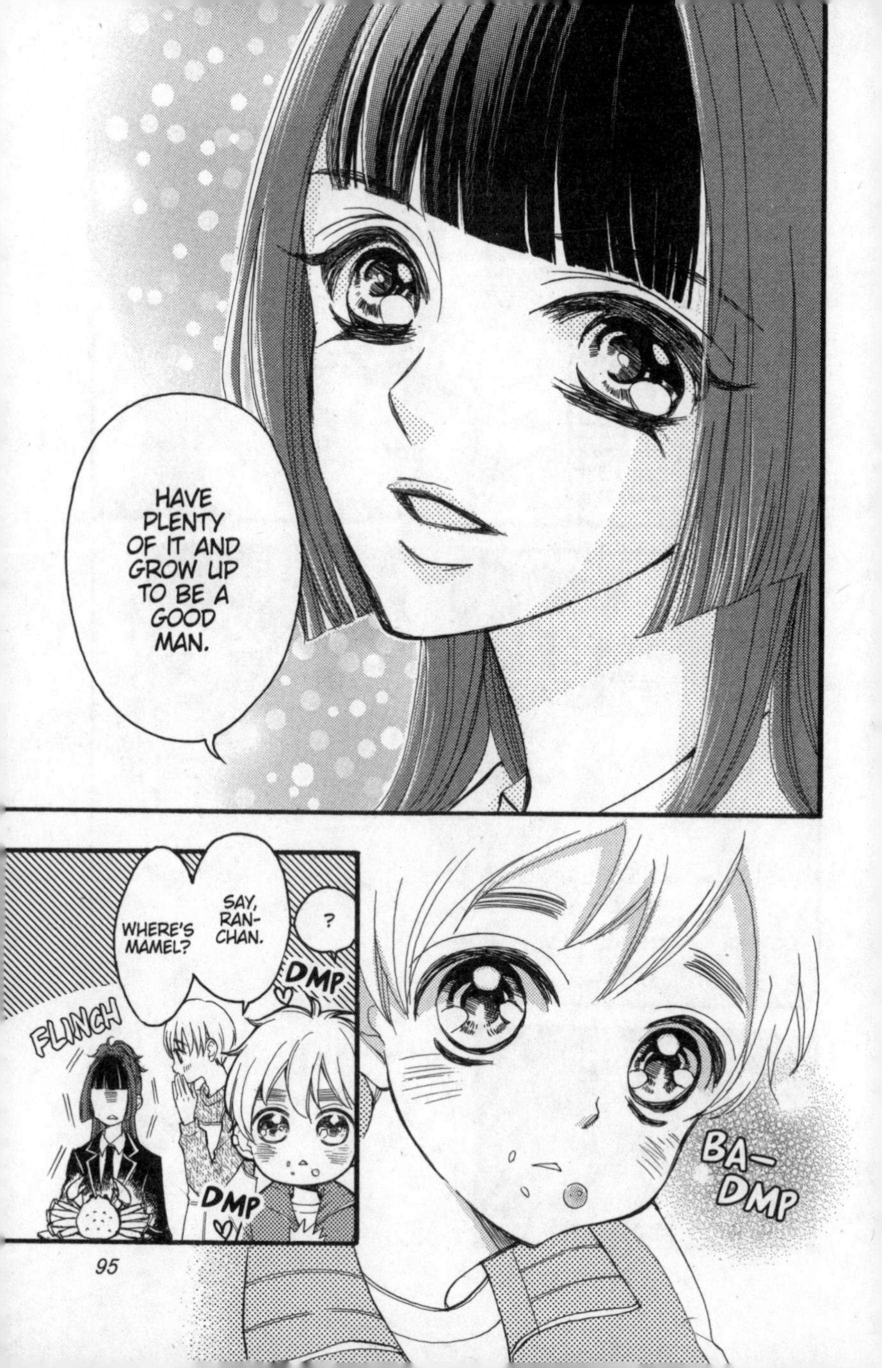
HAVE PLENTY OF IT AND GROW UP TO BE A GOOD MAN.
BA-DMP
?
SAY, RAN-CHAN.
WHERE'S MAMEL?
DMP
FLINCH
DMP

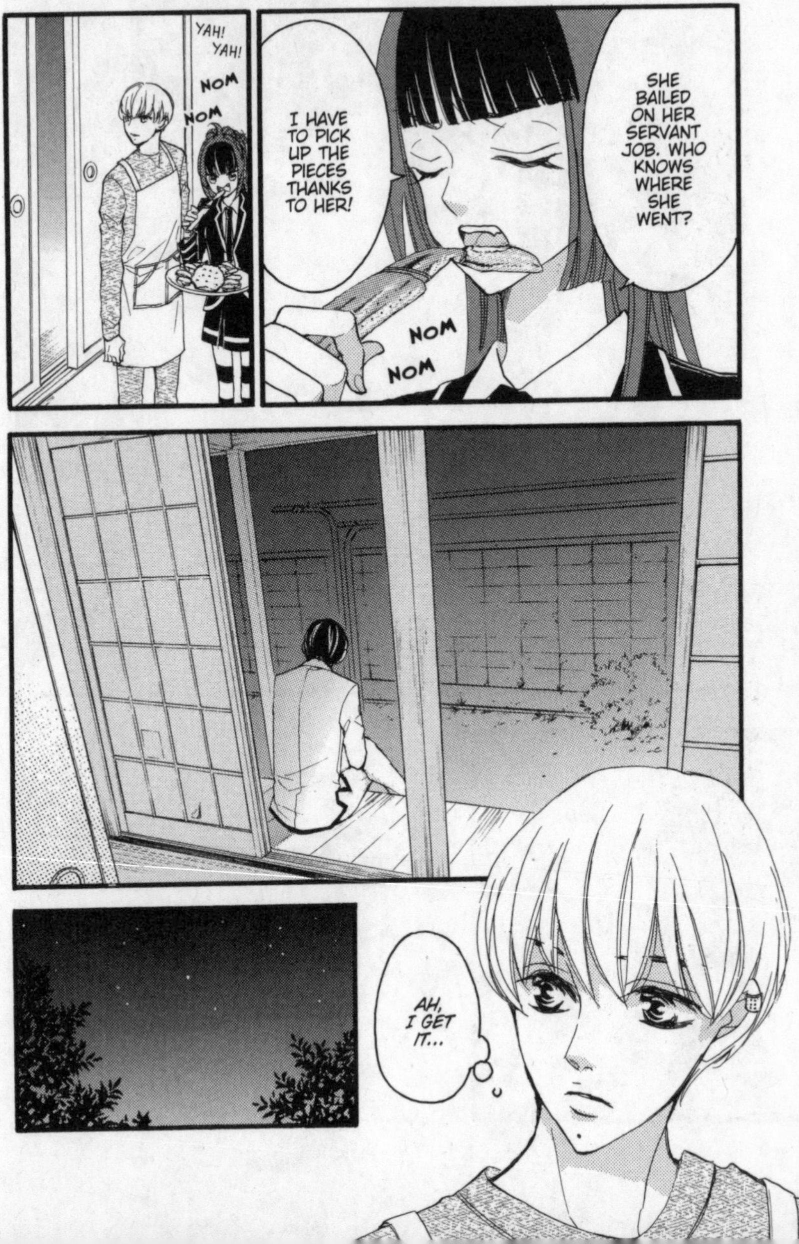
SHE BAILED ON HER SERVANT JOB. WHO KNOWS WHERE SHE WENT?
I HAVE TO PICK UP THE PIECES THANKS TO HER!
NOM NOM
YAH! YAH!
NOM NOM
AH, I GET IT...

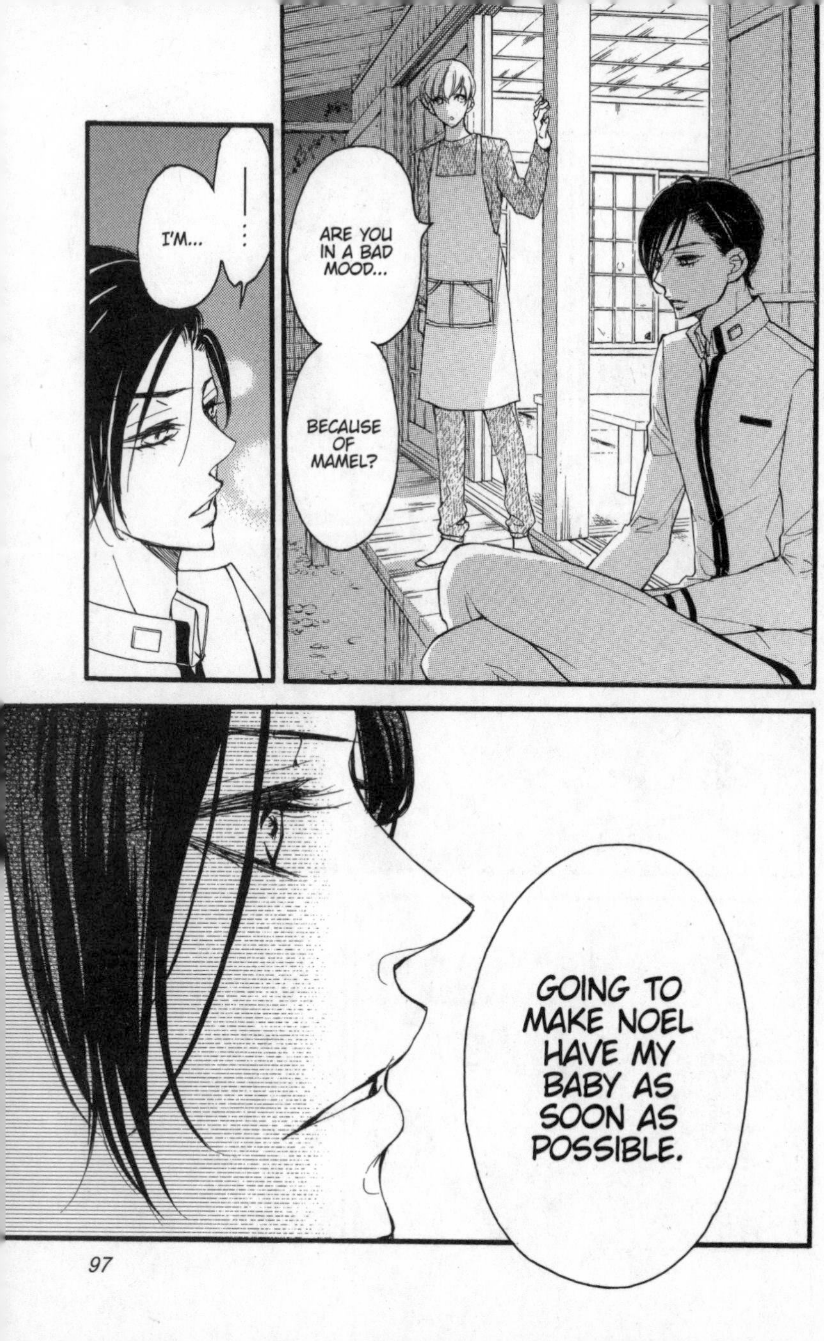
ARE YOU IN A BAD MOOD...
BECAUSE OF MAMEL?
—... I'M...
GOING TO MAKE NOEL HAVE MY BABY AS SOON AS POSSIBLE.

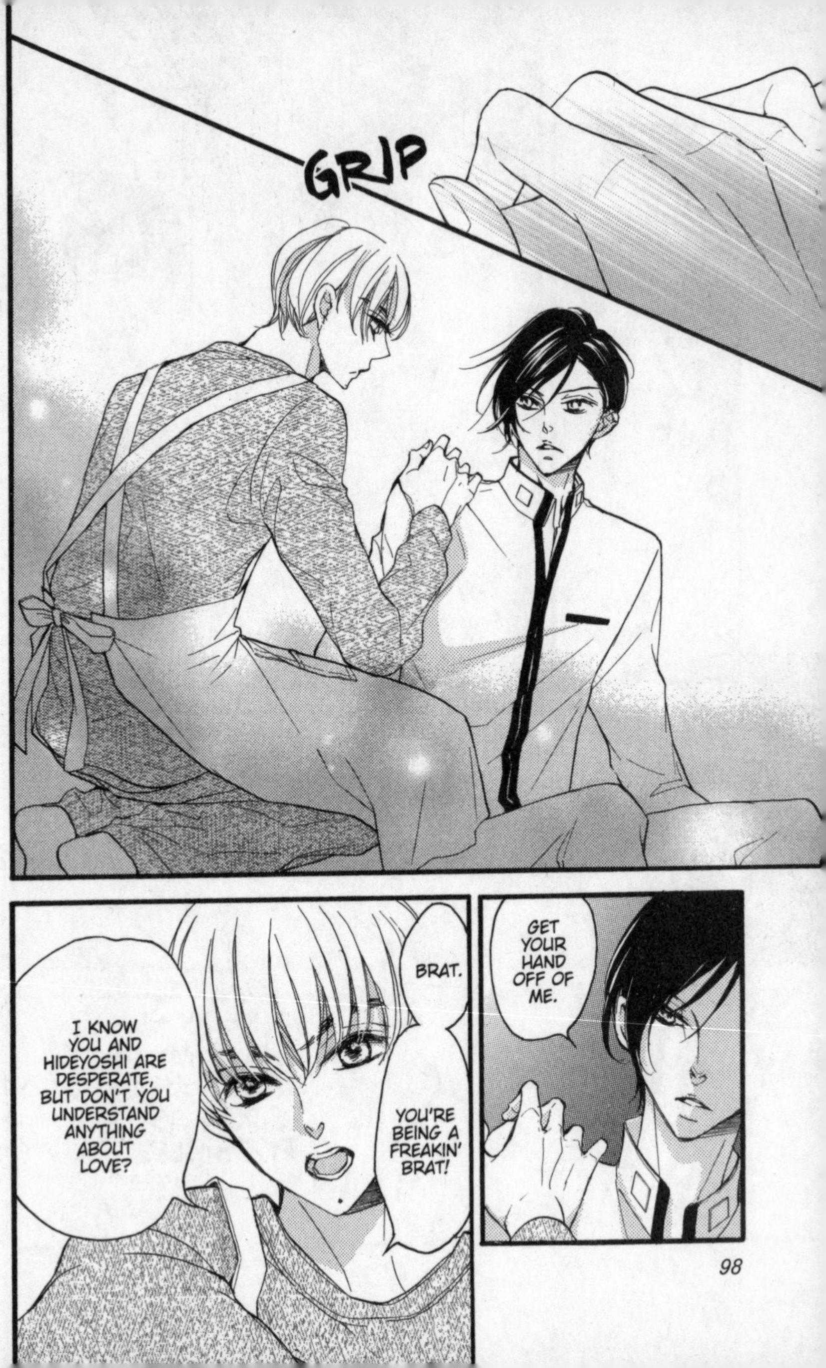
GRIP
GET YOUR HAND OFF OF ME.
BRAT.
YOU'RE BEING A FREAKIN' BRAT!
I KNOW YOU AND HIDEYOSHI ARE DESPERATE, BUT DON'T YOU UNDERSTAND ANYTHING ABOUT LOVE?

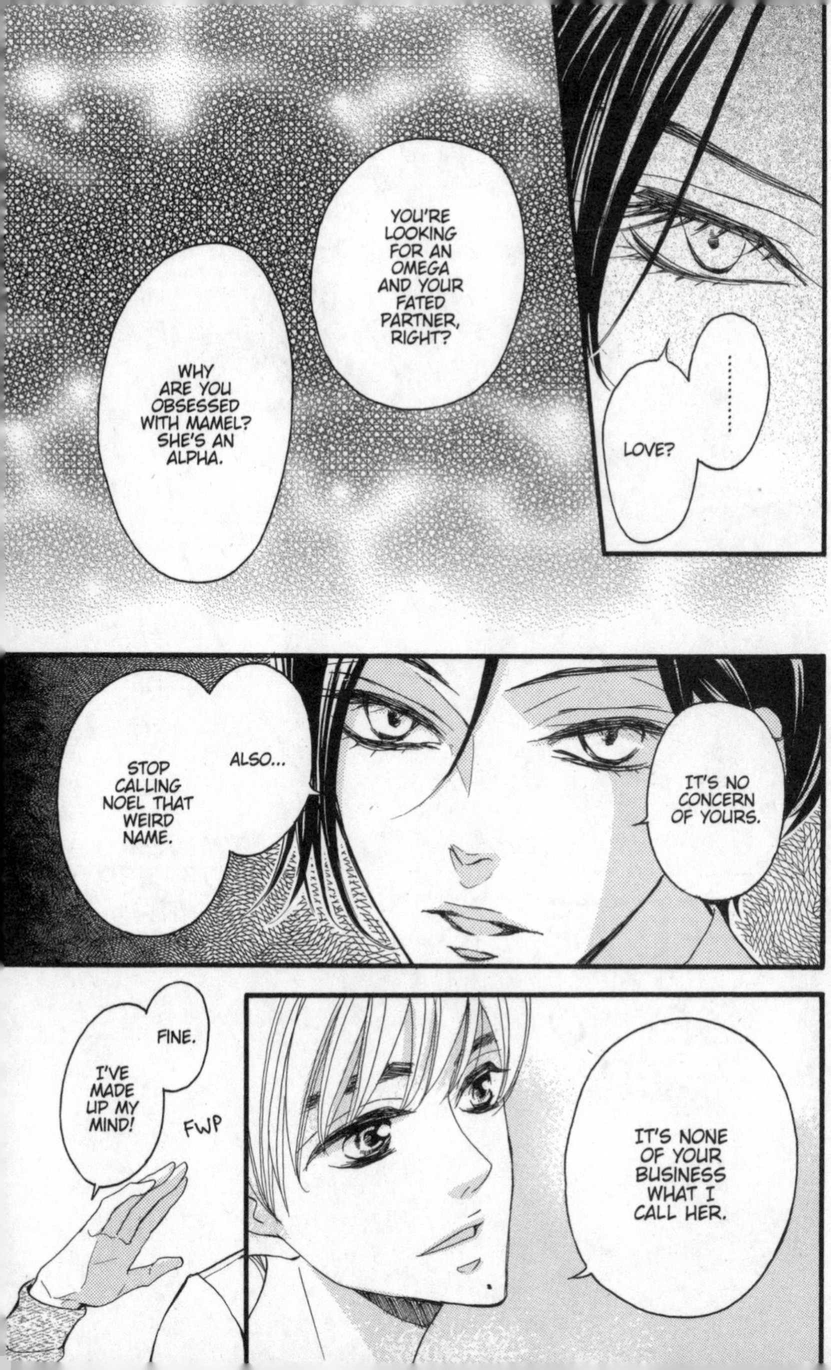
...... LOVE?
YOU'RE LOOKING FOR AN OMEGA AND YOUR FATED PARTNER, RIGHT?
WHY ARE YOU OBSESSED WITH MAMEL? SHE'S AN ALPHA.
IT'S NO CONCERN OF YOURS.
ALSO... STOP CALLING NOEL THAT WEIRD NAME.
IT'S NONE OF YOUR BUSINESS WHAT I CALL HER.
FINE. I'VE MADE UP MY MIND!
FWP

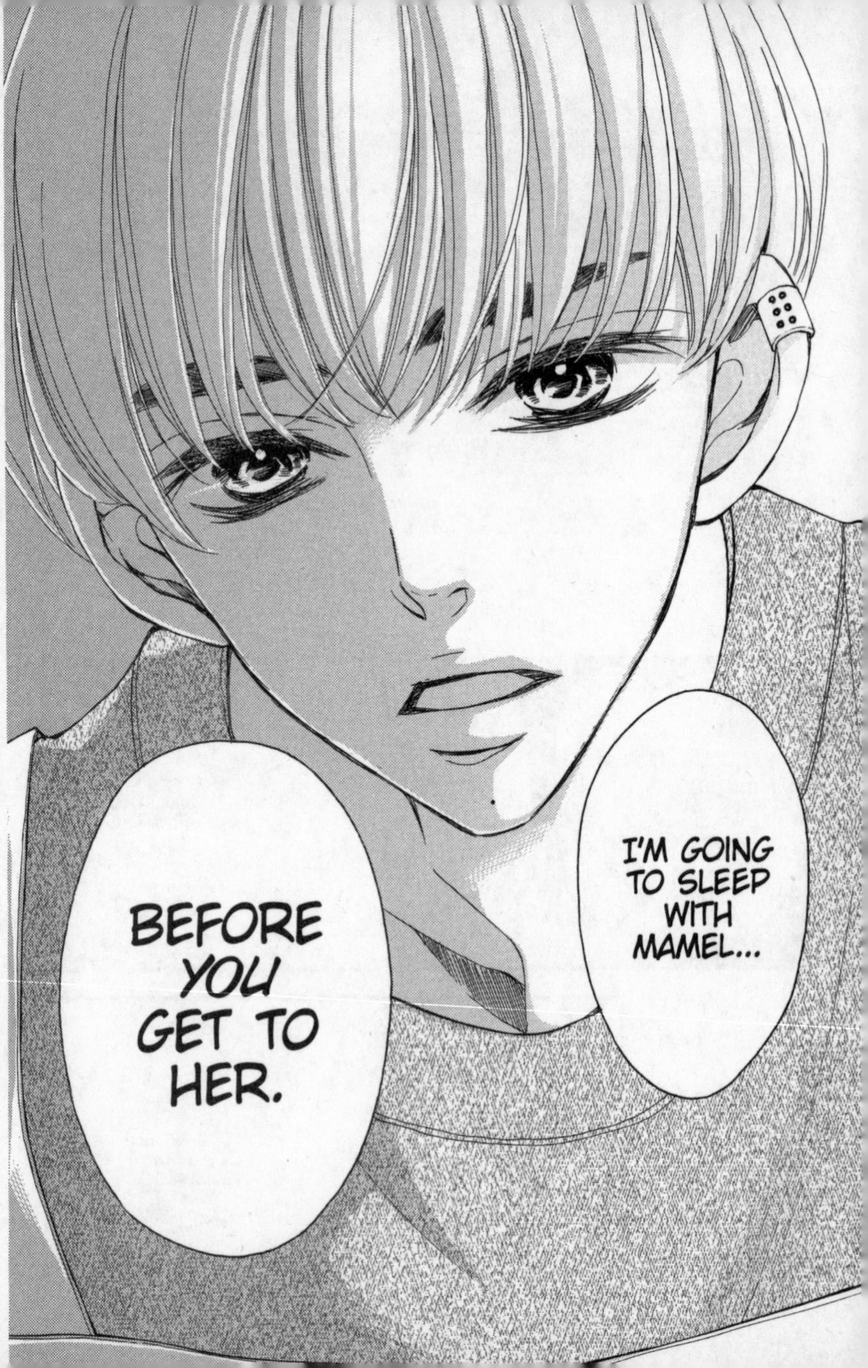
I'M GOING TO SLEEP WITH MAMEL...
BEFORE *YOU* GET TO HER.

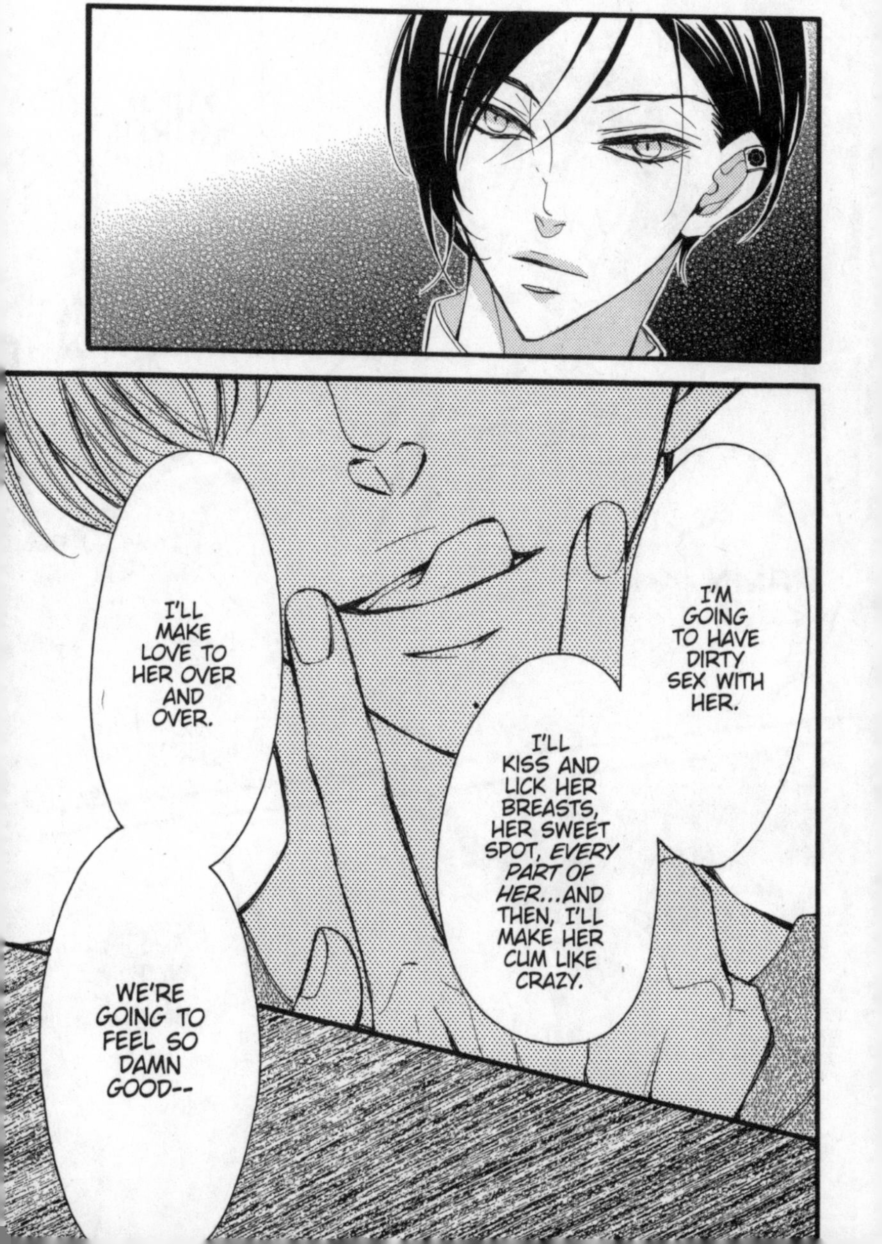
I'M GOING TO HAVE DIRTY SEX WITH HER.
I'LL KISS AND LICK HER BREASTS, HER SWEET SPOT, *EVERY PART OF HER*...AND THEN, I'LL MAKE HER CUM LIKE CRAZY.
I'LL MAKE LOVE TO HER OVER AND OVER.
WE'RE GOING TO FEEL SO DAMN GOOD--

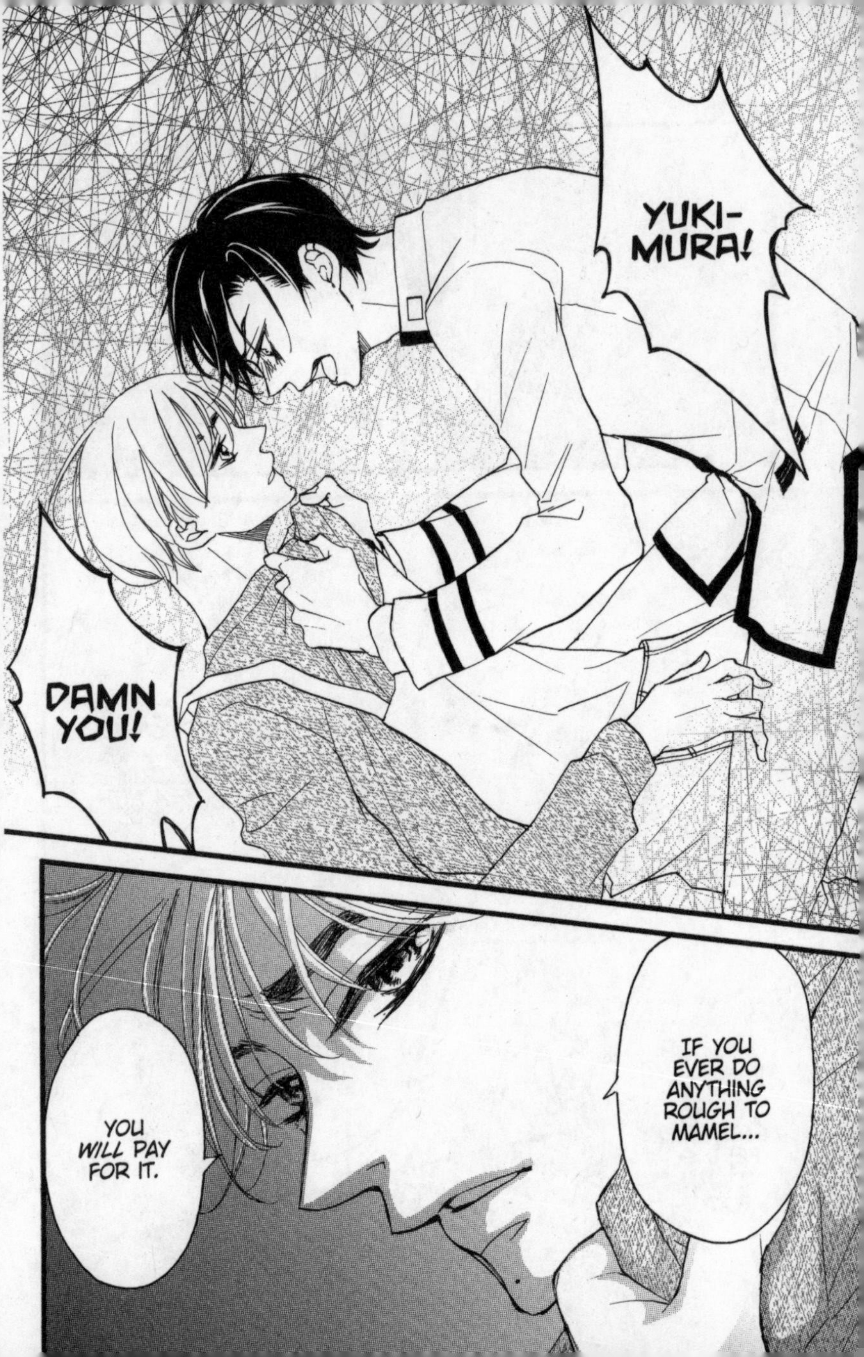
YUKI-MURA!
DAMN YOU!
IF YOU EVER DO ANYTHING ROUGH TO MAMEL...
YOU WILL PAY FOR IT.

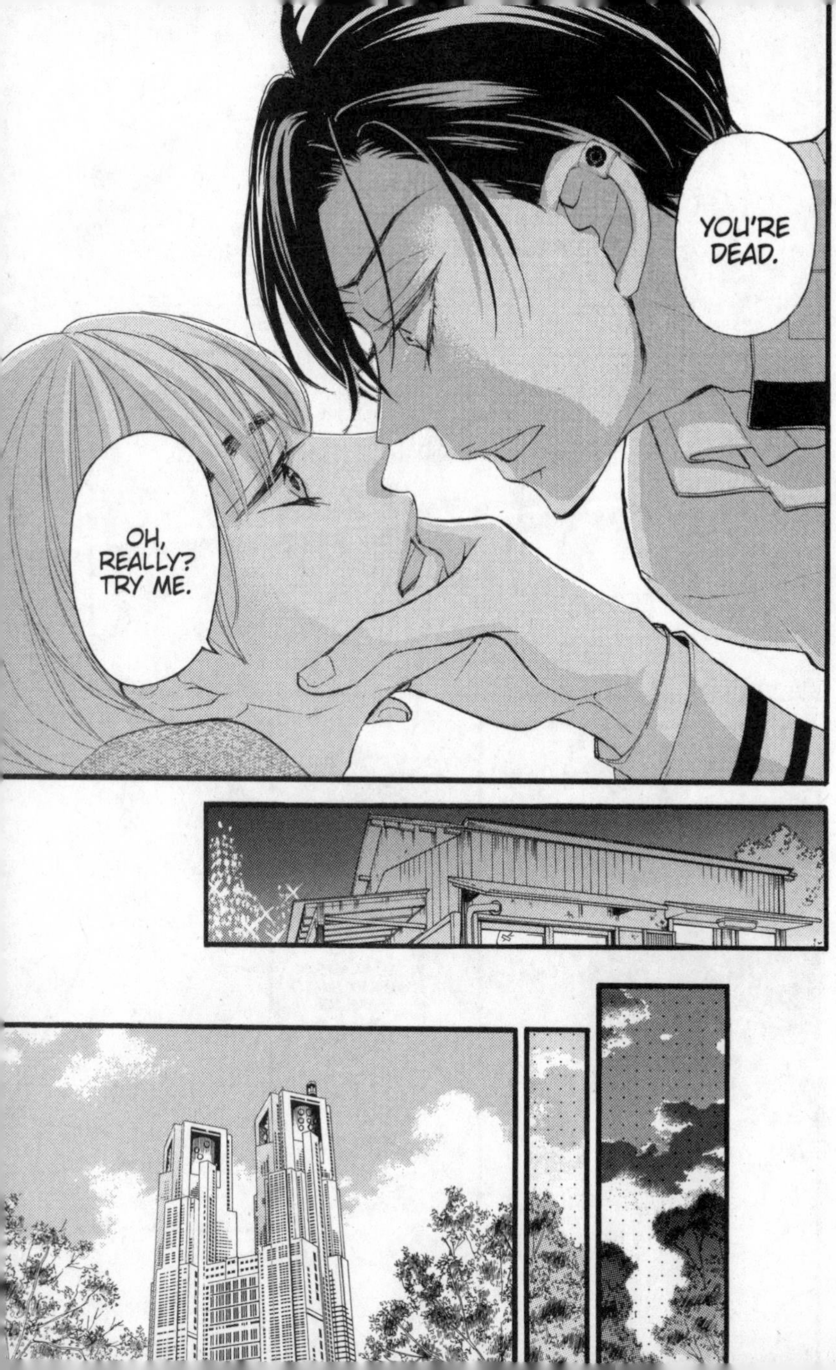
YOU'RE DEAD.
OH, REALLY? TRY ME.

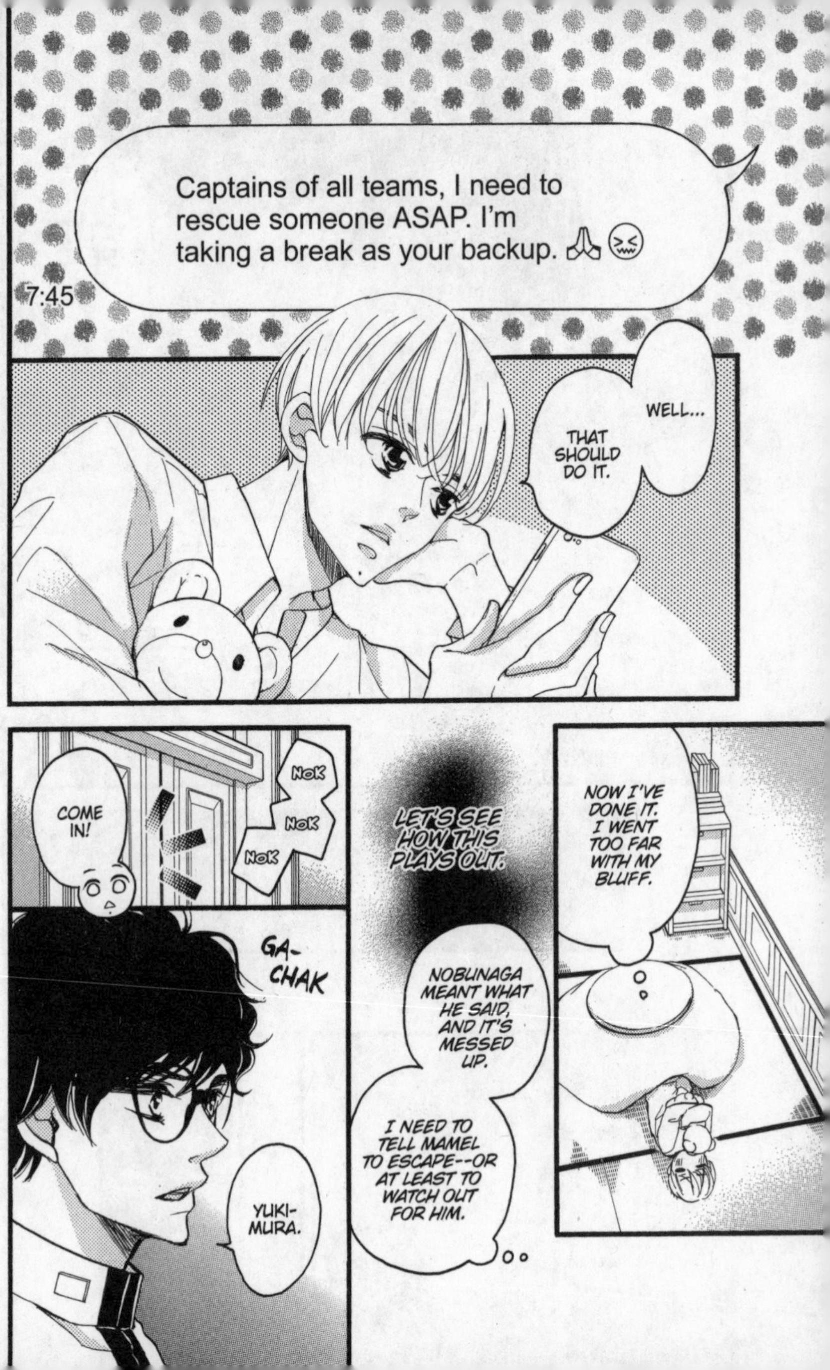
Captains of all teams, I need to rescue someone ASAP. I'm taking a break as your backup. 🙏 😖
7:45
WELL...
THAT SHOULD DO IT.
NOW I'VE DONE IT. I WENT TOO FAR WITH MY BLUFF.
LET'S SEE HOW THIS PLAYS OUT.
NOBUNAGA MEANT WHAT HE SAID, AND IT'S MESSED UP.
I NEED TO TELL MAMEL TO ESCAPE--OR AT LEAST TO WATCH OUT FOR HIM.
NOK
NOK
NOK
COME IN!
GA-CHAK
YUKI-MURA.

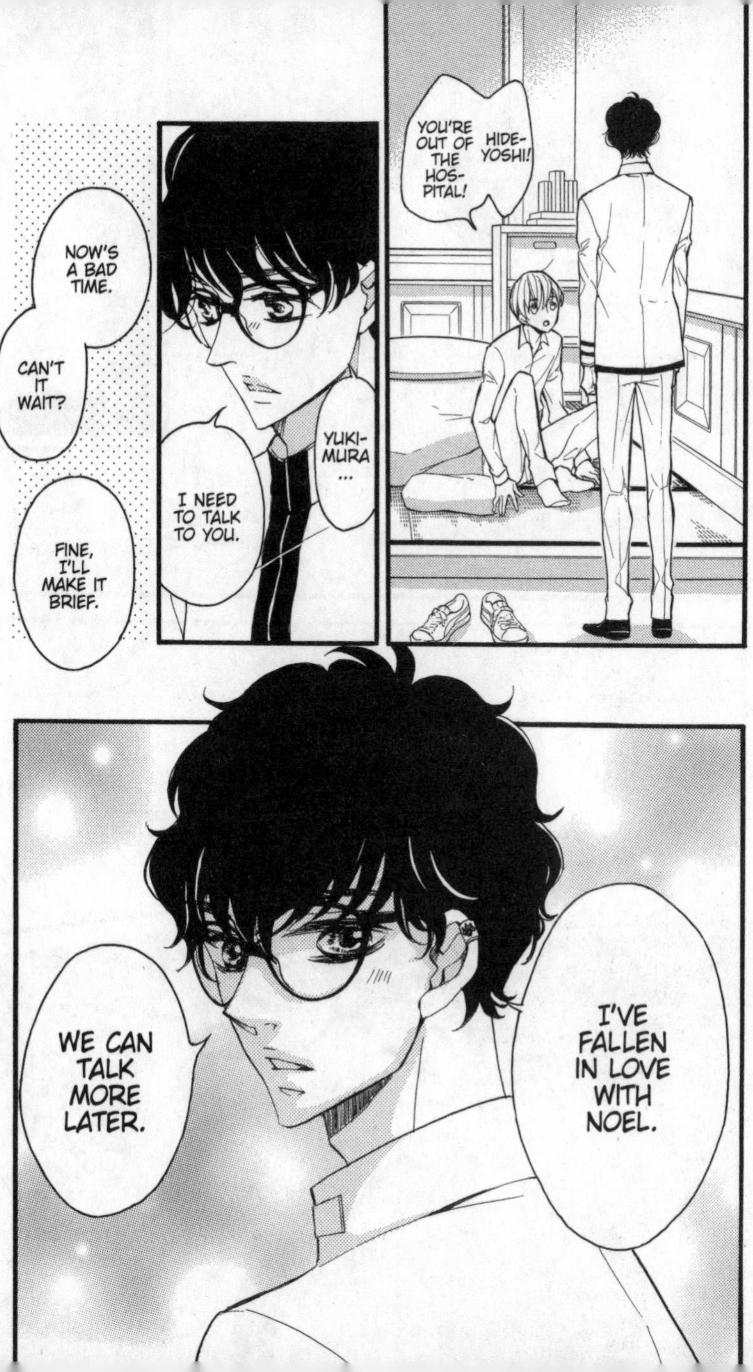
HIDE-YOSHI!
YOU'RE OUT OF THE HOS-PITAL!
YUKI-MURA ...
I NEED TO TALK TO YOU.
NOW'S A BAD TIME.
CAN'T IT WAIT?
FINE, I'LL MAKE IT BRIEF.
I'VE FALLEN IN LOVE WITH NOEL.
WE CAN TALK MORE LATER.

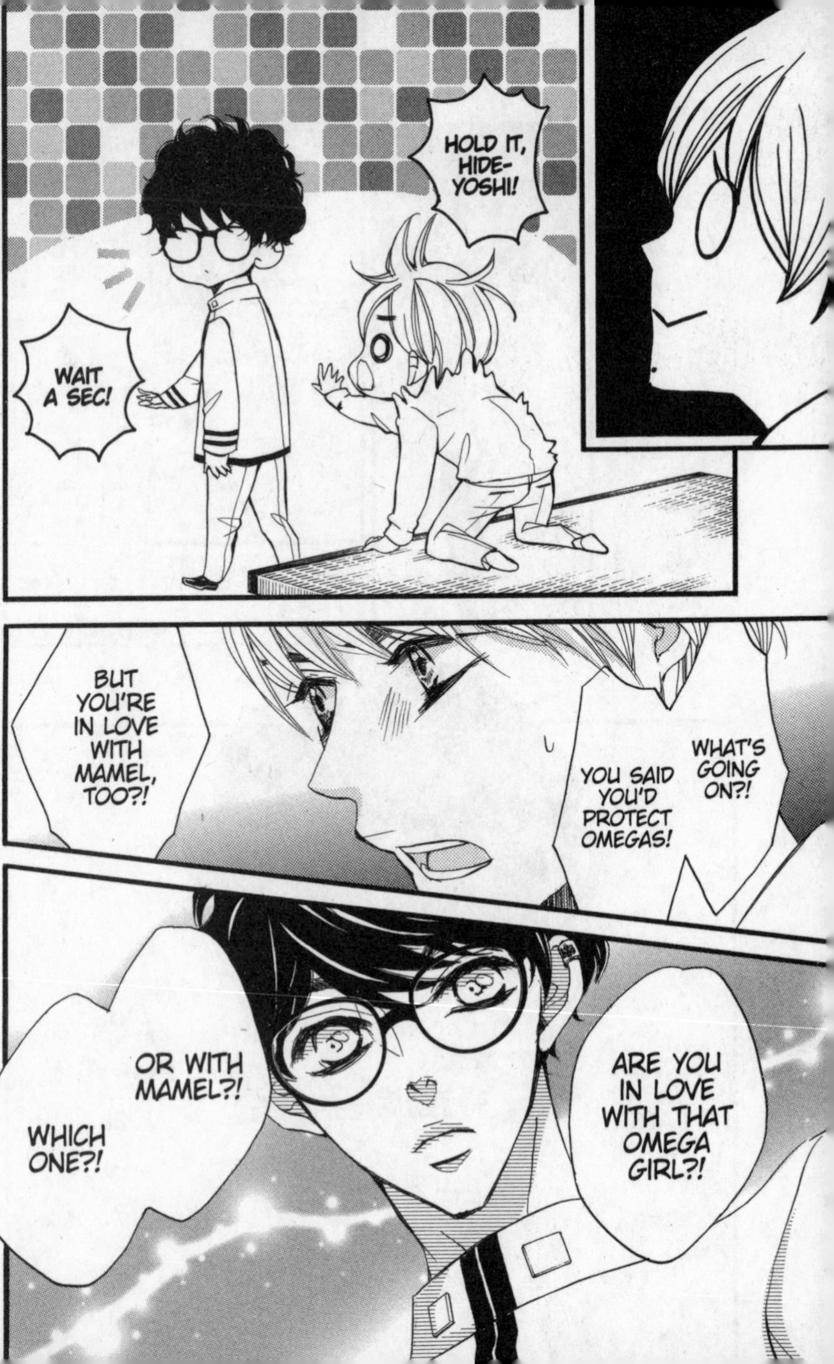
HOLD IT, HIDE-YOSHI!
WAIT A SEC!
WHAT'S GOING ON?!
YOU SAID YOU'D PROTECT OMEGAS!
BUT YOU'RE IN LOVE WITH MAMEL, TOO?!
ARE YOU IN LOVE WITH THAT OMEGA GIRL?!
OR WITH MAMEL?!
WHICH ONE?!

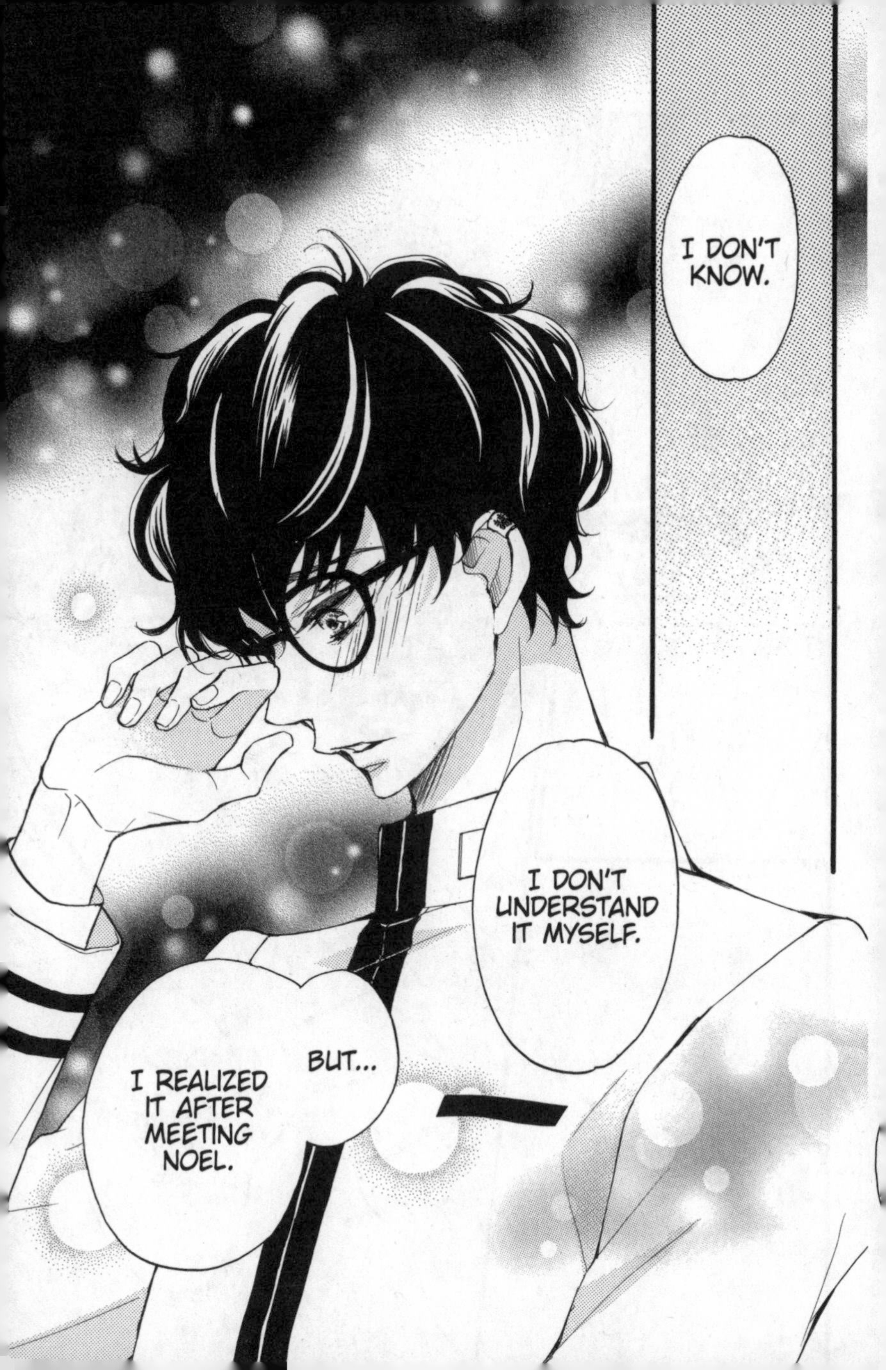
I DON'T KNOW.
I DON'T UNDERSTAND IT MYSELF.
BUT...
I REALIZED IT AFTER MEETING NOEL.

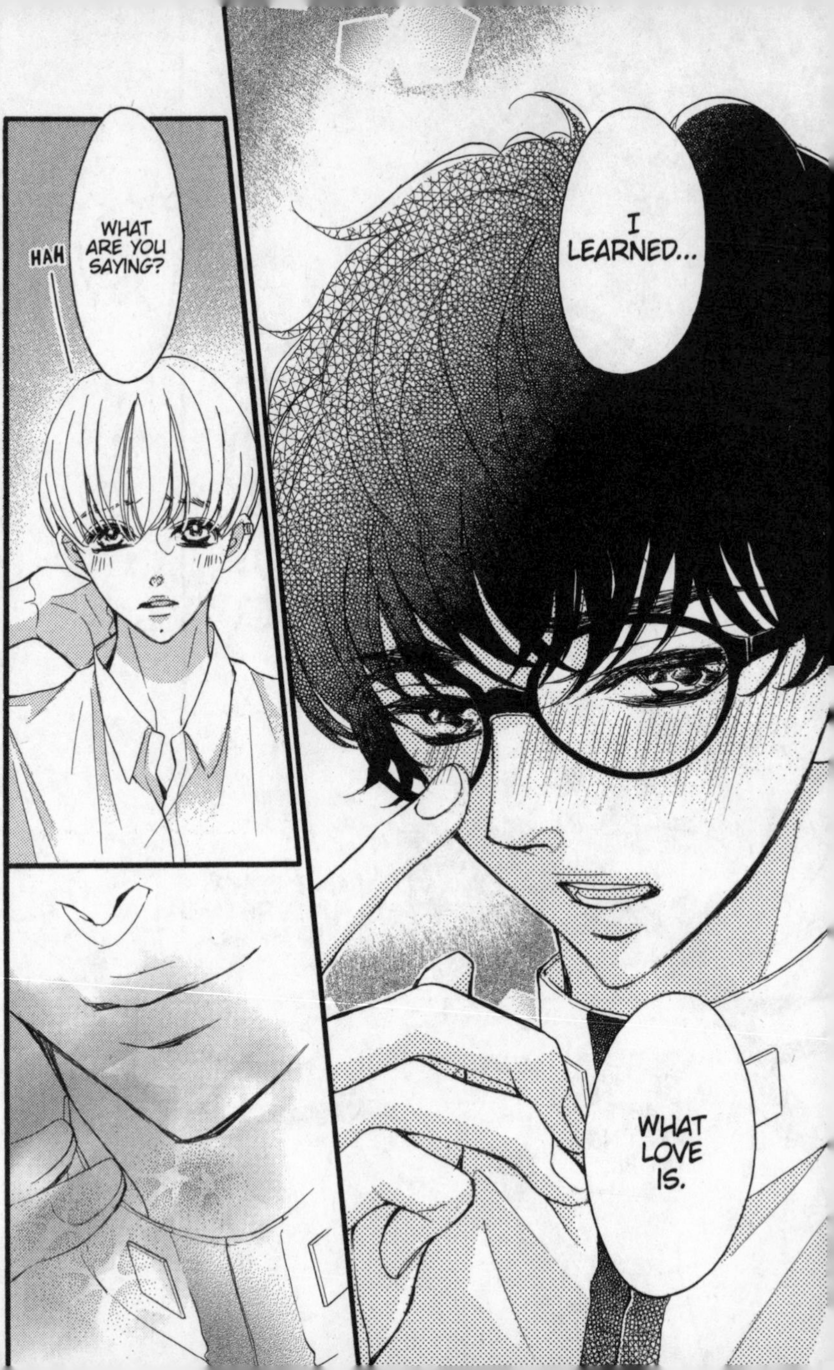
I LEARNED...
WHAT LOVE IS.
WHAT ARE YOU SAYING?
HAH

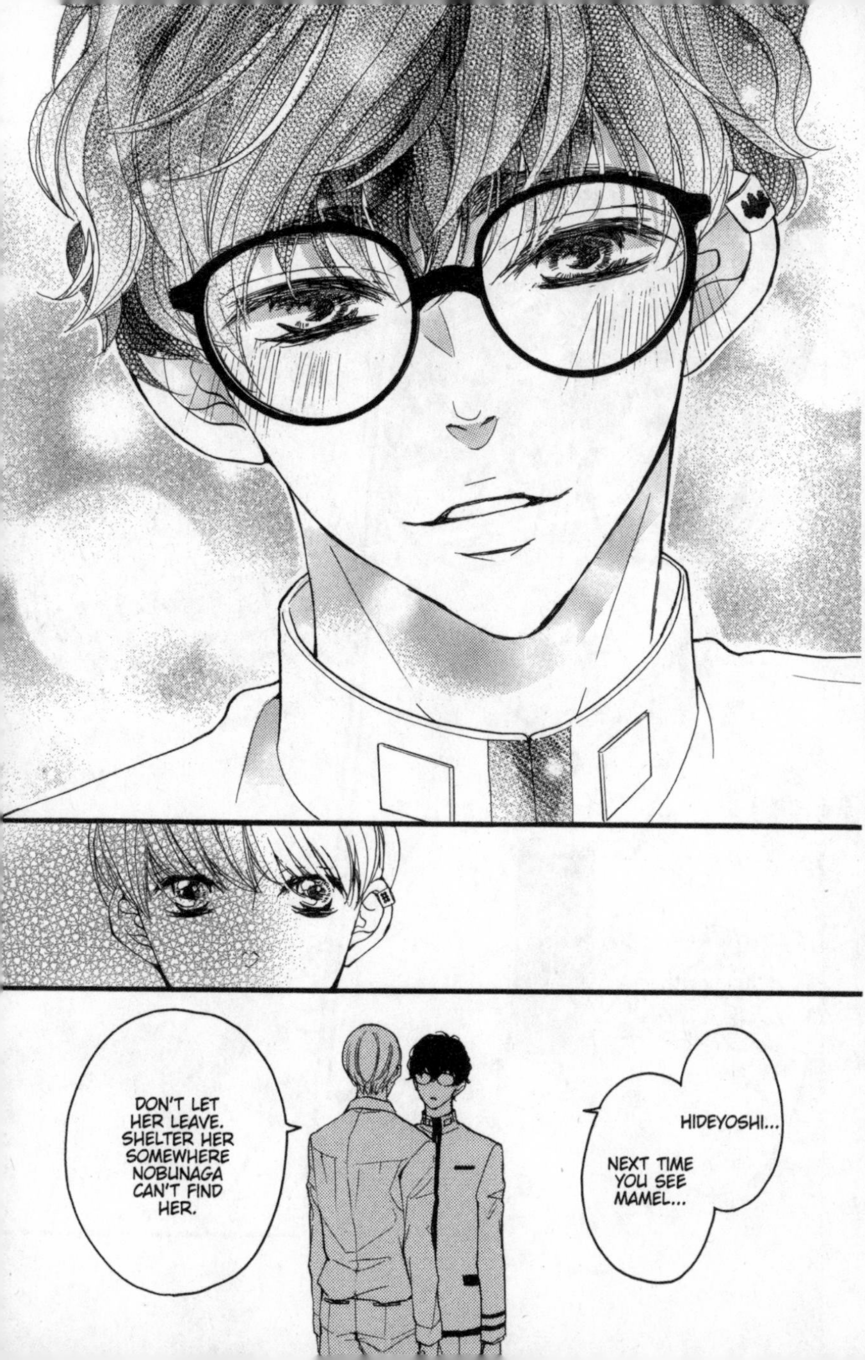
HIDEYOSHI...
NEXT TIME YOU SEE MAMEL...
DON'T LET HER LEAVE. SHELTER HER SOMEWHERE NOBUNAGA CAN'T FIND HER.

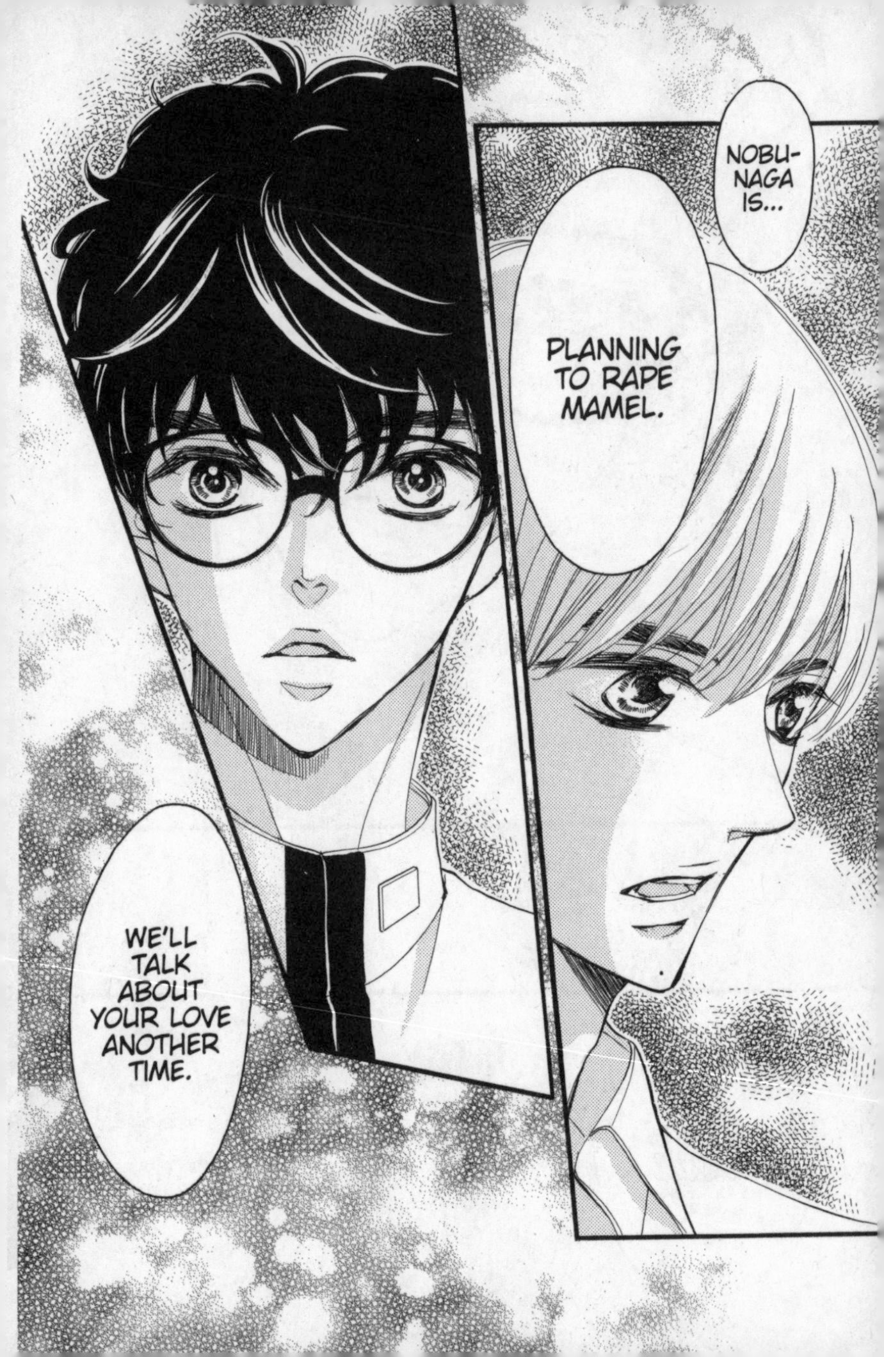
NOBU-NAGA IS...
PLANNING TO RAPE MAMEL.
WE'LL TALK ABOUT YOUR LOVE ANOTHER TIME.

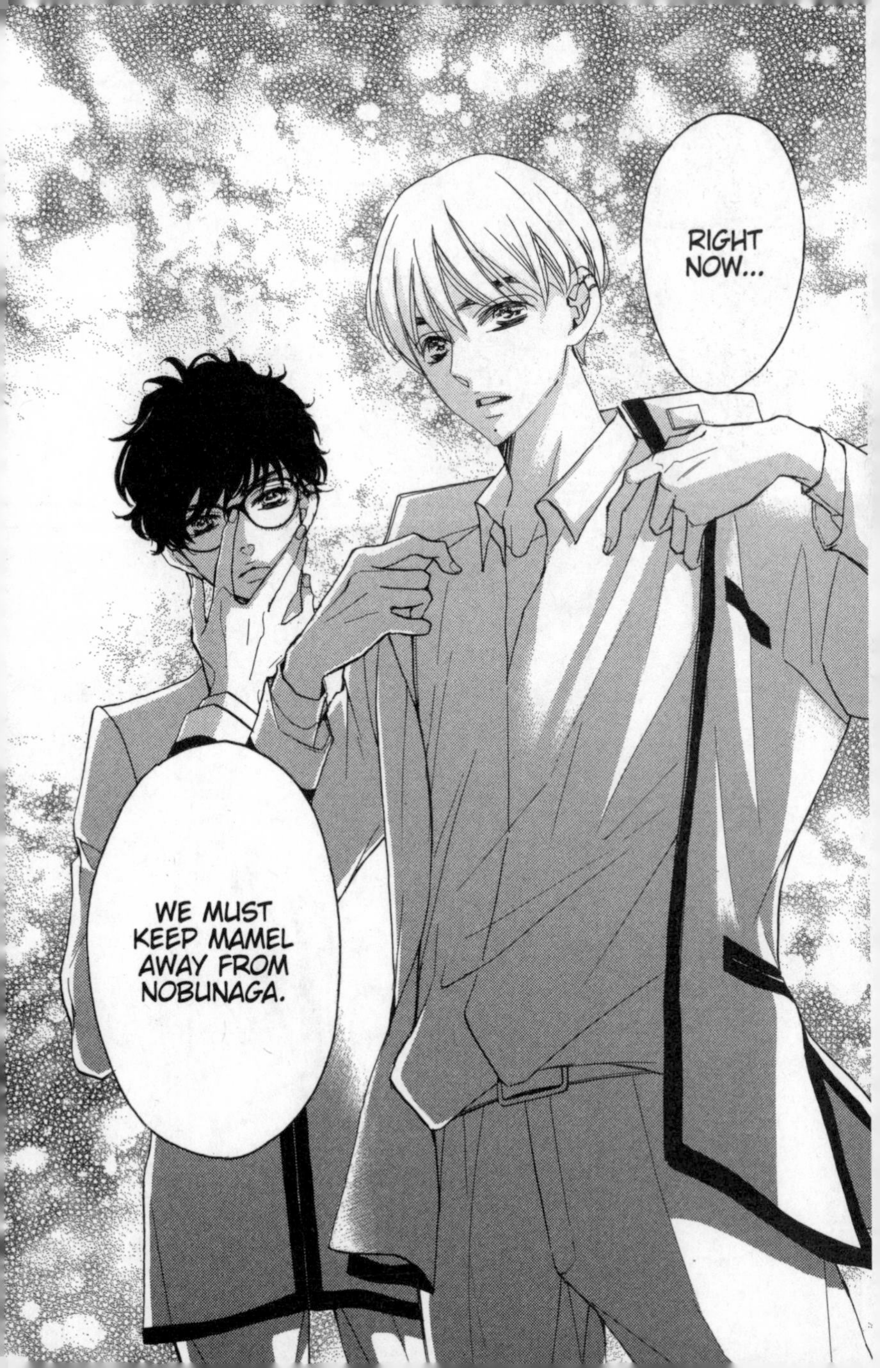
RIGHT NOW...
WE MUST KEEP MAMEL AWAY FROM NOBUNAGA.

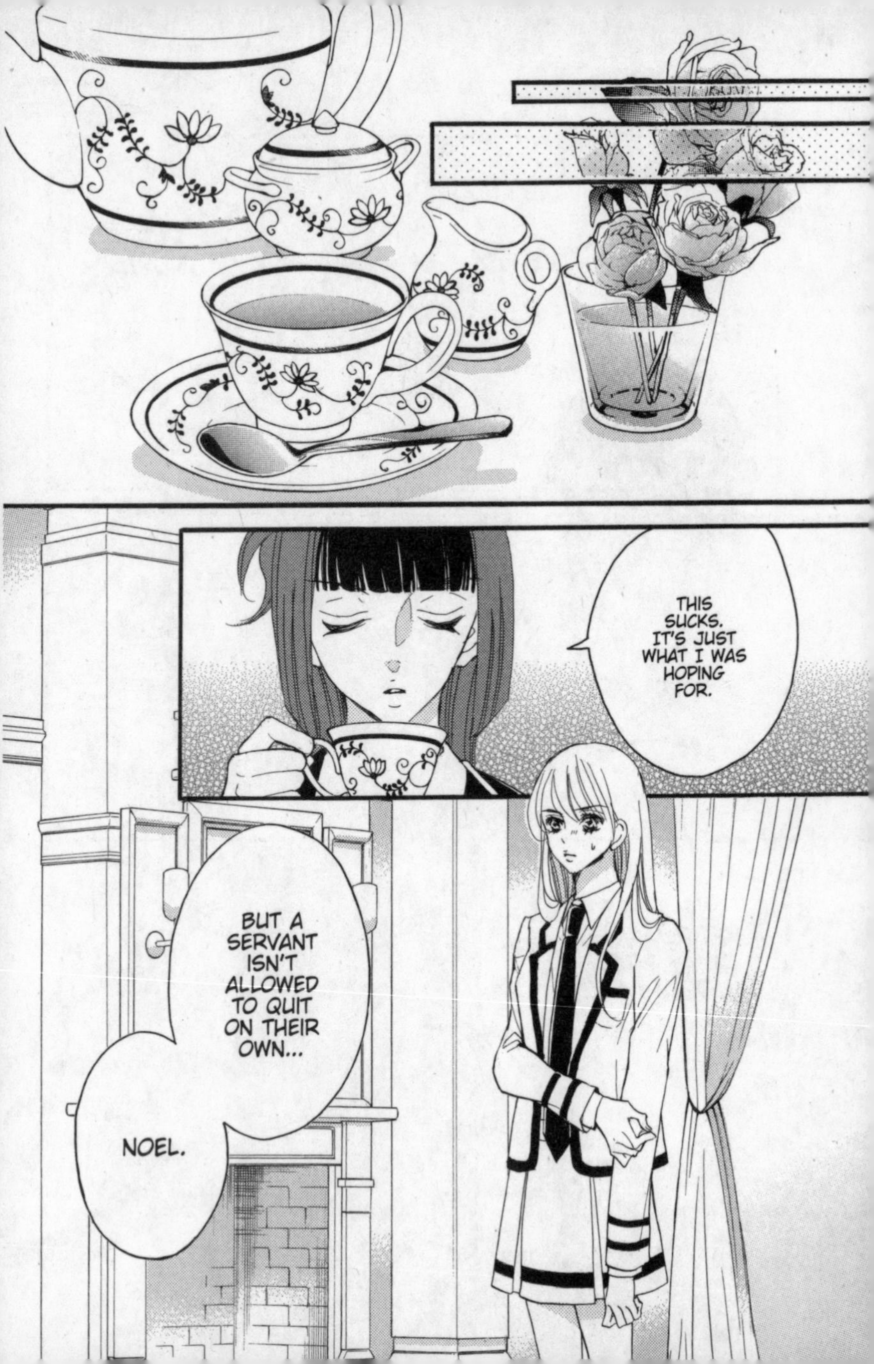
THIS SUCKS. IT'S JUST WHAT I WAS HOPING FOR.
BUT A SERVANT ISN'T ALLOWED TO QUIT ON THEIR OWN...
NOEL.

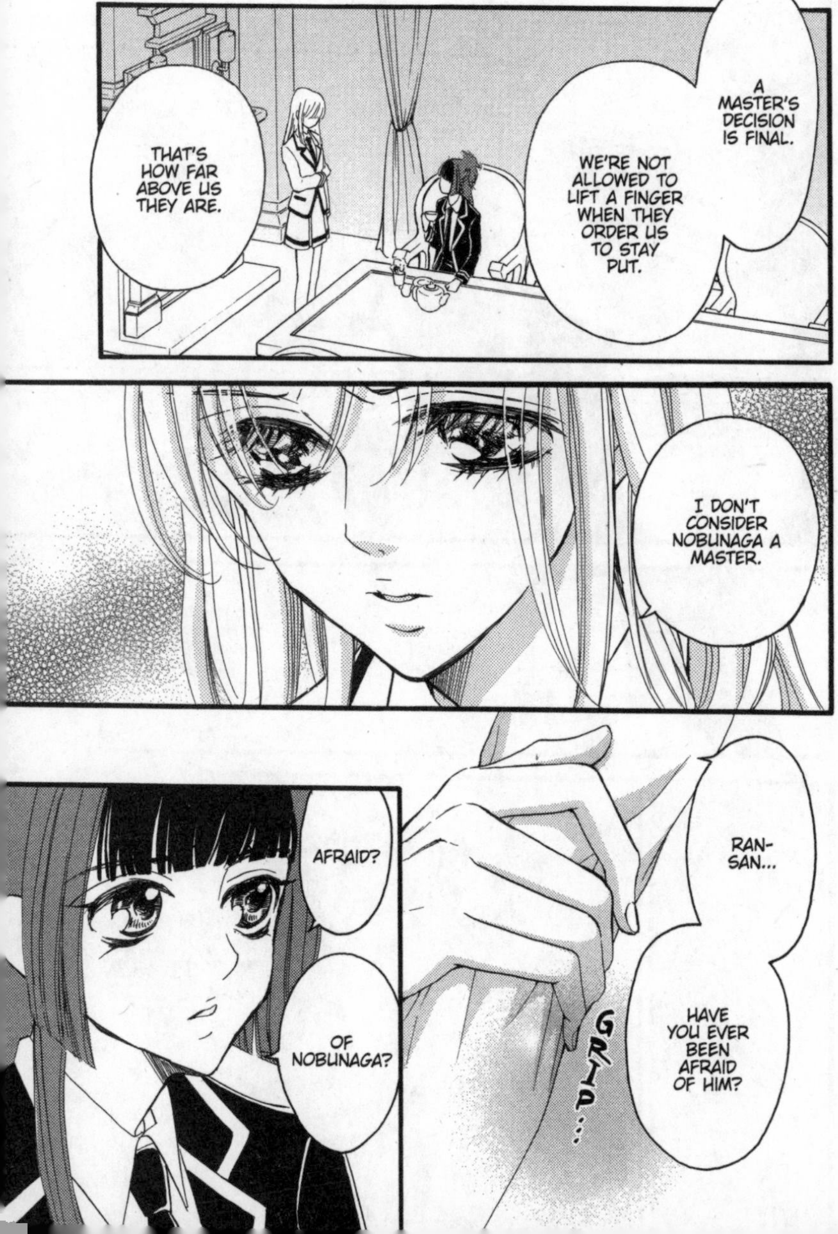
A MASTER'S DECISION IS FINAL.
WE'RE NOT ALLOWED TO LIFT A FINGER WHEN THEY ORDER US TO STAY PUT.
THAT'S HOW FAR ABOVE US THEY ARE.
I DON'T CONSIDER NOBUNAGA A MASTER.
RAN-SAN...
HAVE YOU EVER BEEN AFRAID OF HIM?
GRIP...
AFRAID?
OF NOBUNAGA?

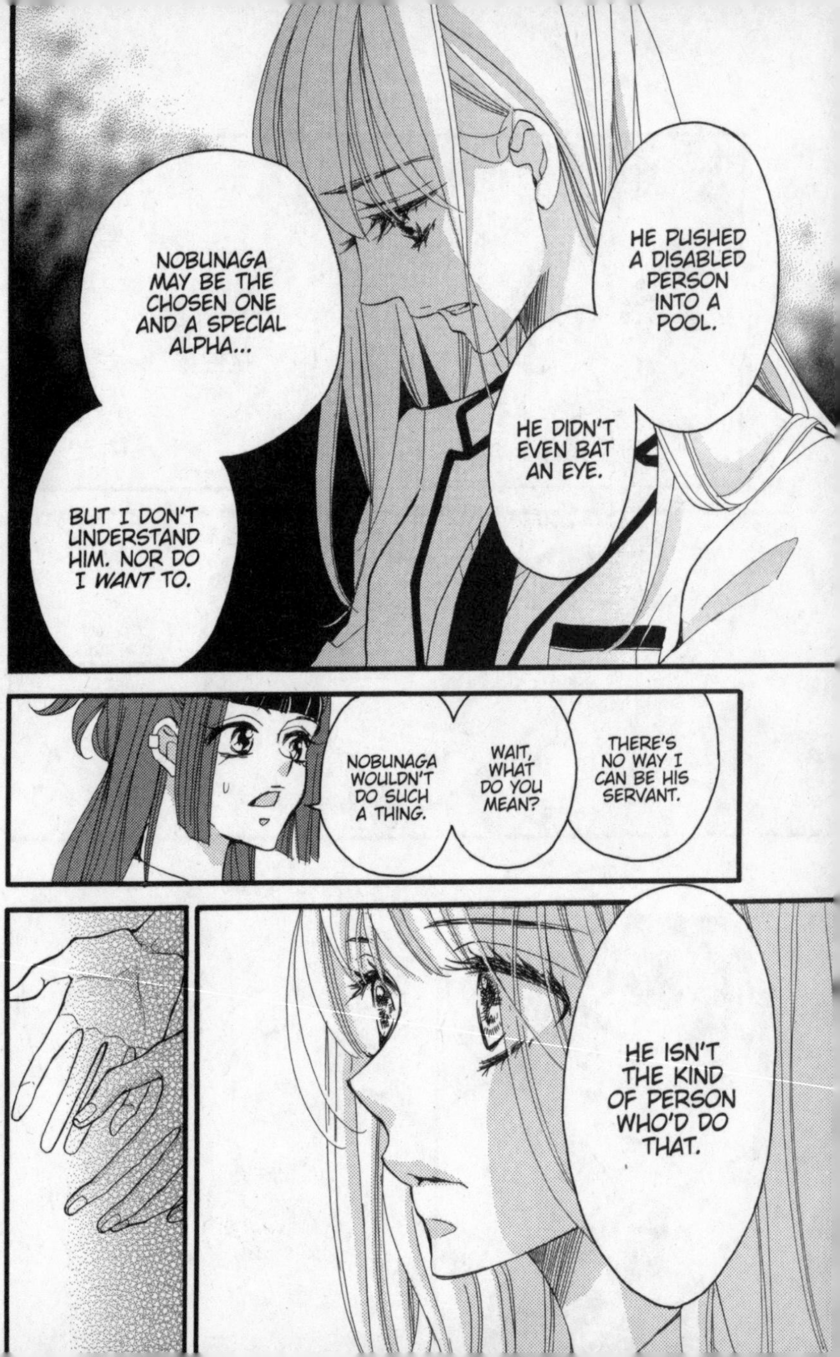
HE PUSHED A DISABLED PERSON INTO A POOL.
HE DIDN'T EVEN BAT AN EYE.
NOBUNAGA MAY BE THE CHOSEN ONE AND A SPECIAL ALPHA...
BUT I DON'T UNDERSTAND HIM. NOR DO I *WANT* TO.
THERE'S NO WAY I CAN BE HIS SERVANT.
WAIT, WHAT DO YOU MEAN?
NOBUNAGA WOULDN'T DO SUCH A THING.
HE ISN'T THE KIND OF PERSON WHO'D DO THAT.

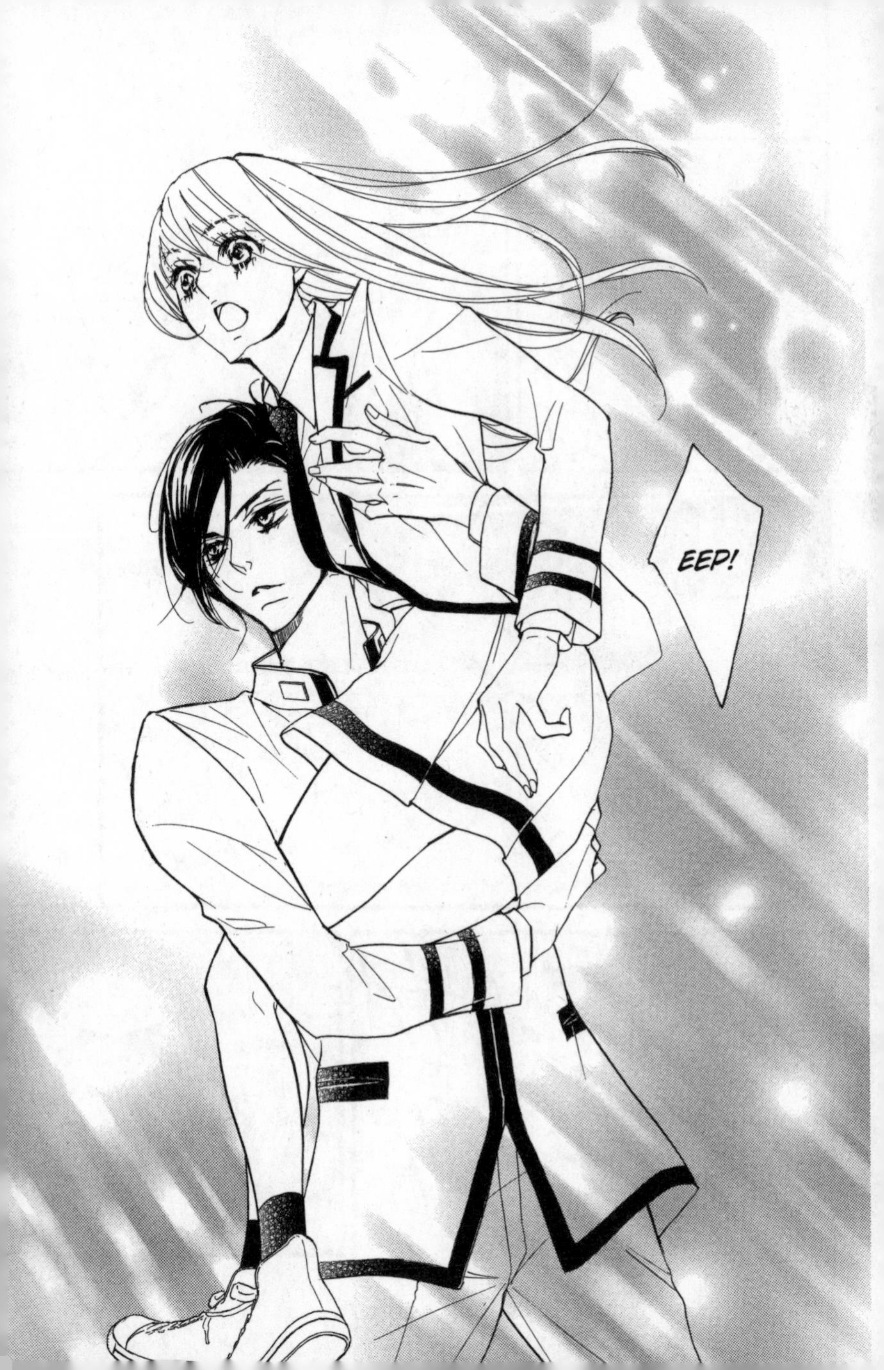
EEP!

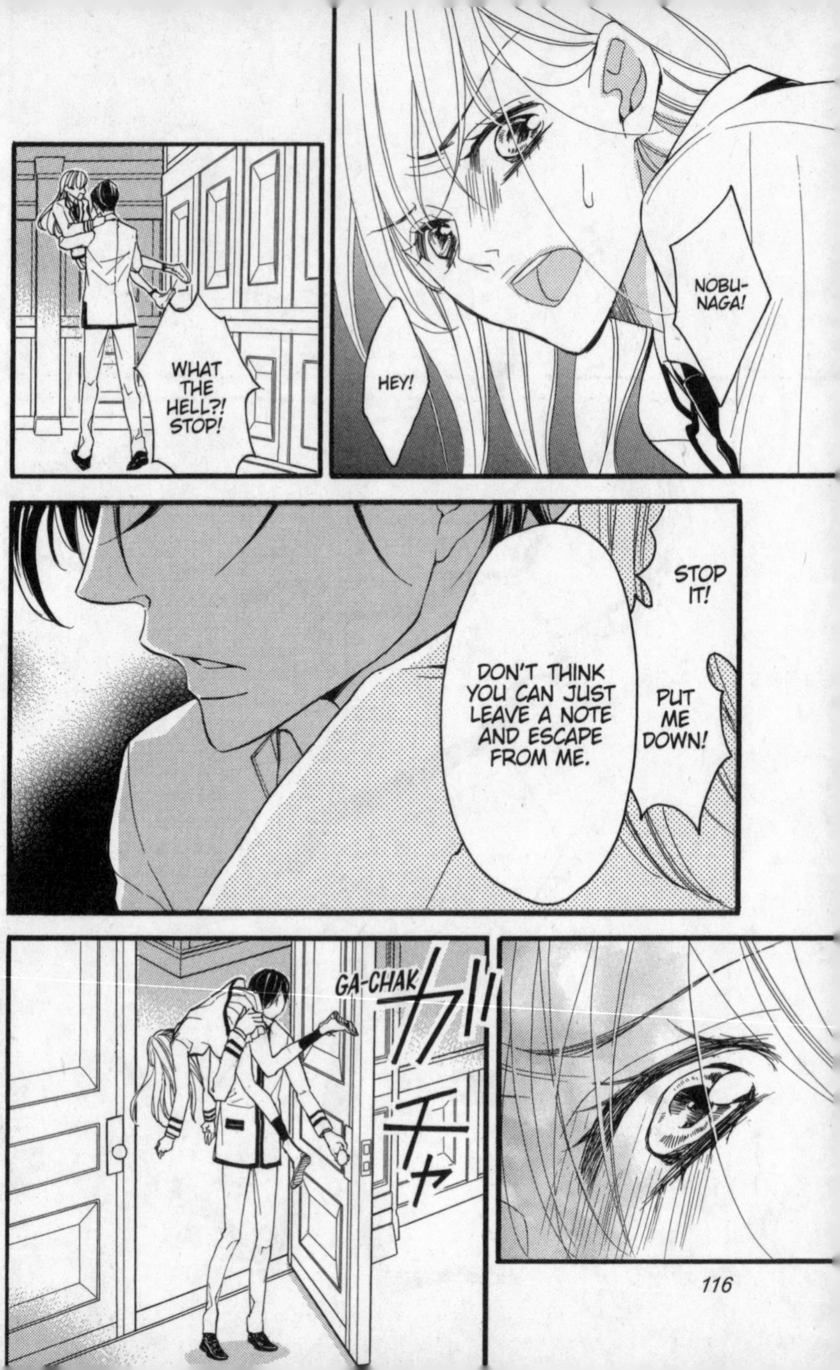
NOBU-NAGA!
HEY!
WHAT THE HELL?! STOP!
STOP IT!
PUT ME DOWN!
DON'T THINK YOU CAN JUST LEAVE A NOTE AND ESCAPE FROM ME.
GA-CHAK
ガチャ

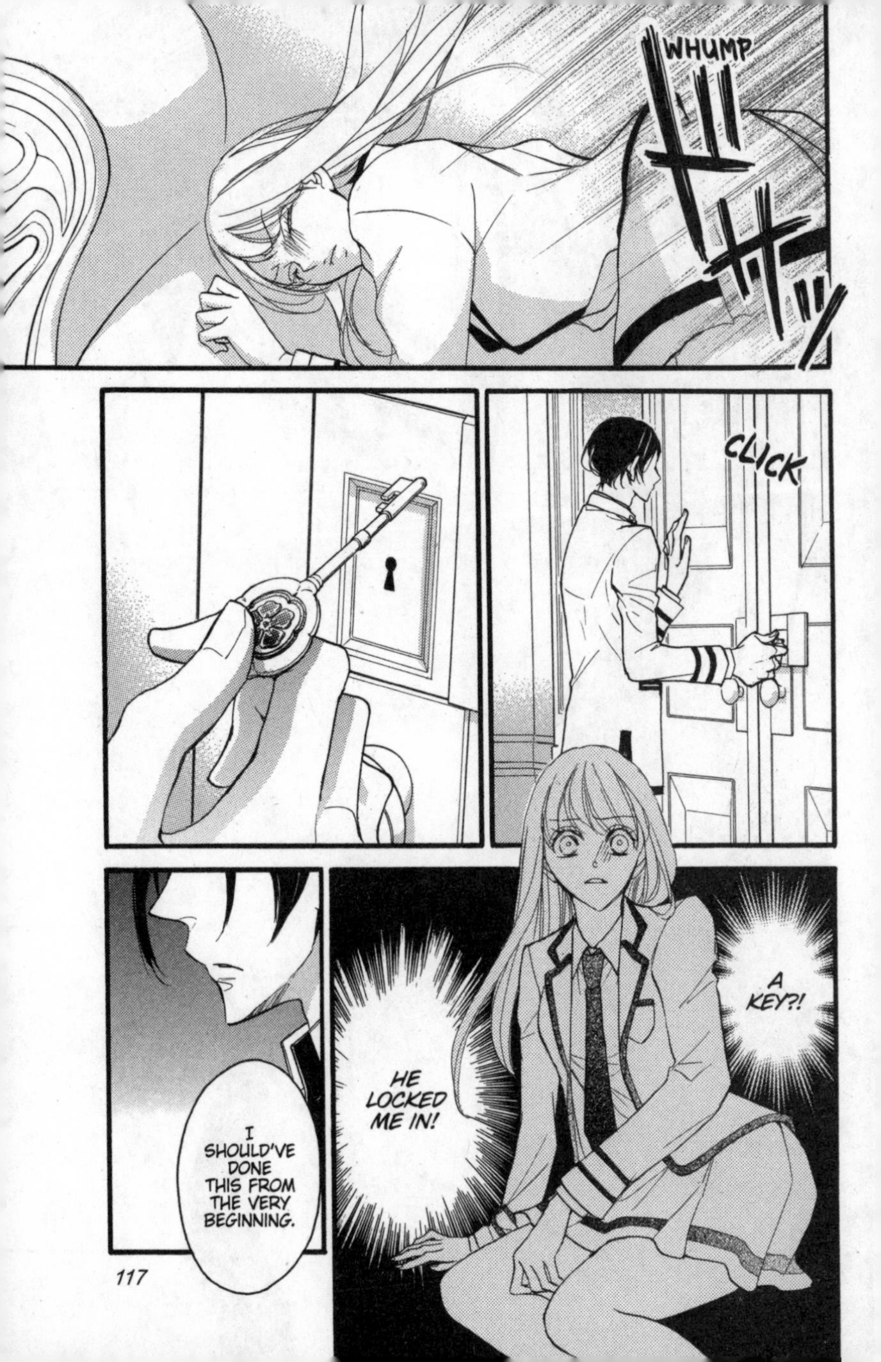
WHUMP
CLICK
A KEY?!
HE LOCKED ME IN!
I SHOULD'VE DONE THIS FROM THE VERY BEGINNING.

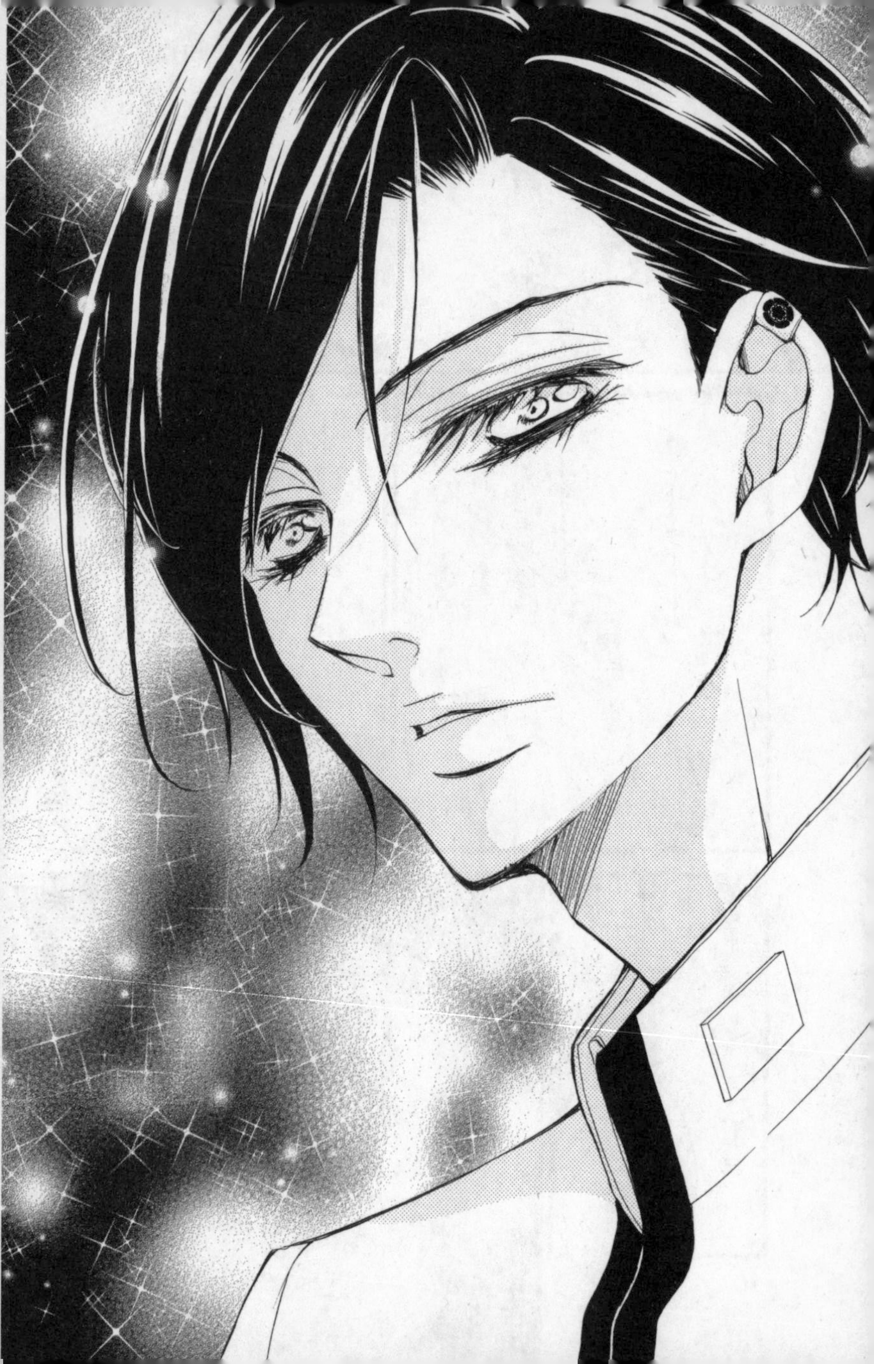

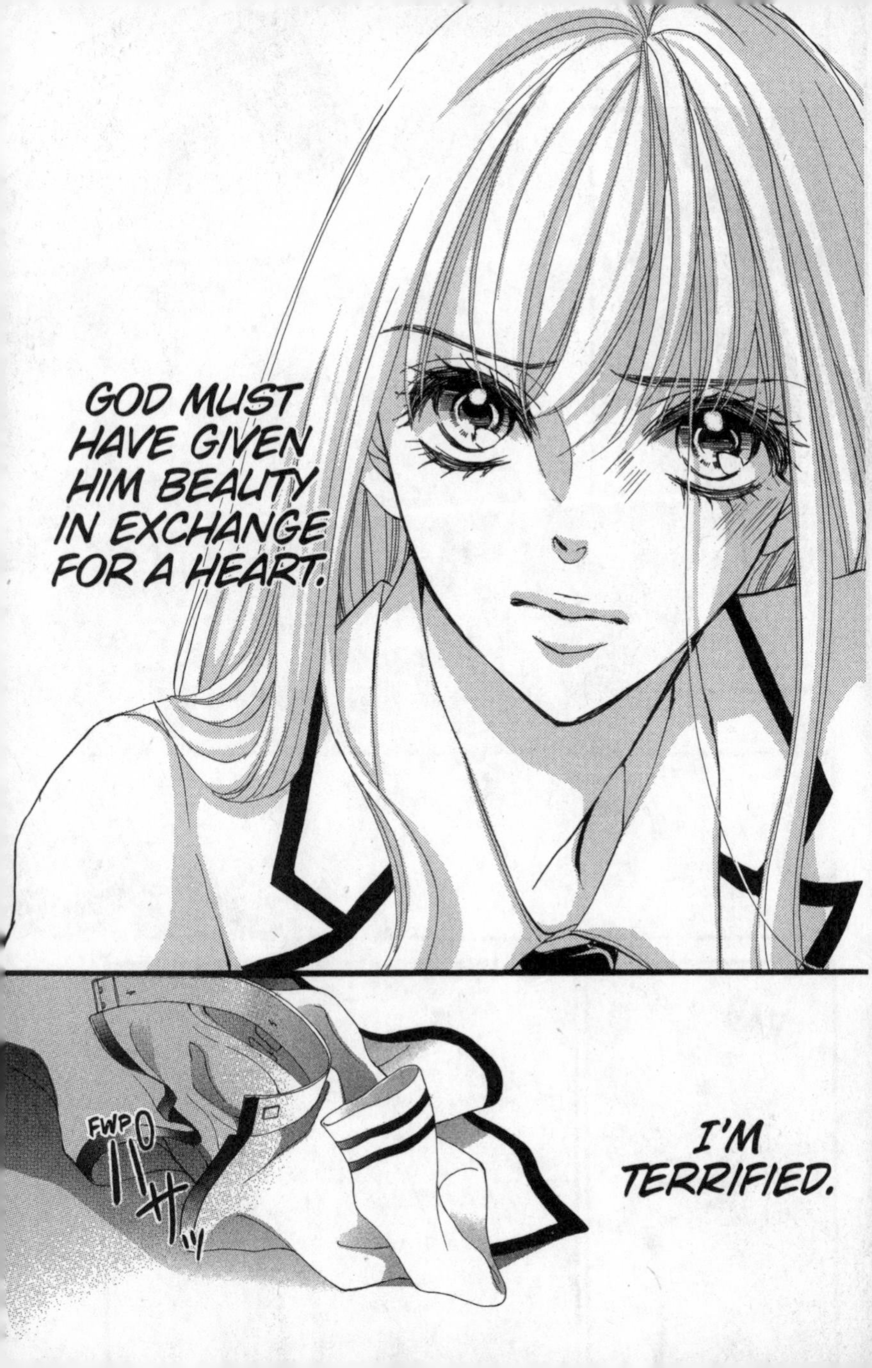
GOD MUST HAVE GIVEN HIM BEAUTY IN EXCHANGE FOR A HEART.
I'M TERRIFIED.
FWP

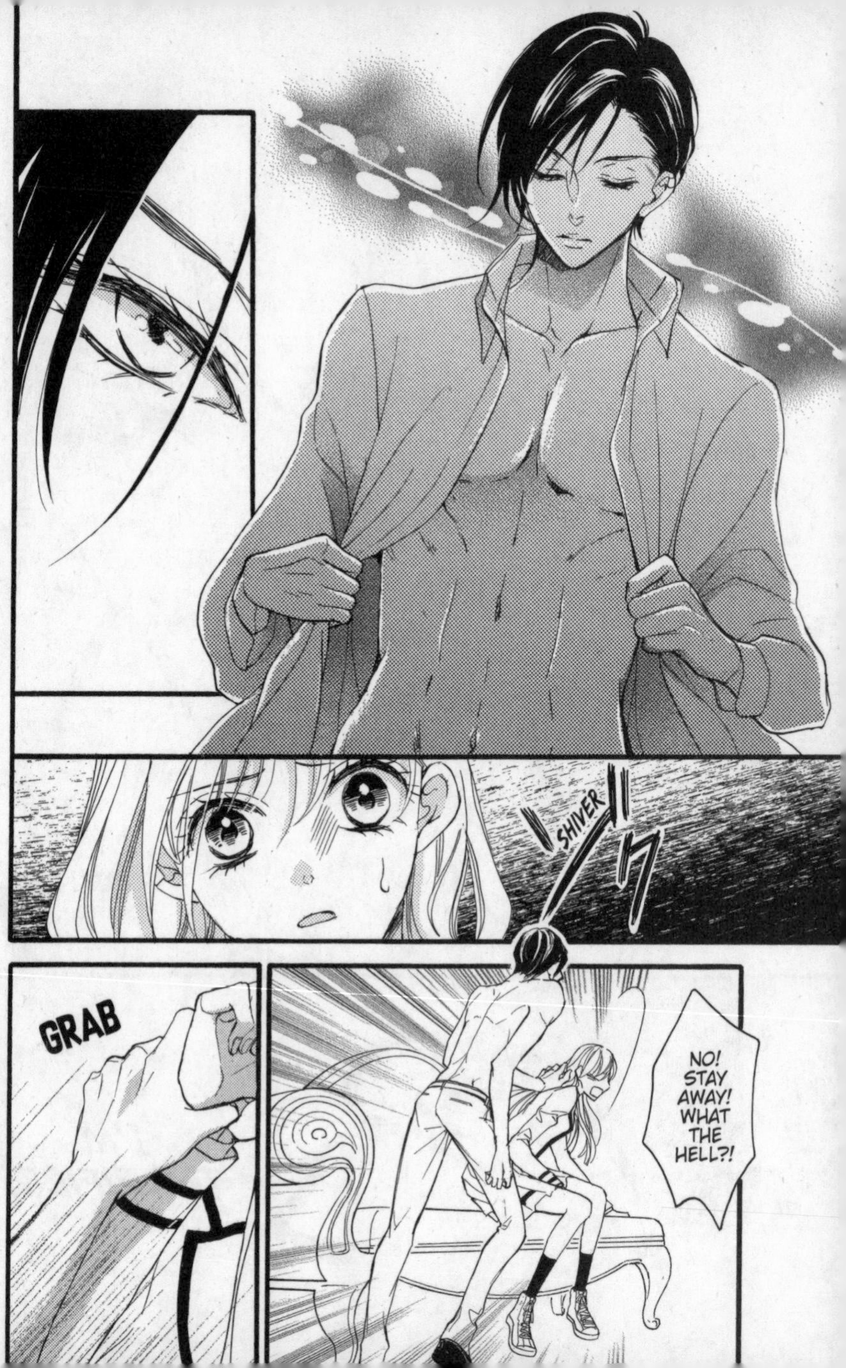
SHIVER
NO! STAY AWAY! WHAT THE HELL?!
GRAB

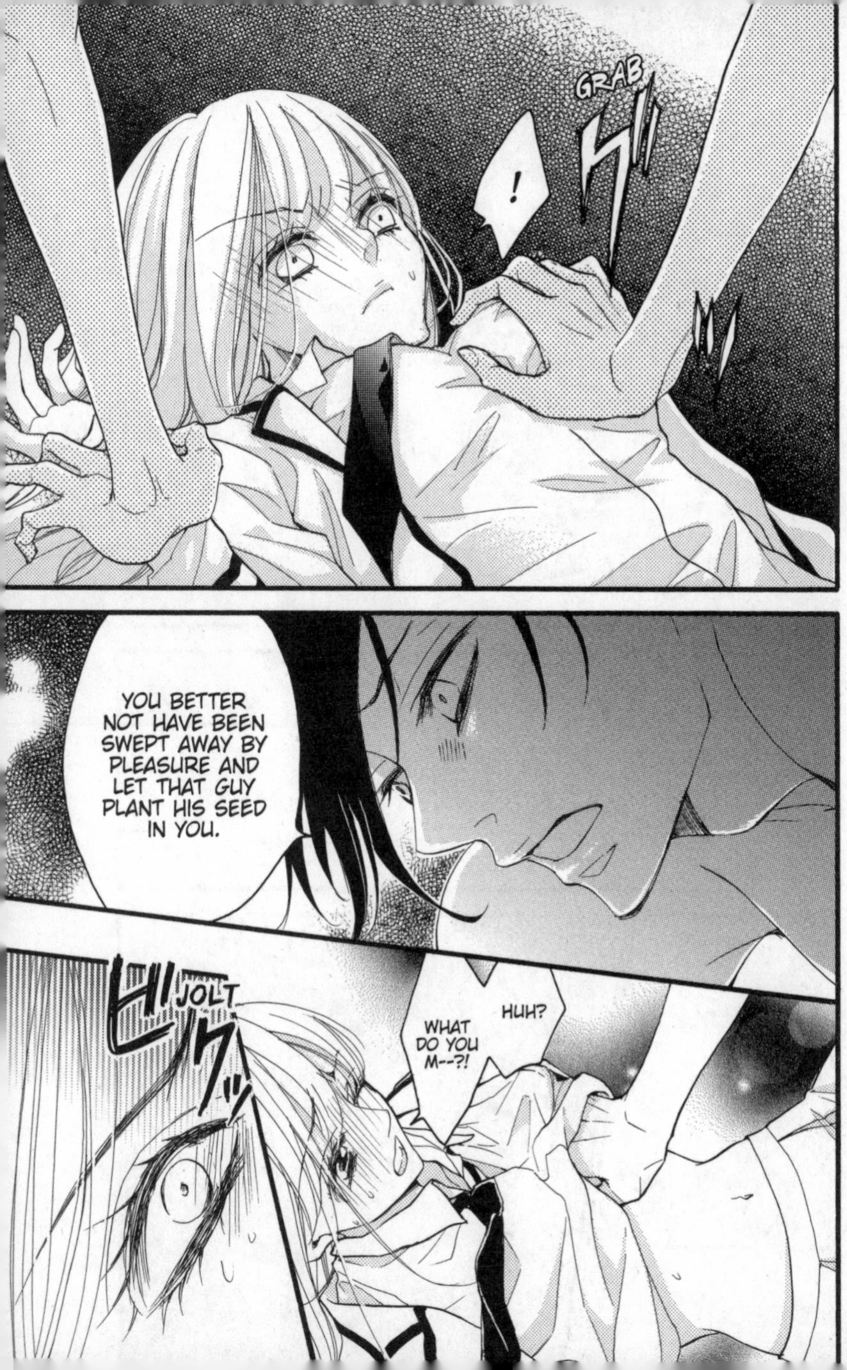
GRAB
!
YOU BETTER NOT HAVE BEEN SWEPT AWAY BY PLEASURE AND LET THAT GUY PLANT HIS SEED IN YOU.
HUH?
WHAT DO YOU M--?!
JOLT

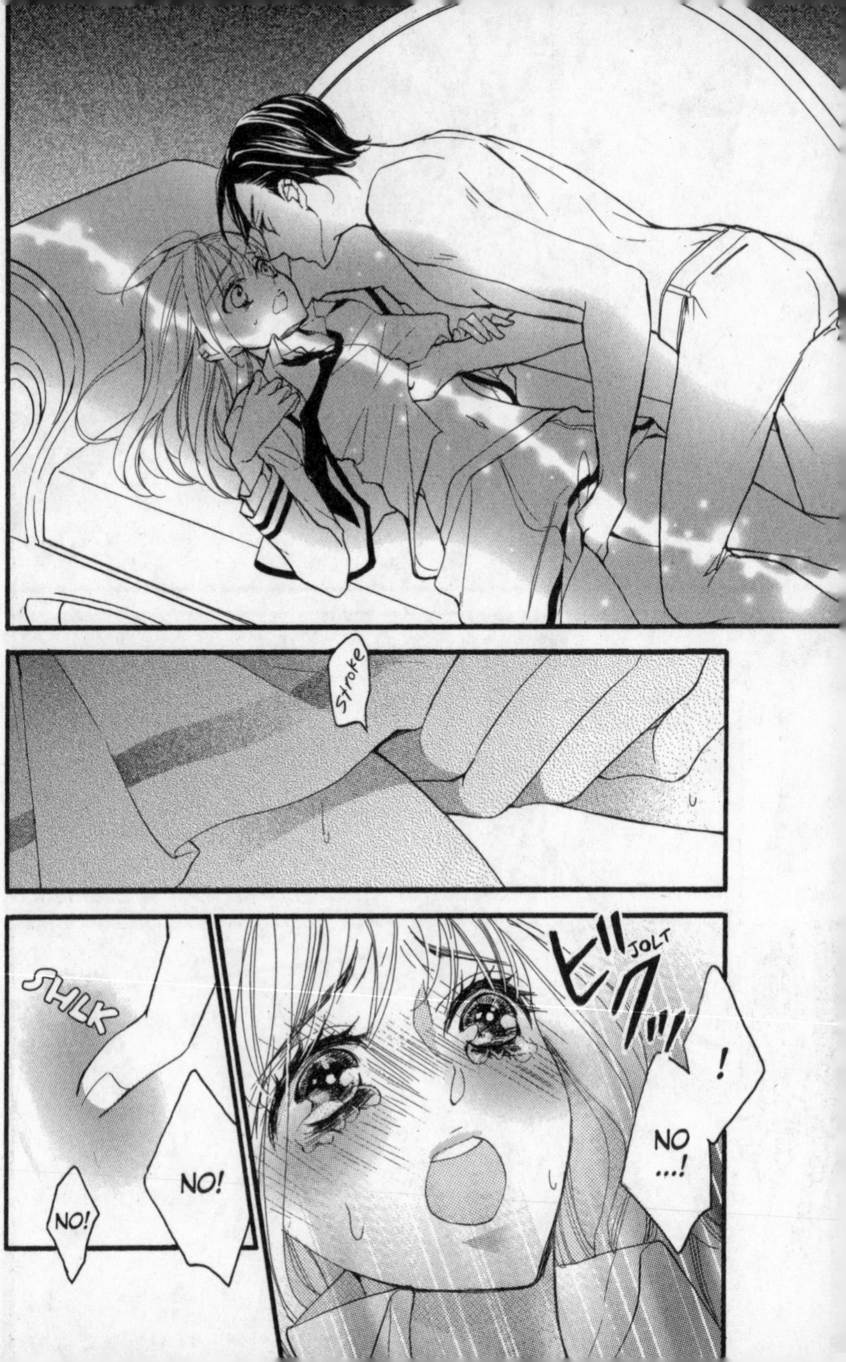

Stroke
JOLT
!
NO ...!
SHLK
NO!
NO!

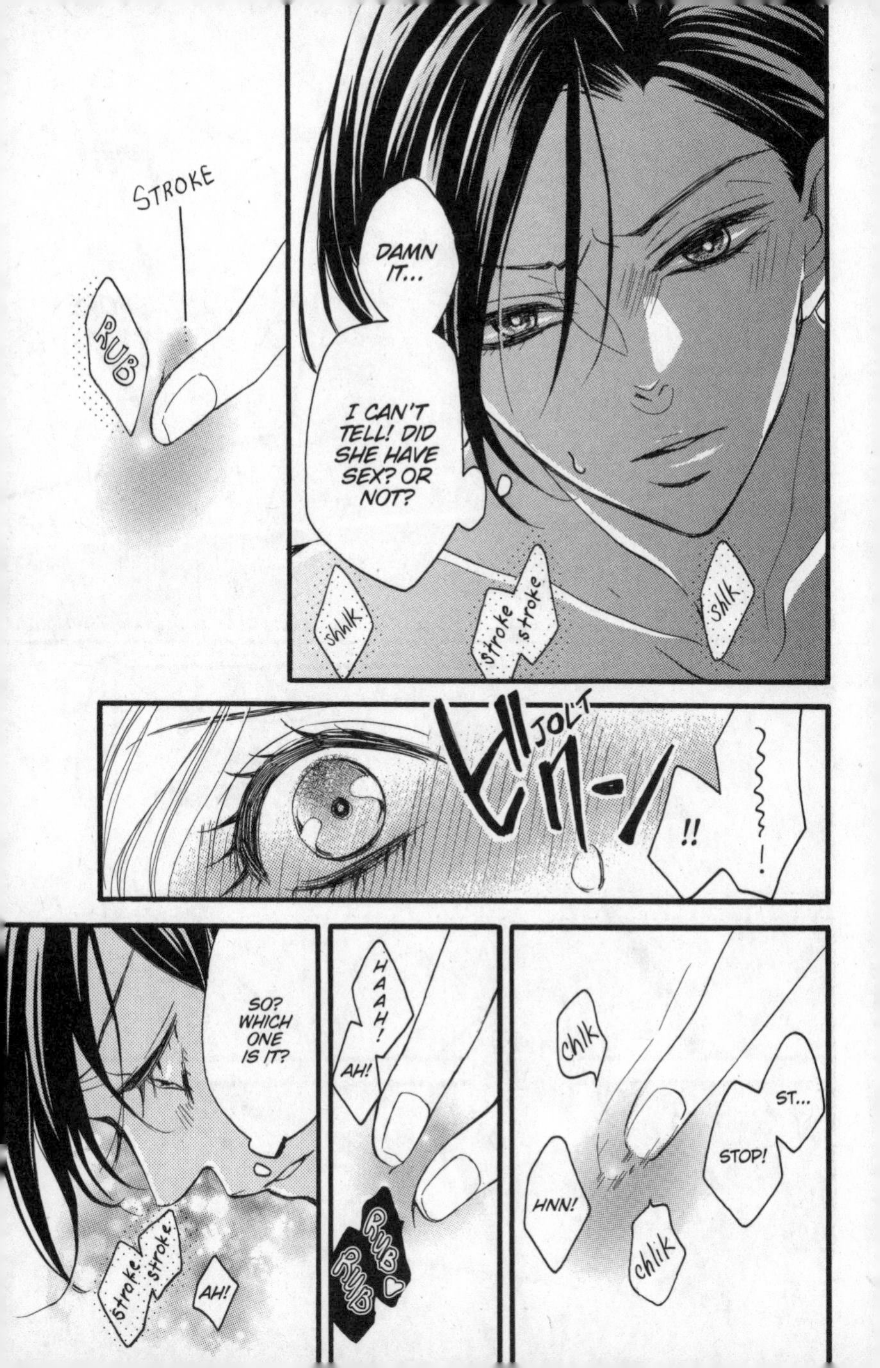
DAMN IT...
I CAN'T TELL! DID SHE HAVE SEX? OR NOT?
shhlk
stroke stroke
shlk
STROKE
RUB
JOLT
!!
~!
chlk
ST... STOP!
HNN!
chlik
HAAAH! AH!
RUB RUB
SO? WHICH ONE IS IT?
stroke stroke
AH!

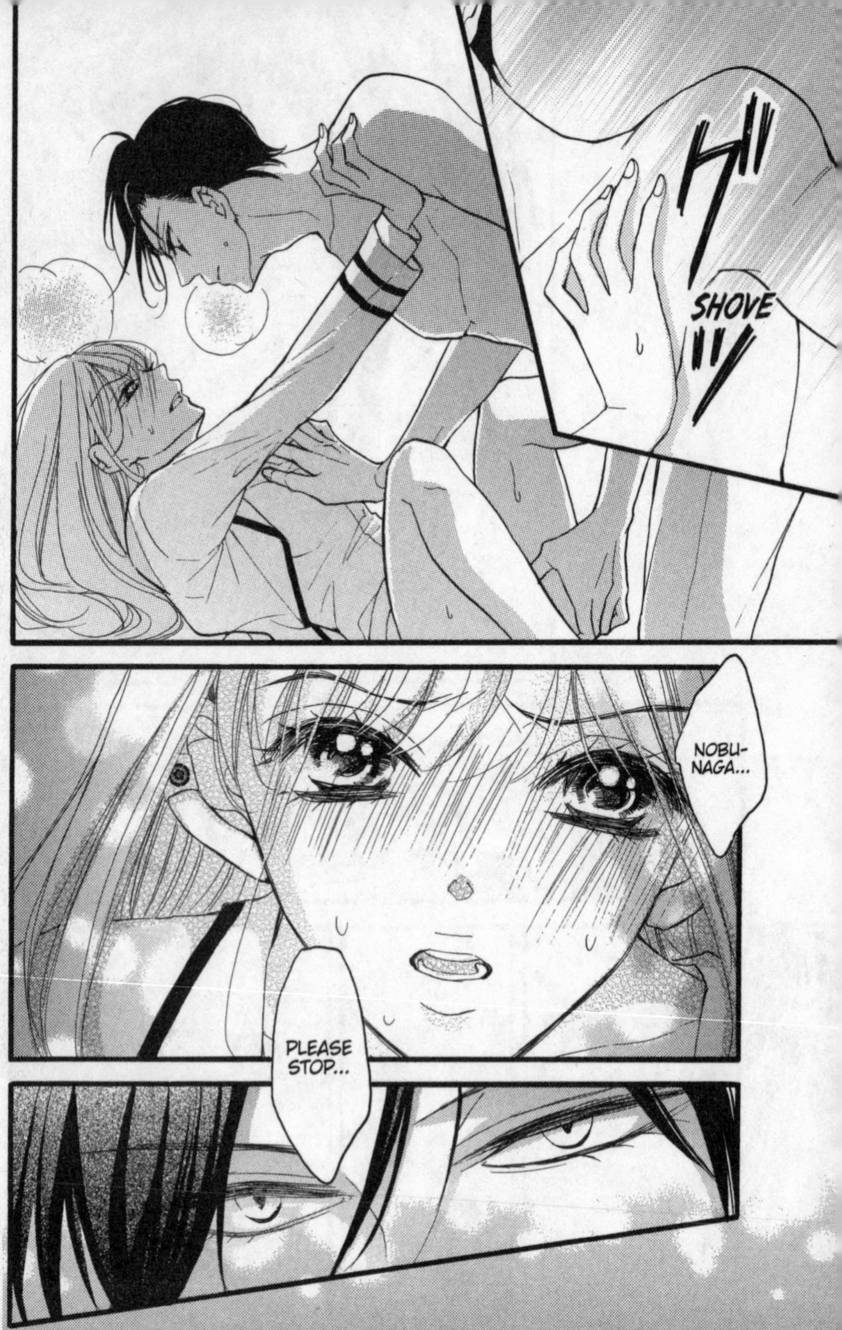
SHOVE
NOBU-NAGA...
PLEASE STOP...

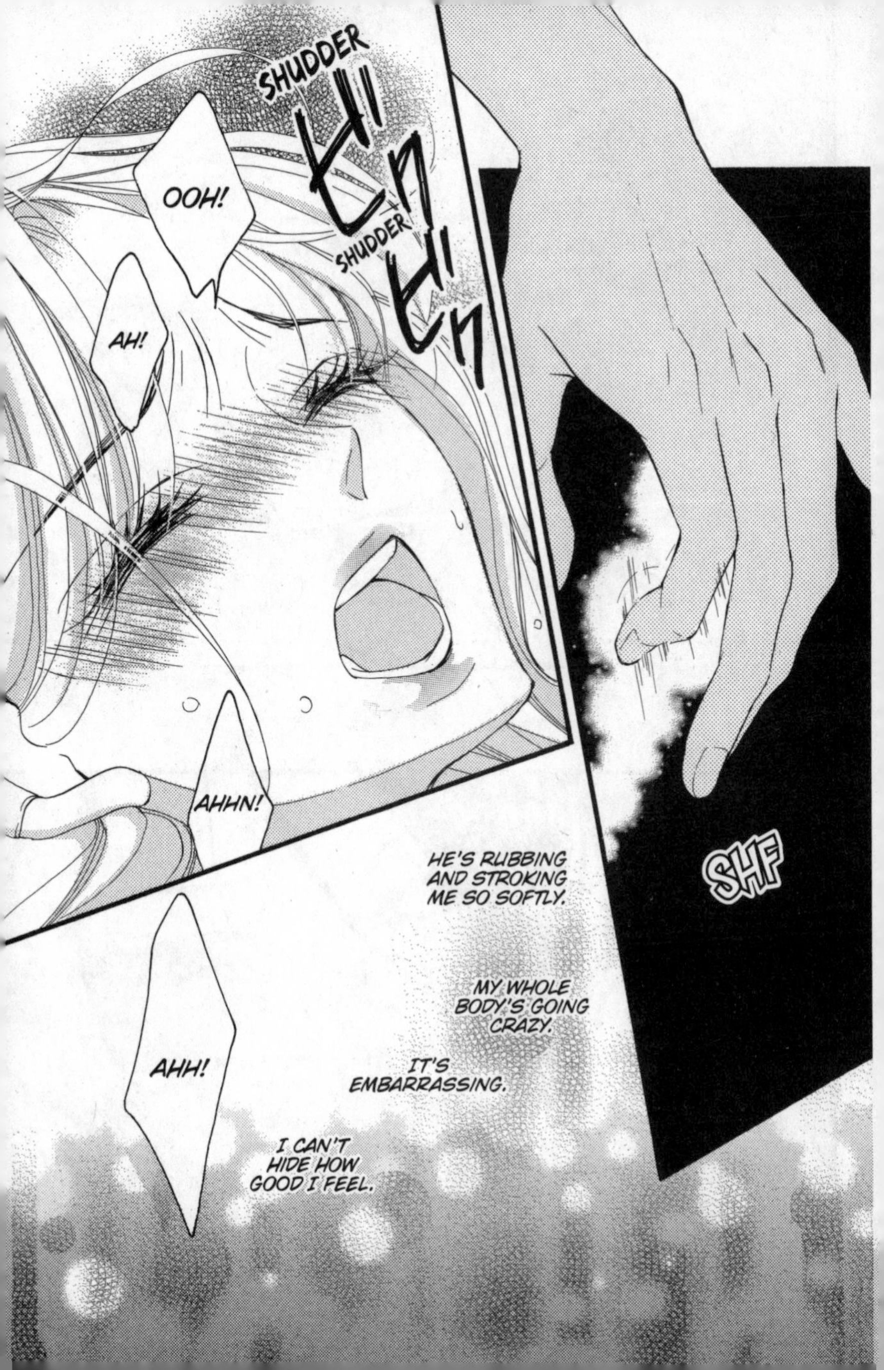
SHF
SHUDDER
SHUDDER
OOH!
AH!
AHHN!
HE'S RUBBING AND STROKING ME SO SOFTLY.
MY WHOLE BODY'S GOING CRAZY.
IT'S EMBARRASSING.
AHH!
I CAN'T HIDE HOW GOOD I FEEL.

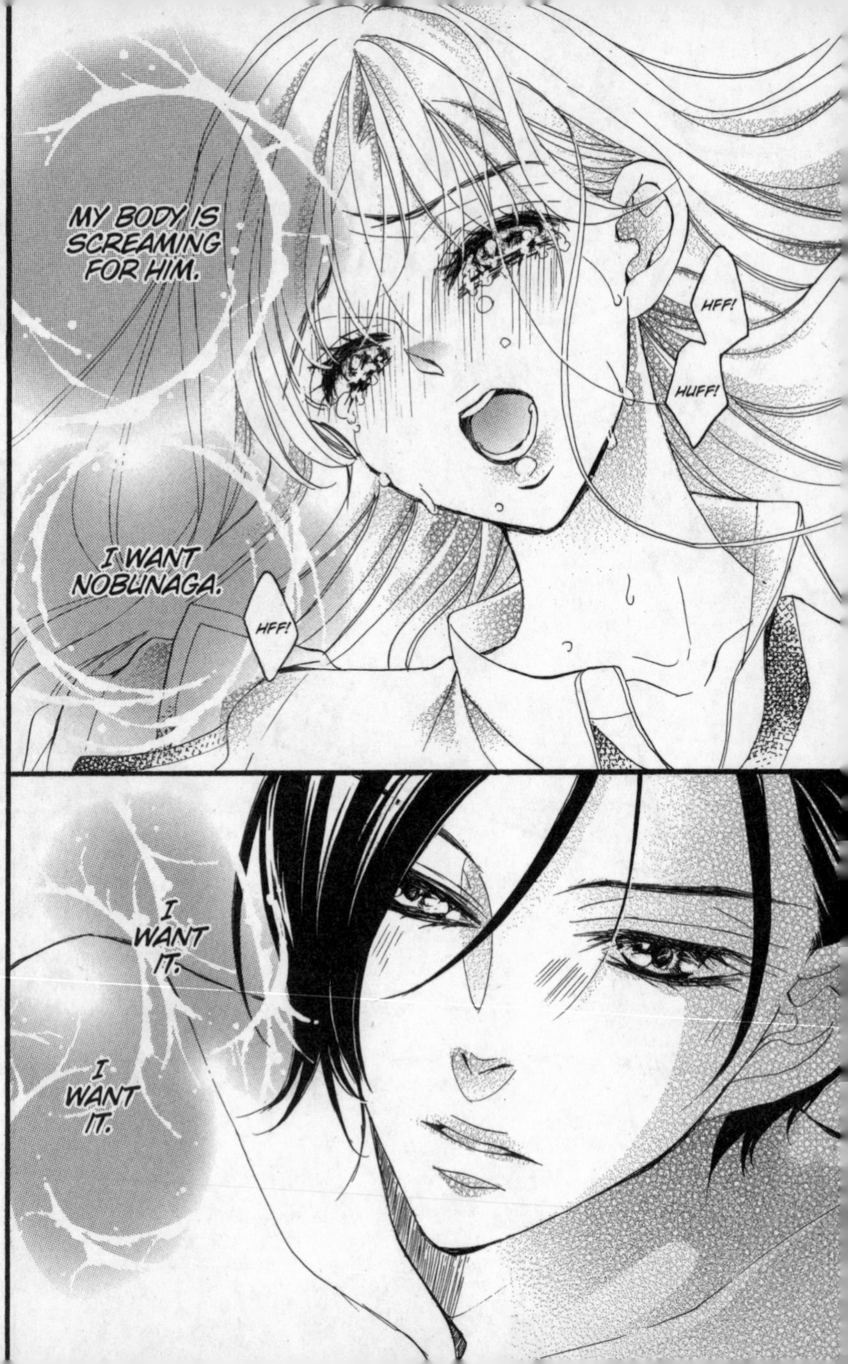
MY BODY IS SCREAMING FOR HIM.
HFF!
HUFF!
I WANT NOBUNAGA.
HFF!
I WANT IT.
I WANT IT.

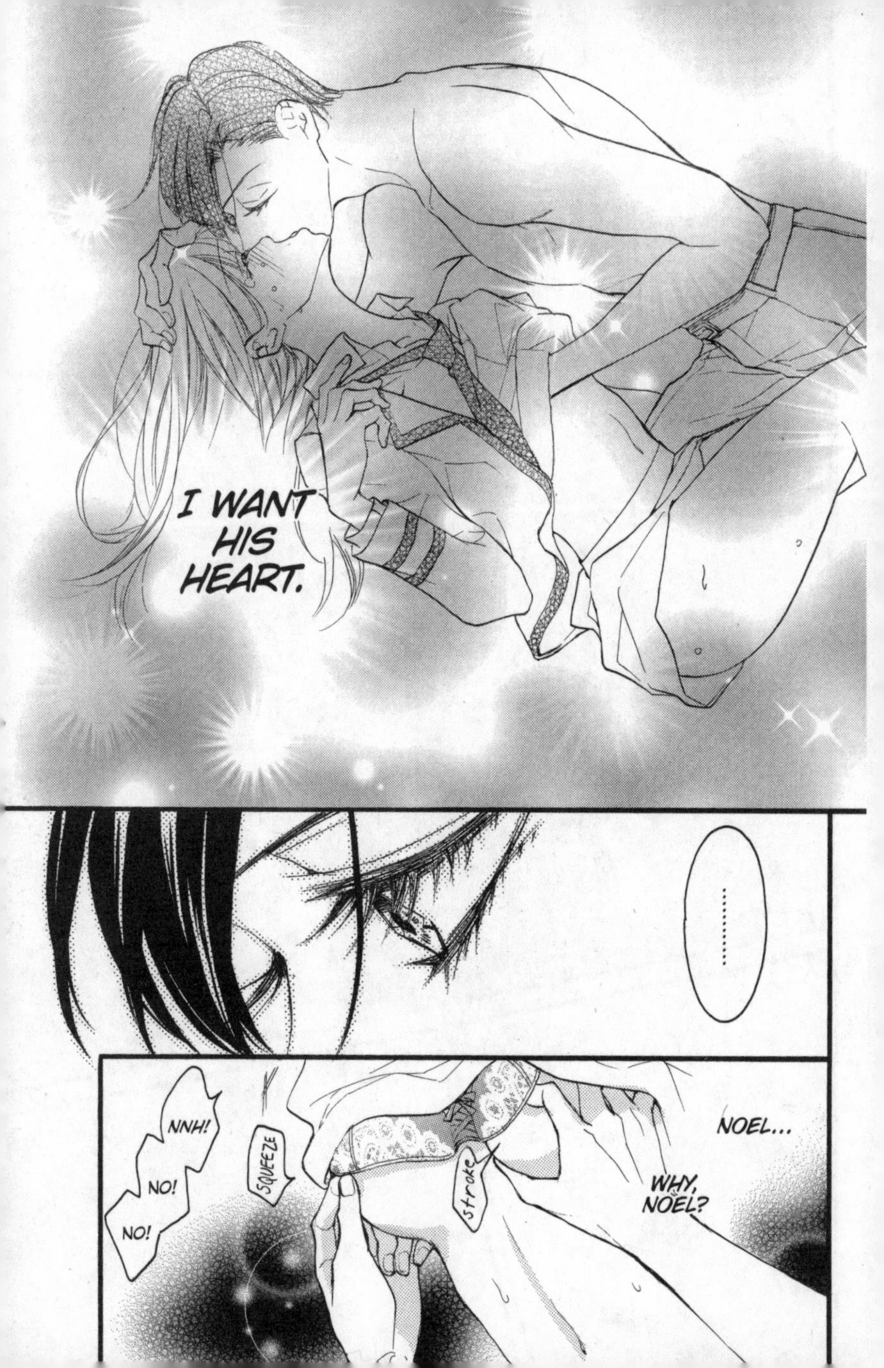
I WANT HIS HEART.
......
NOEL...
WHY, NOEL?
stroke
SQUEEZE
NNH!
NO!
NO!

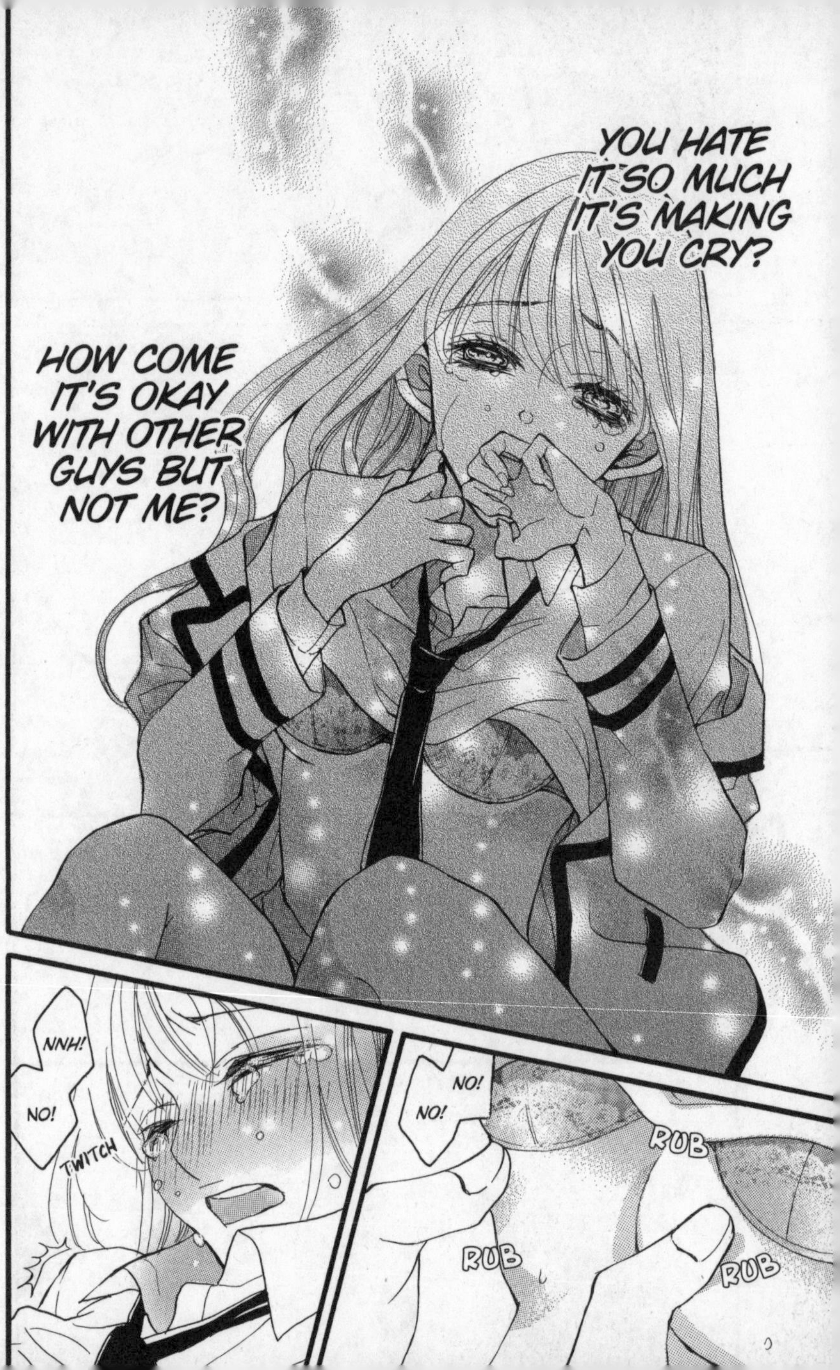
YOU HATE IT SO MUCH IT'S MAKING YOU CRY?
HOW COME IT'S OKAY WITH OTHER GUYS BUT NOT ME?
NO!
NO!
RUB
RUB
RUB
NNH!
NO!
TWITCH

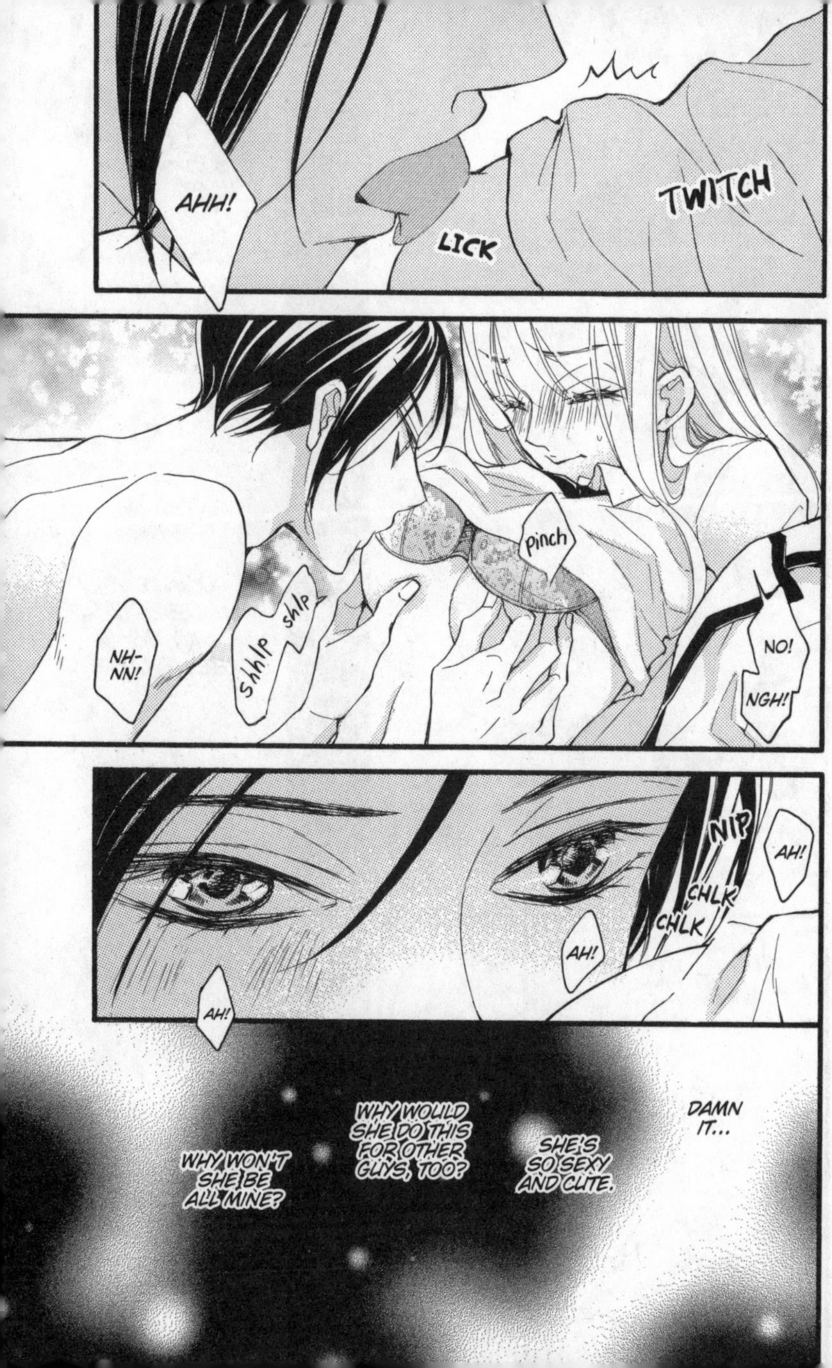
TWITCH
LICK
AHH!
NO! NGH!
pinch
shhlp
shhlp
NH-NN!
AH!
NIP
CHLK
CHLK
AH!
AH!
DAMN IT...
SHE'S SO SEXY AND CUTE.
WHY WOULD SHE DO THIS FOR OTHER GUYS, TOO?
WHY WON'T SHE BE ALL MINE?

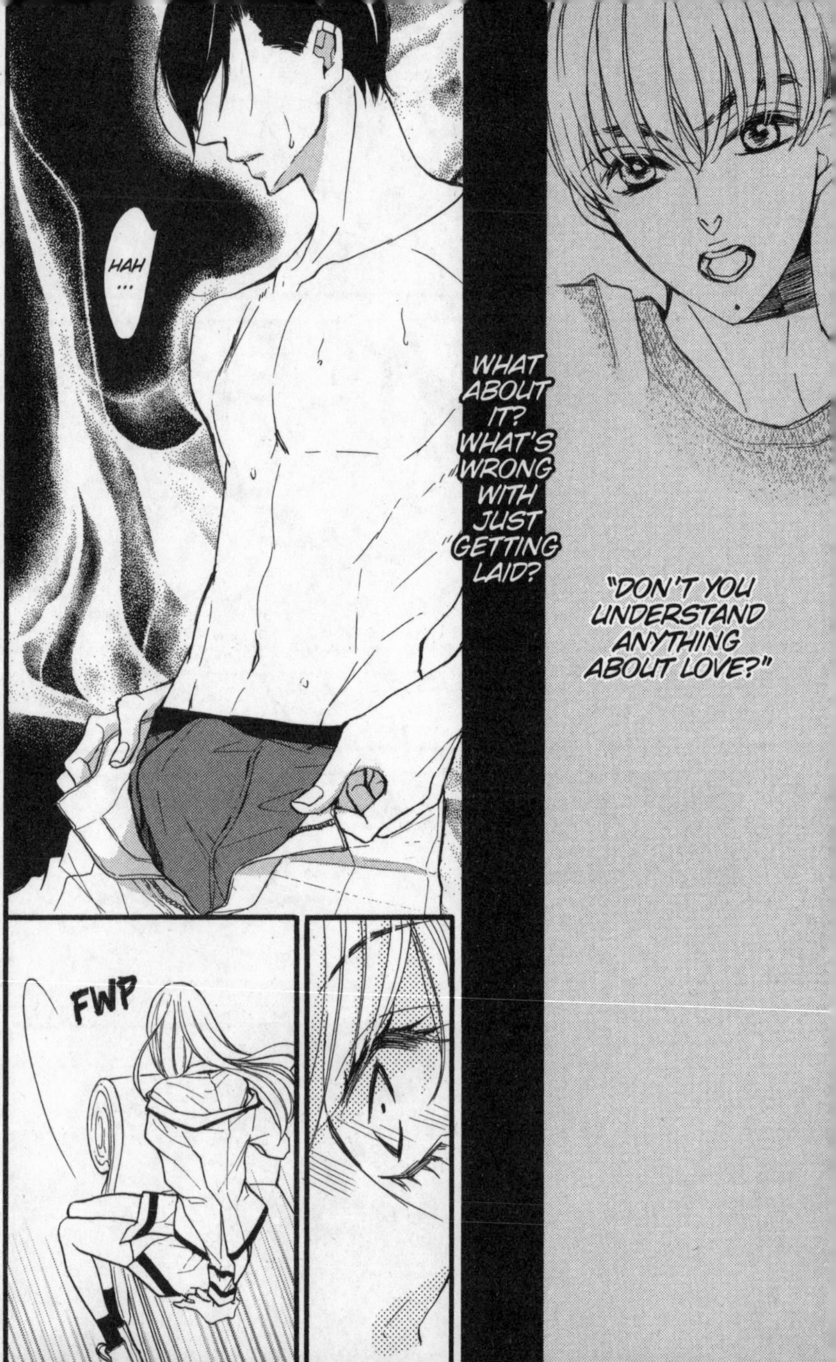
"DON'T YOU UNDERSTAND ANYTHING ABOUT LOVE?"
WHAT ABOUT IT? WHAT'S WRONG WITH JUST GETTING LAID?
HAH ...
FWP

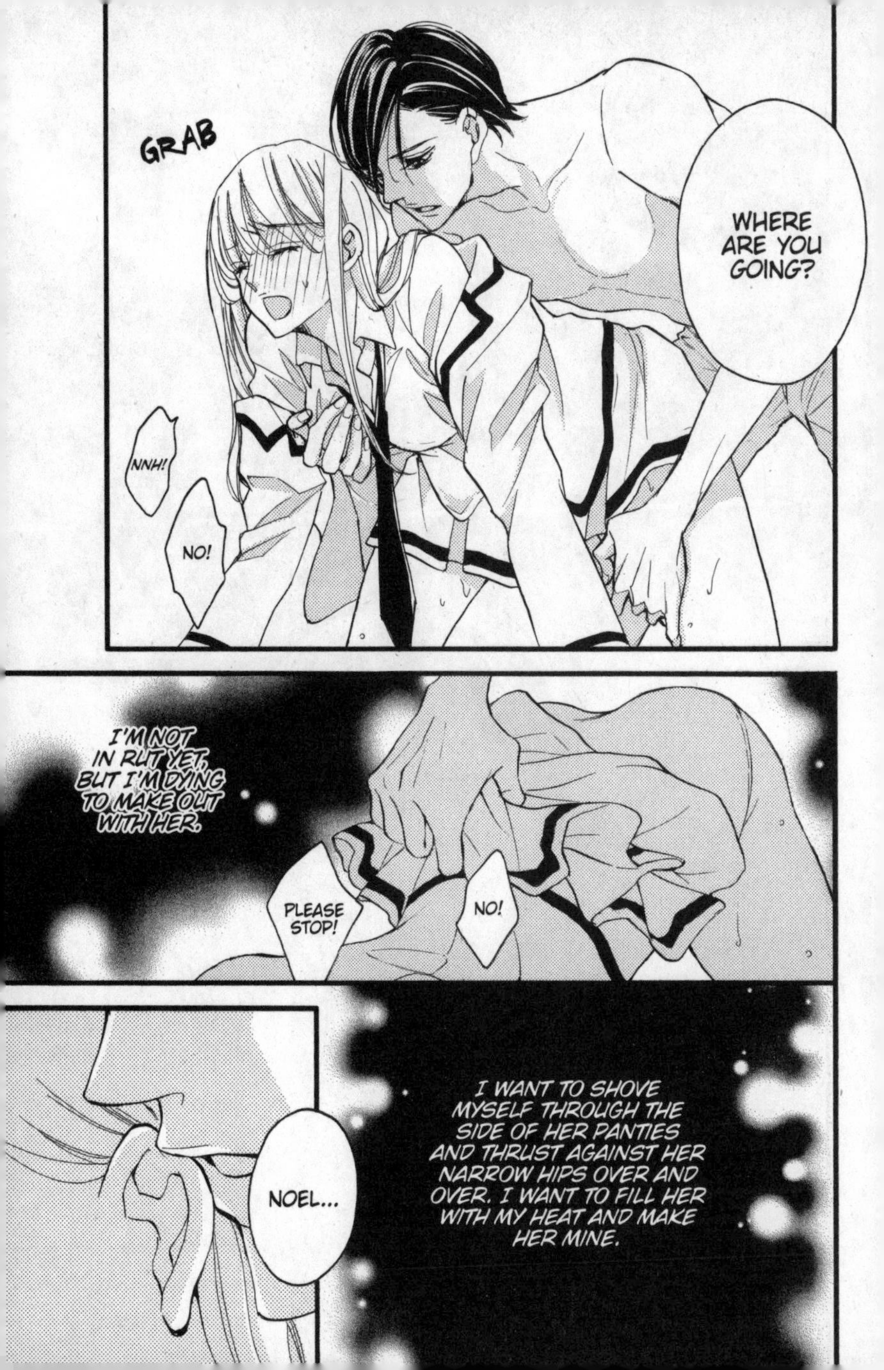
WHERE ARE YOU GOING?
GRAB
NNH!
NO!
I'M NOT IN RUT YET, BUT I'M DYING TO MAKE OUT WITH HER.
NO!
PLEASE STOP!
I WANT TO SHOVE MYSELF THROUGH THE SIDE OF HER PANTIES AND THRUST AGAINST HER NARROW HIPS OVER AND OVER. I WANT TO FILL HER WITH MY HEAT AND MAKE HER MINE.
NOEL...

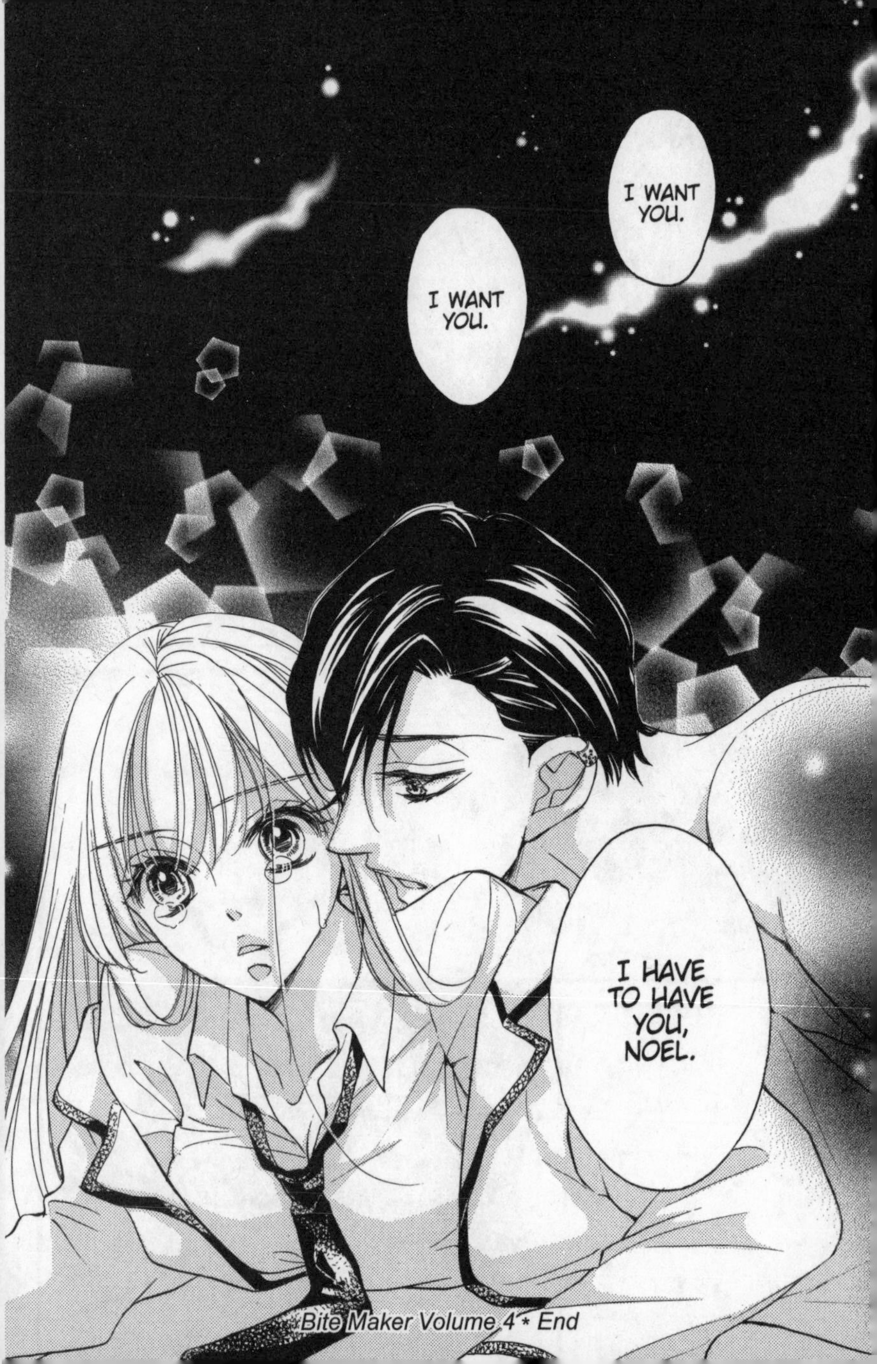
I WANT YOU.
I WANT YOU.
I HAVE TO HAVE YOU, NOEL.
Bite Maker Volume 4 • End

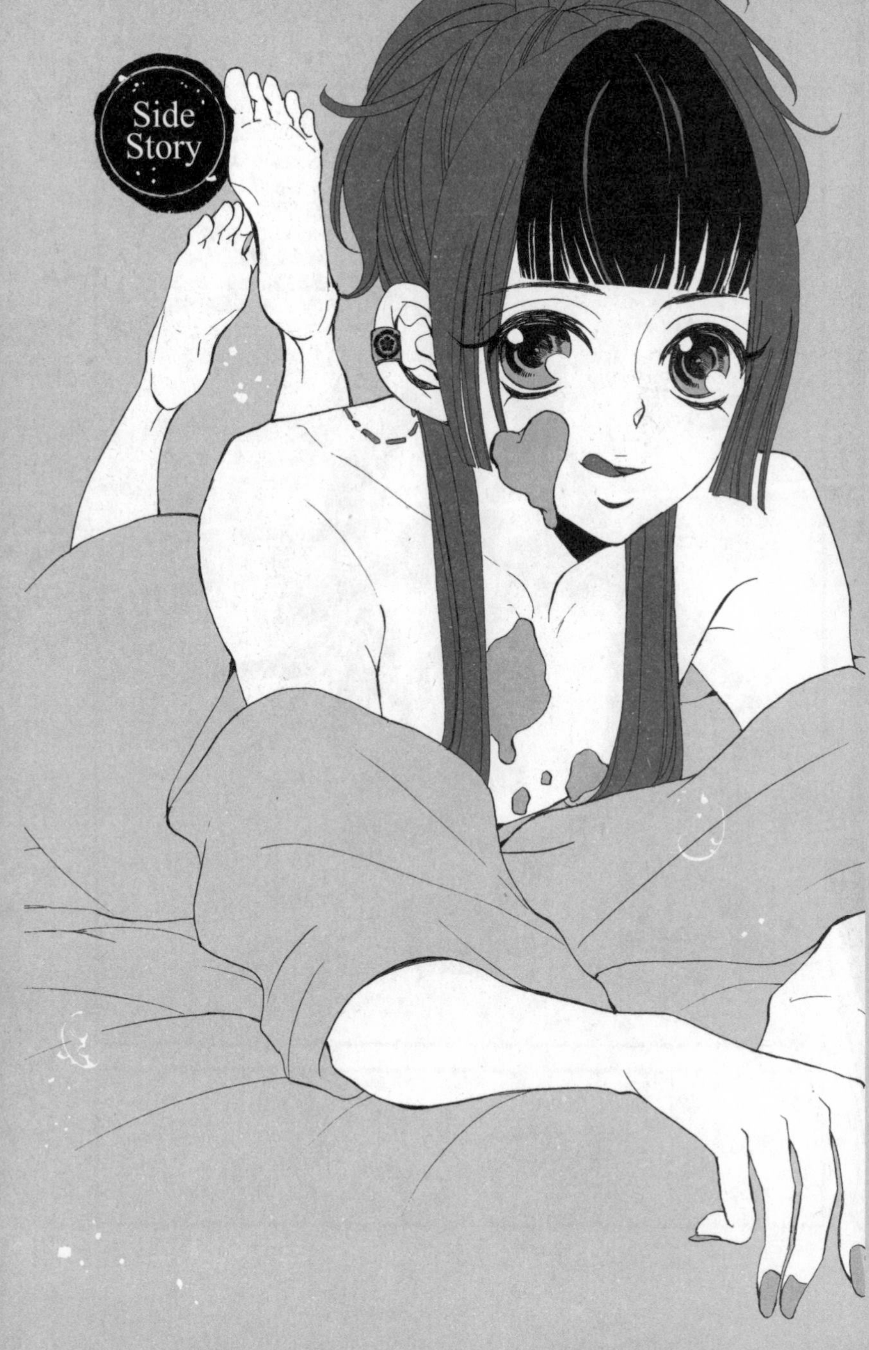
Side
Story

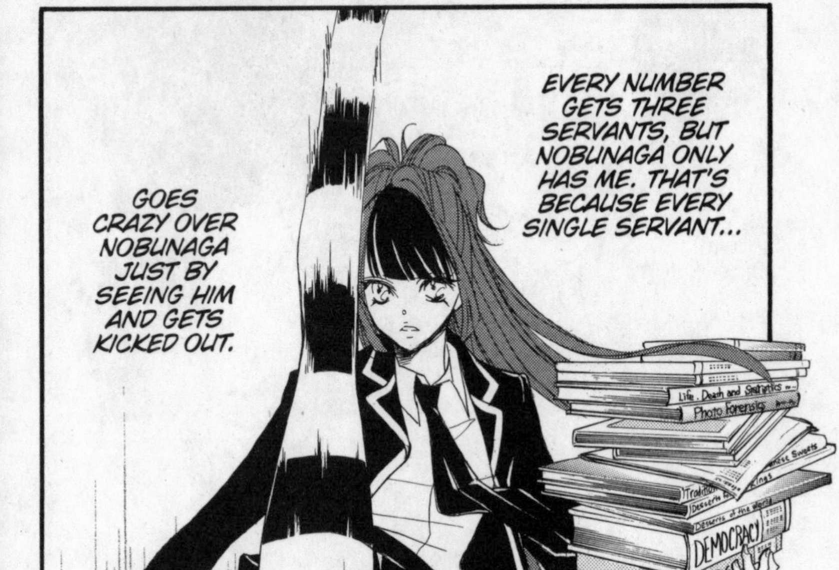
EVERY NUMBER GETS THREE SERVANTS, BUT NOBUNAGA ONLY HAS ME. THAT'S BECAUSE EVERY SINGLE SERVANT...
GOES CRAZY OVER NOBUNAGA JUST BY SEEING HIM AND GETS KICKED OUT.
Photo Forensics
DEMOCRACY
WORDS

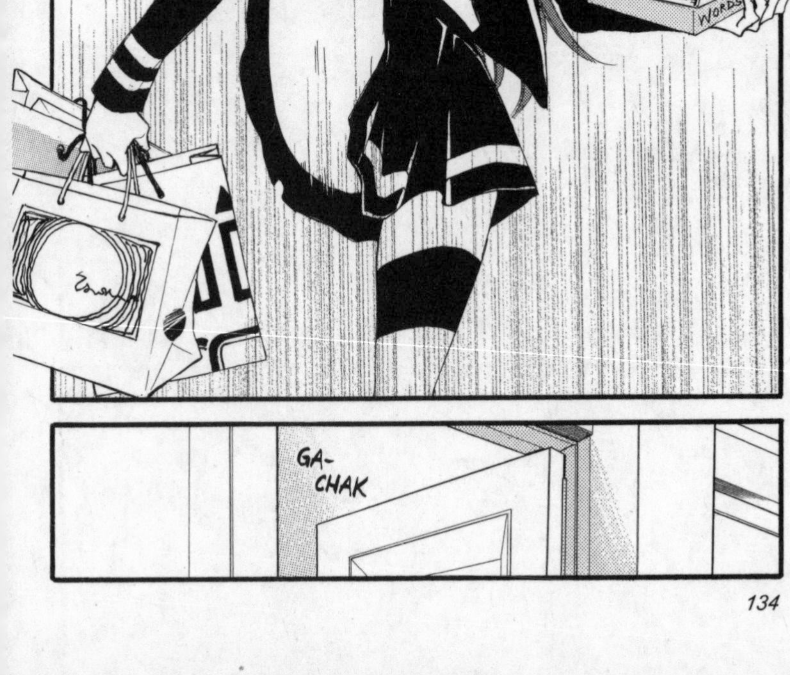
GA-CHAK

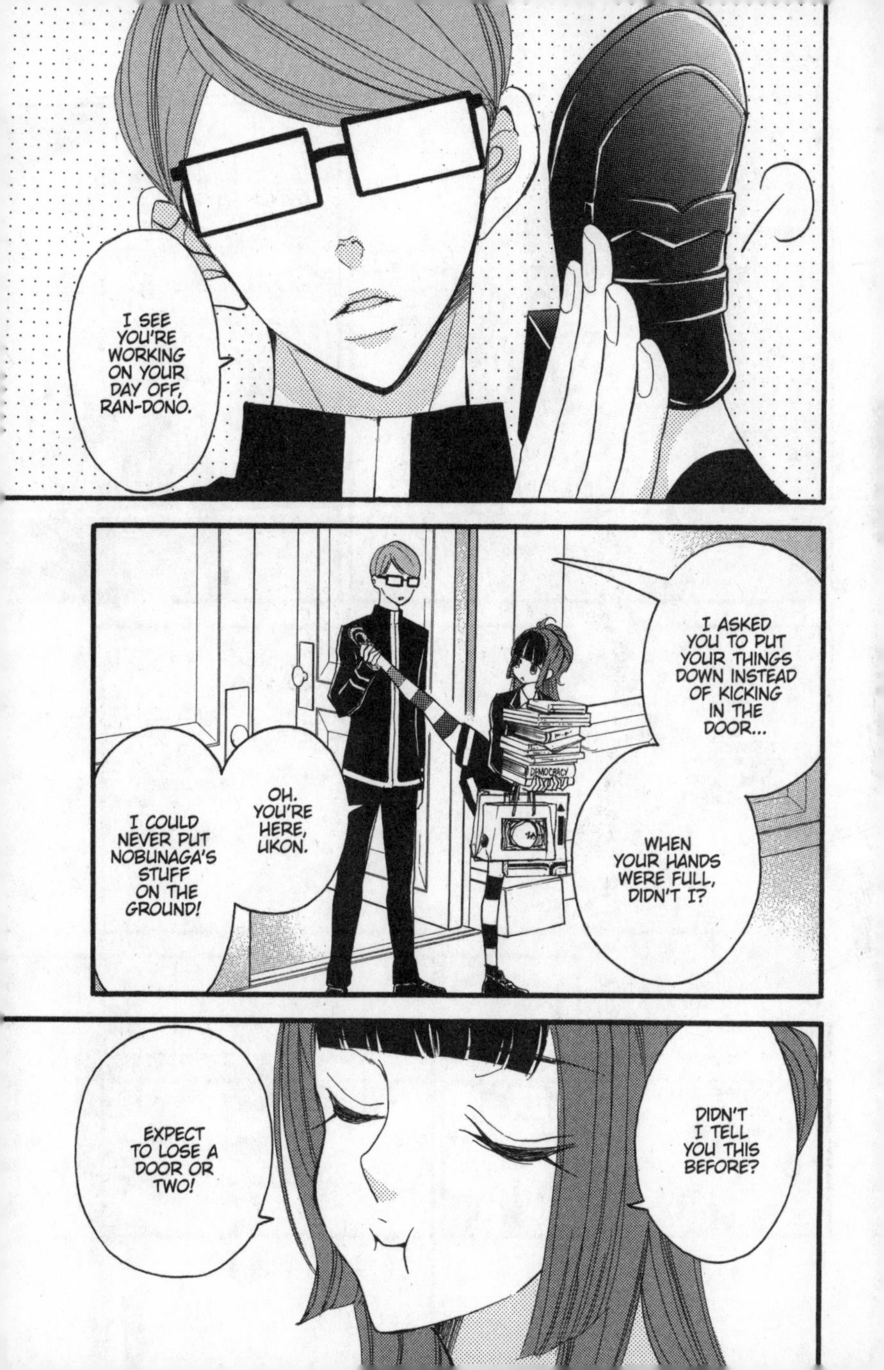
I SEE YOU'RE WORKING ON YOUR DAY OFF, RAN-DONO.
I ASKED YOU TO PUT YOUR THINGS DOWN INSTEAD OF KICKING IN THE DOOR...
WHEN YOUR HANDS WERE FULL, DIDN'T I?
DEMOCRACY
OH. YOU'RE HERE, UKON.
I COULD NEVER PUT NOBUNAGA'S STUFF ON THE GROUND!
DIDN'T I TELL YOU THIS BEFORE?
EXPECT TO LOSE A DOOR OR TWO!

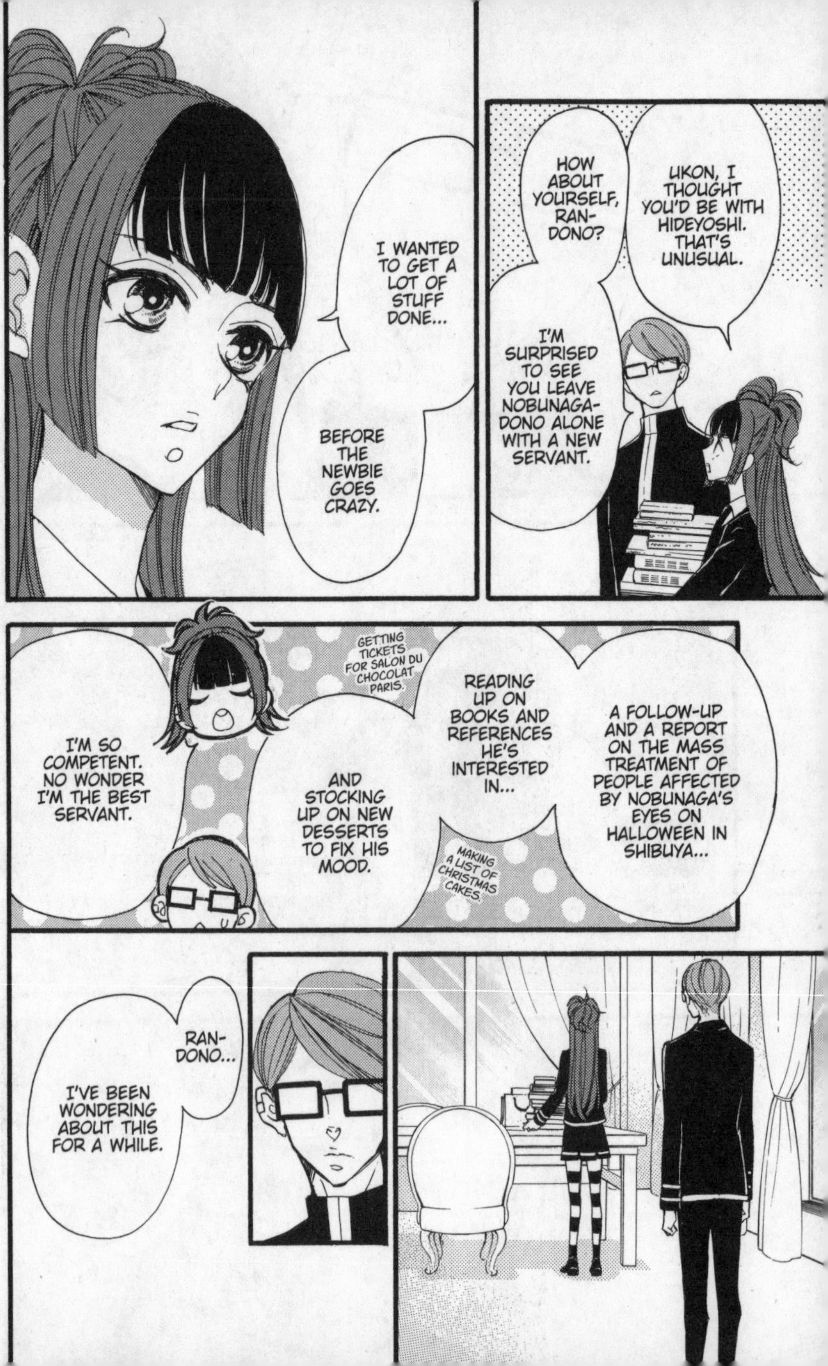
UKON, I THOUGHT YOU'D BE WITH HIDEYOSHI. THAT'S UNUSUAL.
HOW ABOUT YOURSELF, RAN-DONO?
I'M SURPRISED TO SEE YOU LEAVE NOBUNAGA-DONO ALONE WITH A NEW SERVANT.
I WANTED TO GET A LOT OF STUFF DONE...
BEFORE THE NEWBIE GOES CRAZY.
A FOLLOW-UP AND A REPORT ON THE MASS TREATMENT OF PEOPLE AFFECTED BY NOBUNAGA'S EYES ON HALLOWEEN IN SHIBUYA...
READING UP ON BOOKS AND REFERENCES HE'S INTERESTED IN...
GETTING TICKETS FOR SALON DU CHOCOLAT PARIS.
MAKING A LIST OF CHRISTMAS CAKES.
AND STOCKING UP ON NEW DESSERTS TO FIX HIS MOOD.
I'M SO COMPETENT. NO WONDER I'M THE BEST SERVANT.
RAN-DONO...
I'VE BEEN WONDERING ABOUT THIS FOR A WHILE.

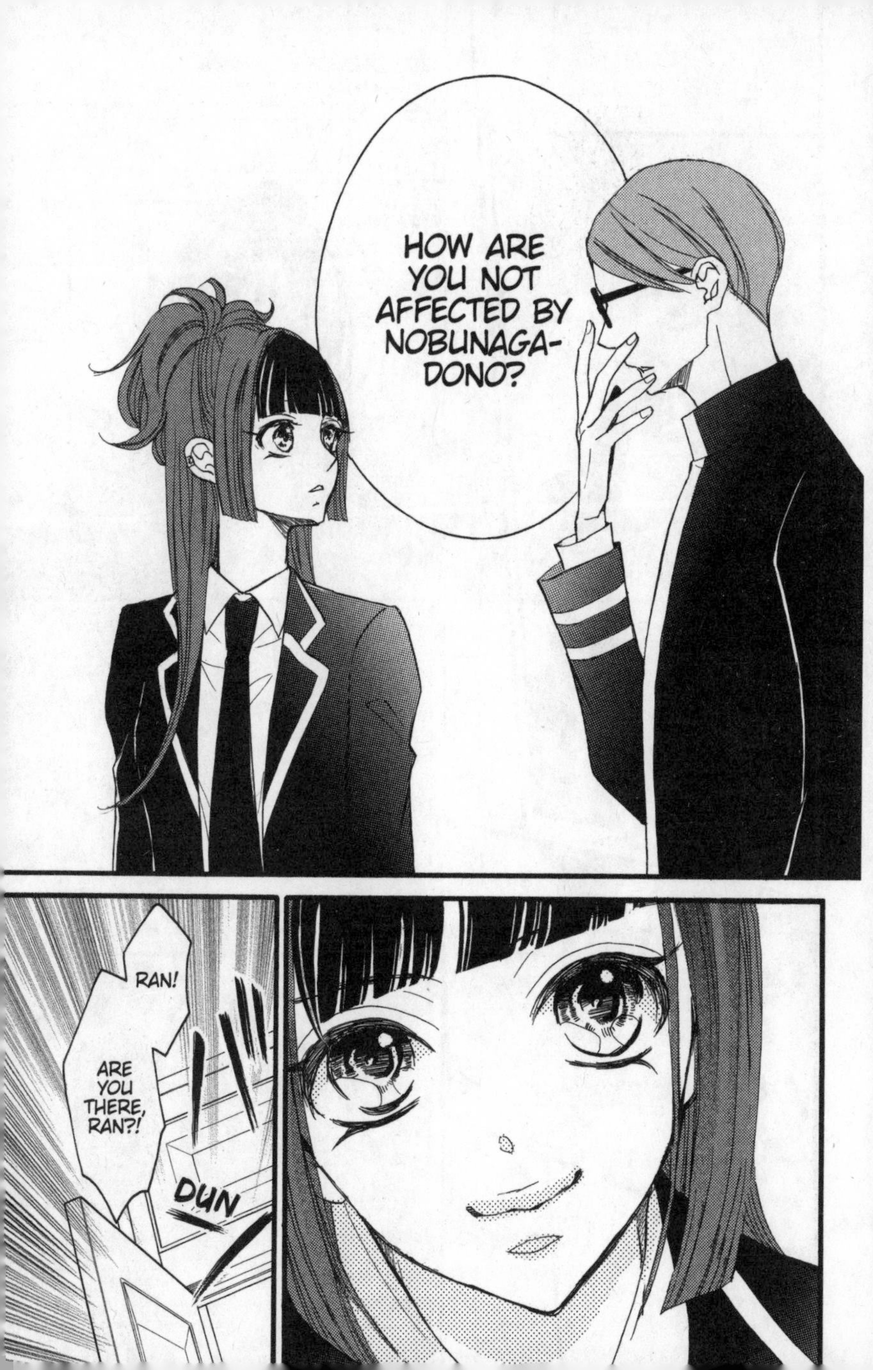
HOW ARE YOU NOT AFFECTED BY NOBUNAGA-DONO?
RAN!
ARE YOU THERE, RAN?!
DUN

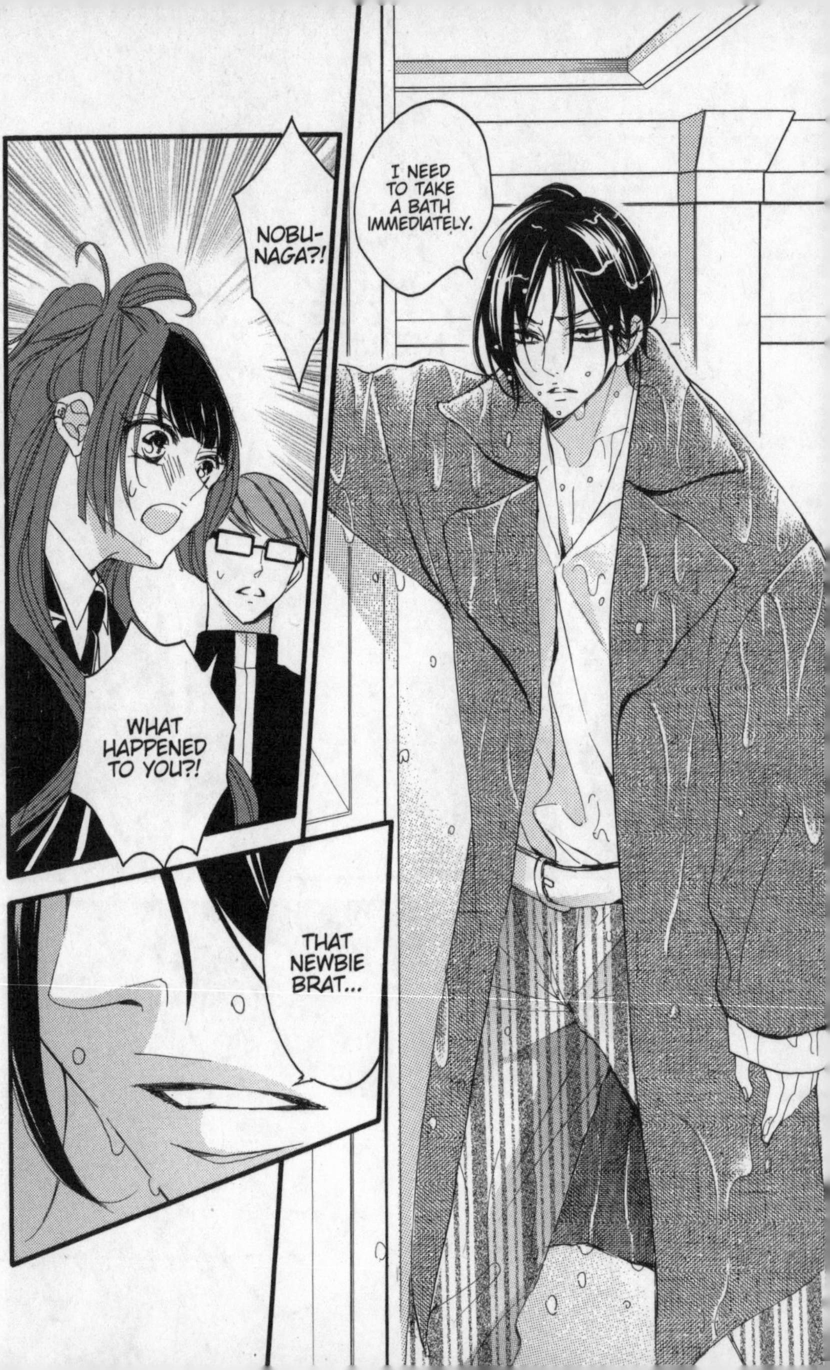
I NEED TO TAKE A BATH IMMEDIATELY.
NOBU-NAGA?!
WHAT HAPPENED TO YOU?!
THAT NEWBIE BRAT...

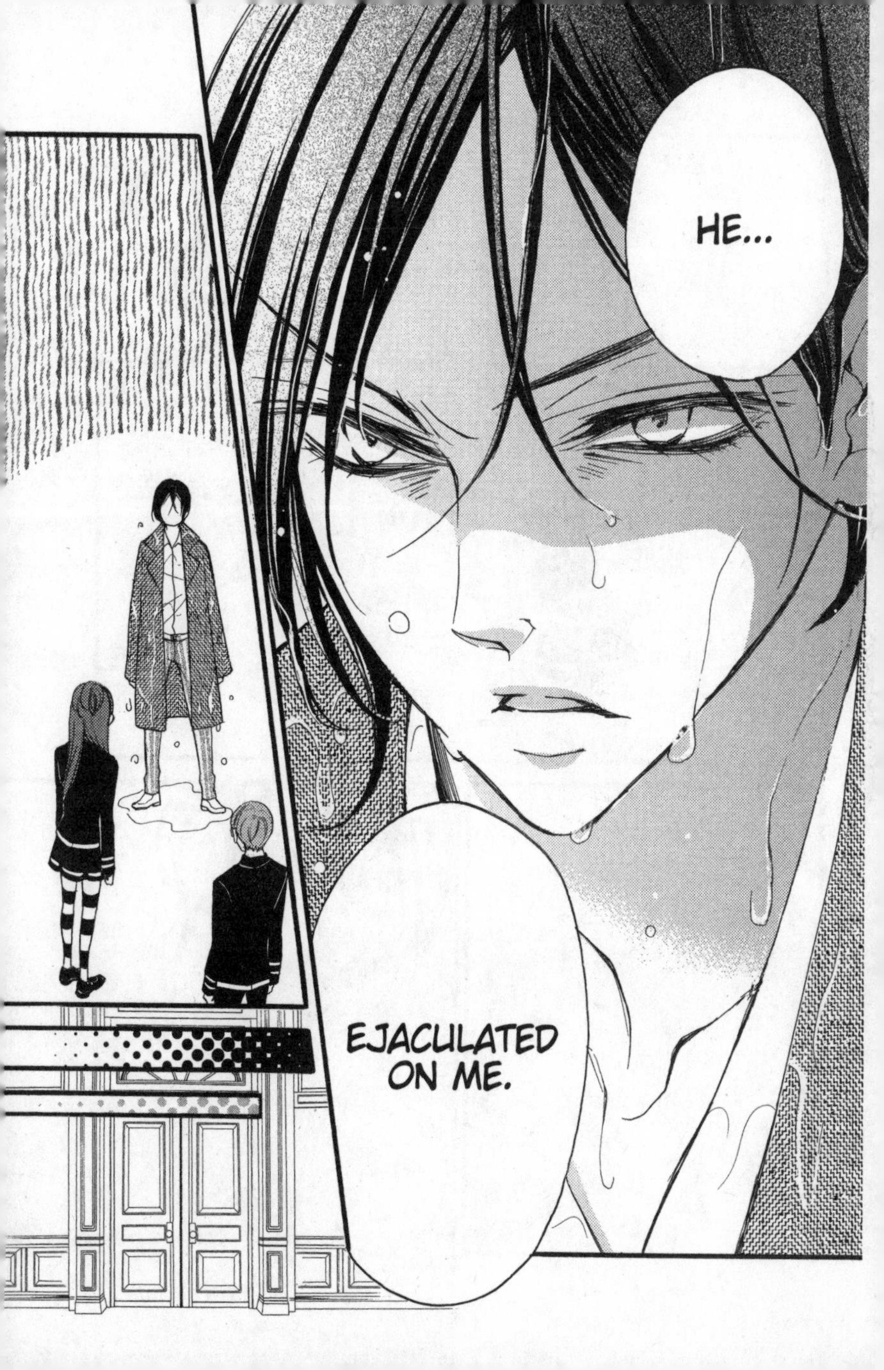
HE...
EJACULATED ON ME.

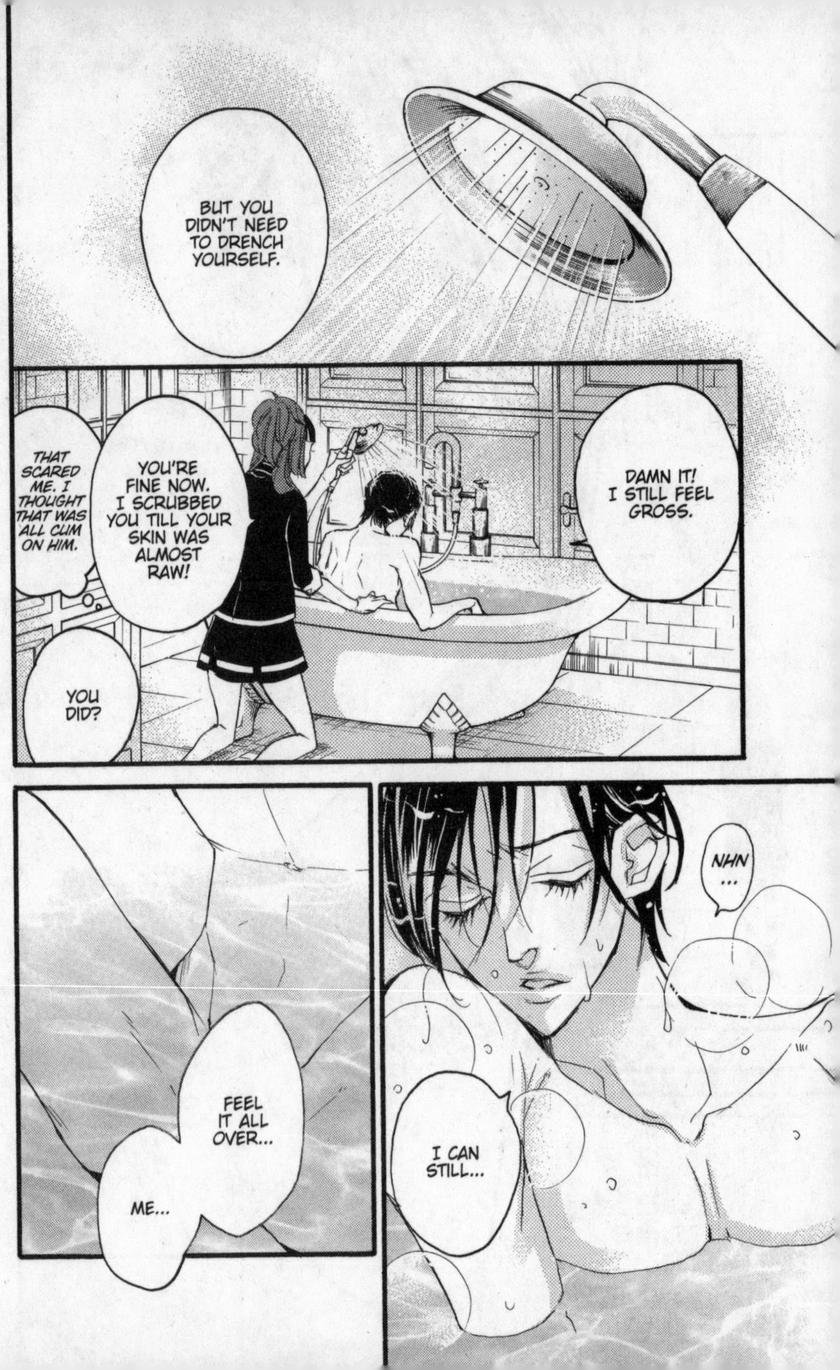
BUT YOU DIDN'T NEED TO DRENCH YOURSELF.
DAMN IT! I STILL FEEL GROSS.
YOU'RE FINE NOW. I SCRUBBED YOU TILL YOUR SKIN WAS ALMOST RAW!
THAT SCARED ME. I THOUGHT THAT WAS ALL CUM ON HIM.
YOU DID?
NHN ...
I CAN STILL...
FEEL IT ALL OVER...
ME...

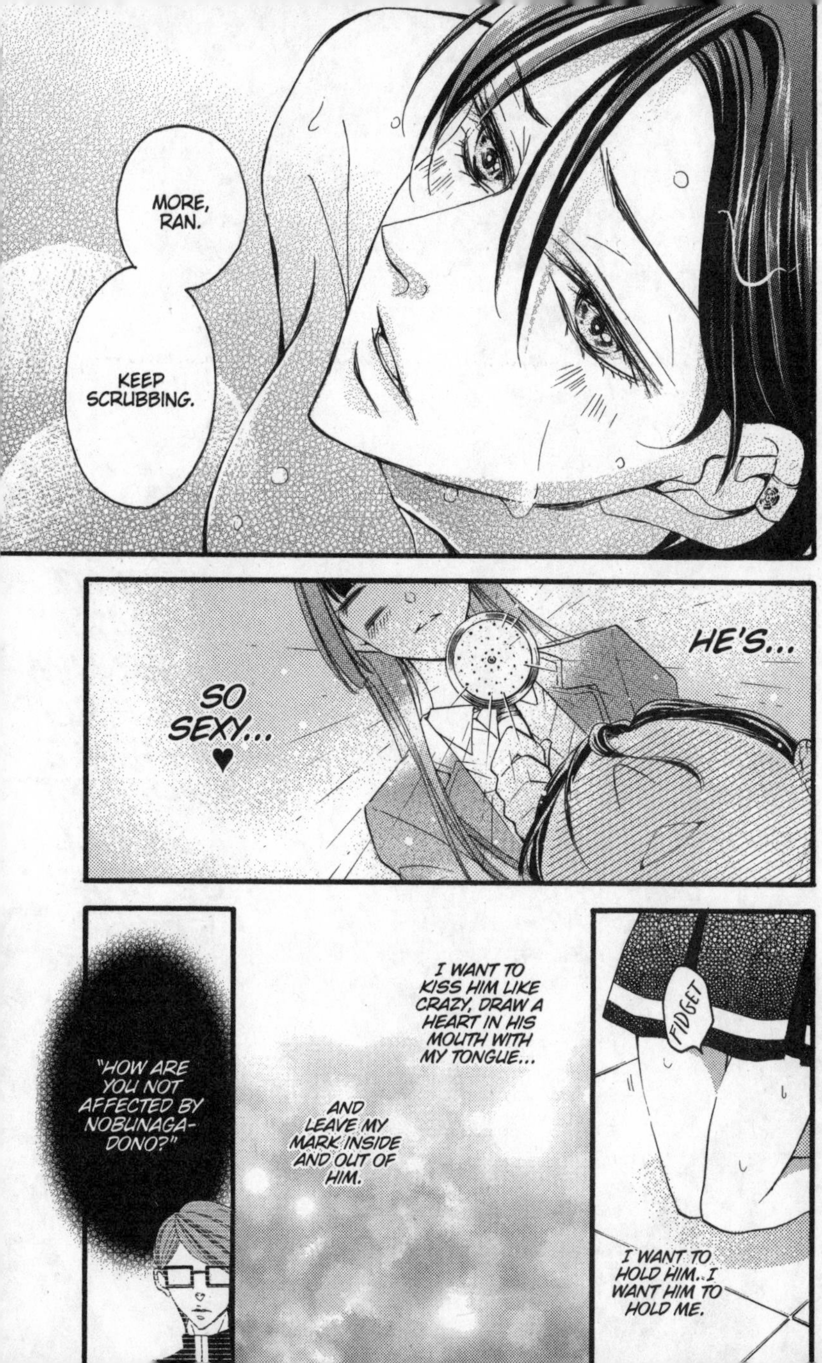
MORE, RAN.
KEEP SCRUBBING.
HE'S...
SO SEXY... ♥
FIDGET
I WANT TO HOLD HIM..I WANT HIM TO HOLD ME.
I WANT TO KISS HIM LIKE CRAZY, DRAW A HEART IN HIS MOUTH WITH MY TONGUE...
AND LEAVE MY MARK INSIDE AND OUT OF HIM.
"HOW ARE YOU NOT AFFECTED BY NOBUNAGA-DONO?"

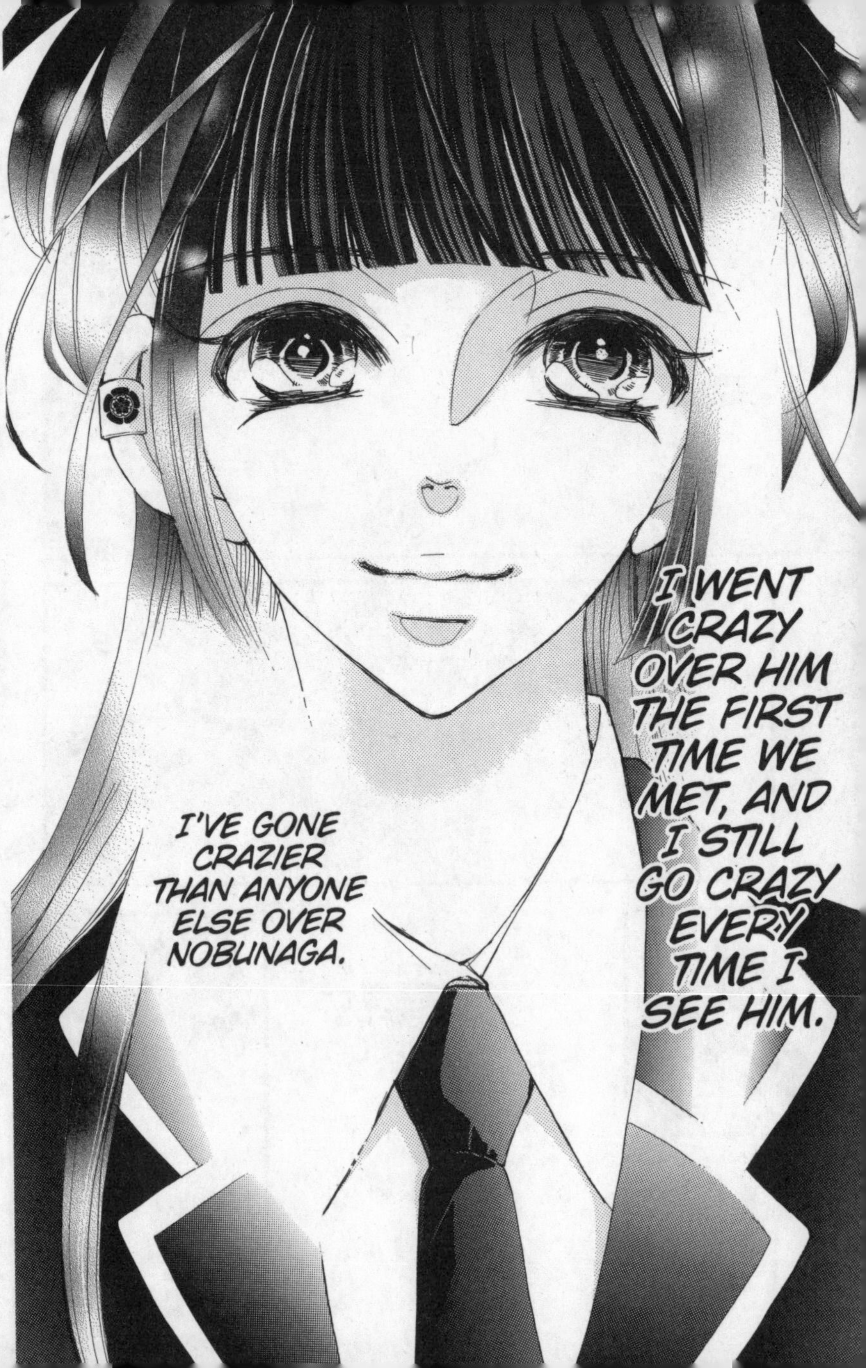
I WENT CRAZY OVER HIM THE FIRST TIME WE MET, AND I STILL GO CRAZY EVERY TIME I SEE HIM.
I'VE GONE CRAZIER THAN ANYONE ELSE OVER NOBUNAGA.

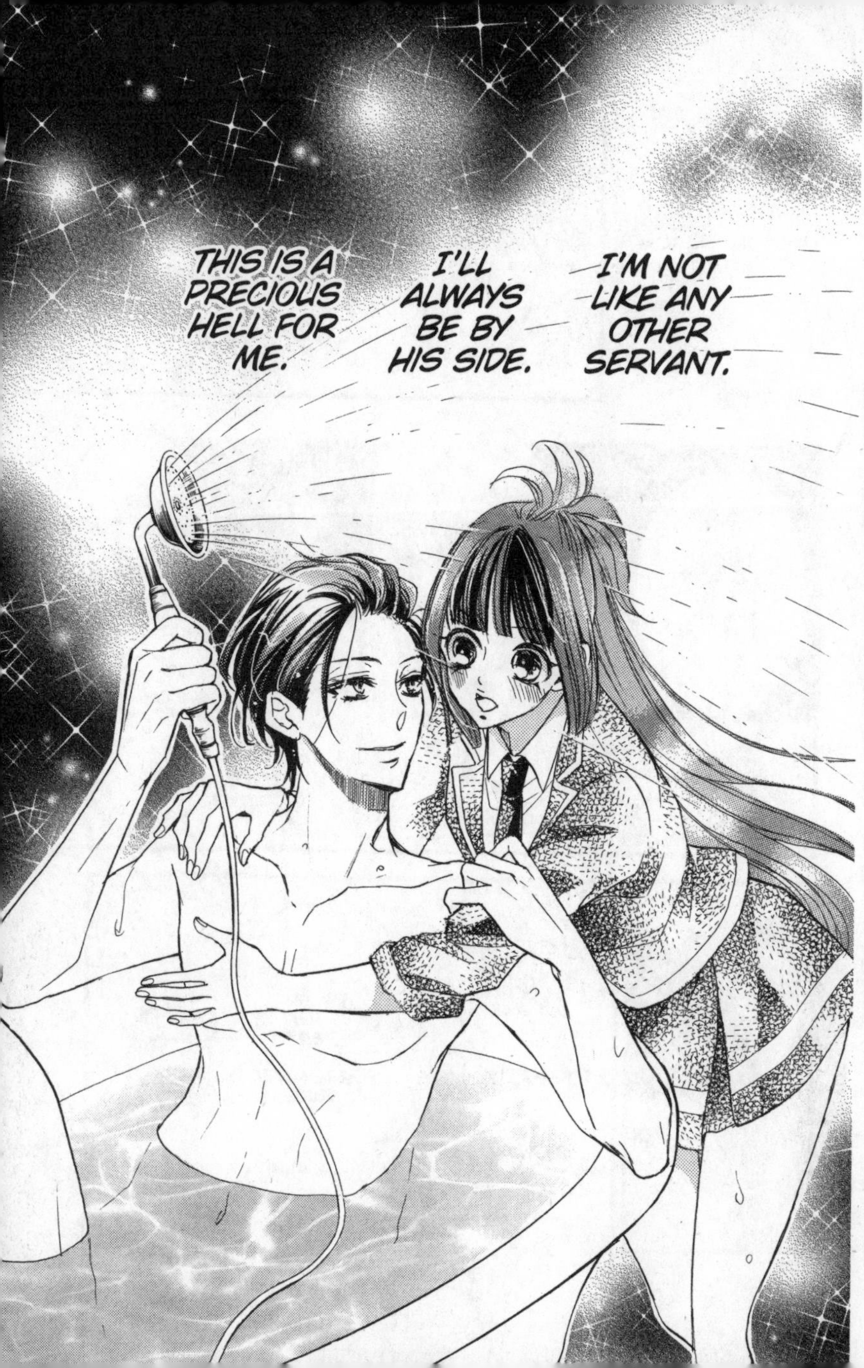
I'M NOT LIKE ANY OTHER SERVANT.
I'LL ALWAYS BE BY HIS SIDE.
THIS IS A PRECIOUS HELL FOR ME.

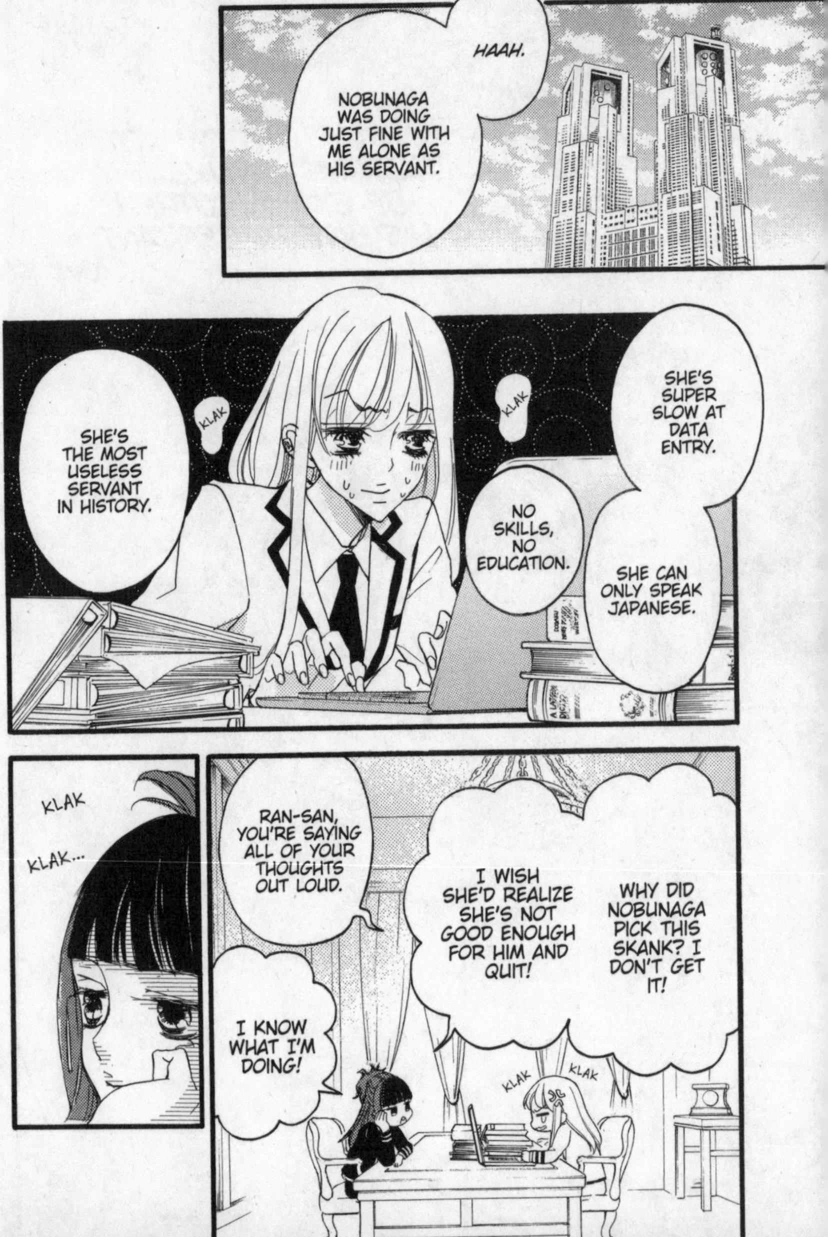
HAAH.
NOBUNAGA WAS DOING JUST FINE WITH ME ALONE AS HIS SERVANT.
SHE'S SUPER SLOW AT DATA ENTRY.
KLAK
NO SKILLS, NO EDUCATION.
SHE CAN ONLY SPEAK JAPANESE.
KLAK
SHE'S THE MOST USELESS SERVANT IN HISTORY.
WHY DID NOBUNAGA PICK THIS SKANK? I DON'T GET IT!
I WISH SHE'D REALIZE SHE'S NOT GOOD ENOUGH FOR HIM AND QUIT!
RAN-SAN, YOU'RE SAYING ALL OF YOUR THOUGHTS OUT LOUD.
I KNOW WHAT I'M DOING!
KLAK
KLAK
KLAK
KLAK...

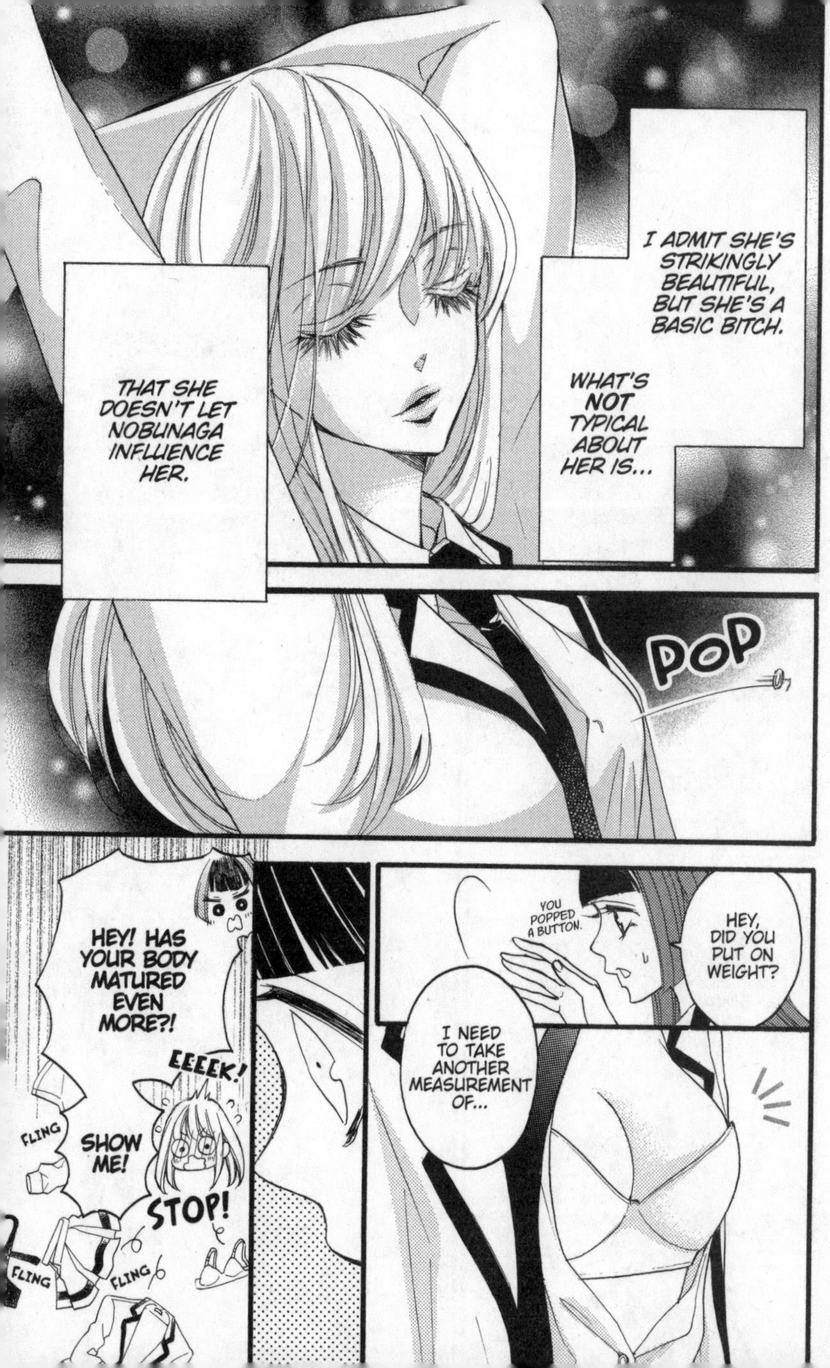
I ADMIT SHE'S STRIKINGLY BEAUTIFUL, BUT SHE'S A BASIC BITCH.
WHAT'S NOT TYPICAL ABOUT HER IS...
THAT SHE DOESN'T LET NOBUNAGA INFLUENCE HER.
POP
HEY, DID YOU PUT ON WEIGHT?
YOU POPPED A BUTTON.
I NEED TO TAKE ANOTHER MEASUREMENT OF...
HEY! HAS YOUR BODY MATURED EVEN MORE?!
EEEEK!
SHOW ME!
FLING
STOP!
FLING
FLING

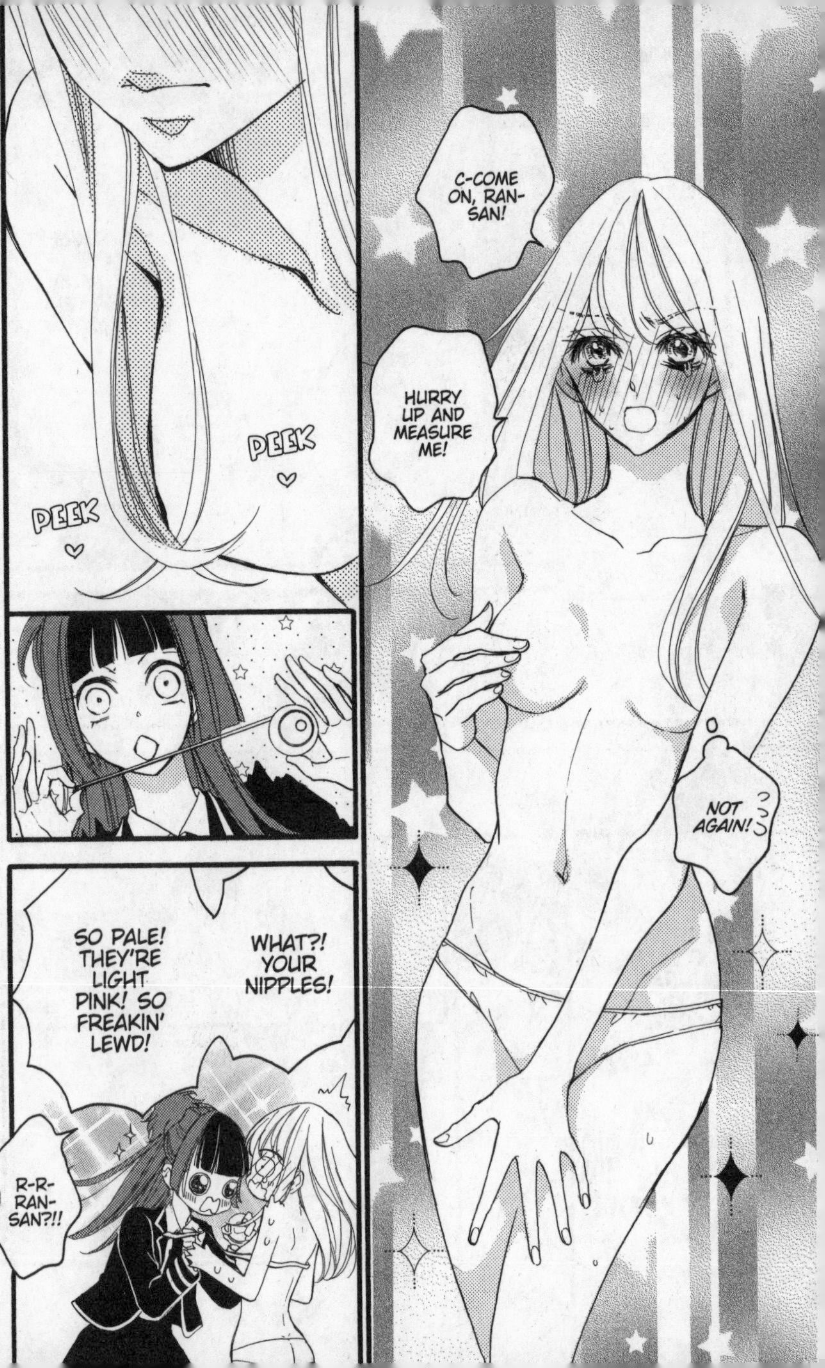
C-COME ON, RAN-SAN!
HURRY UP AND MEASURE ME!
NOT AGAIN!
PEEK
PEEK
WHAT?! YOUR NIPPLES!
SO PALE! THEY'RE LIGHT PINK! SO FREAKIN' LEWD!
R-R-RAN-SAN?!!

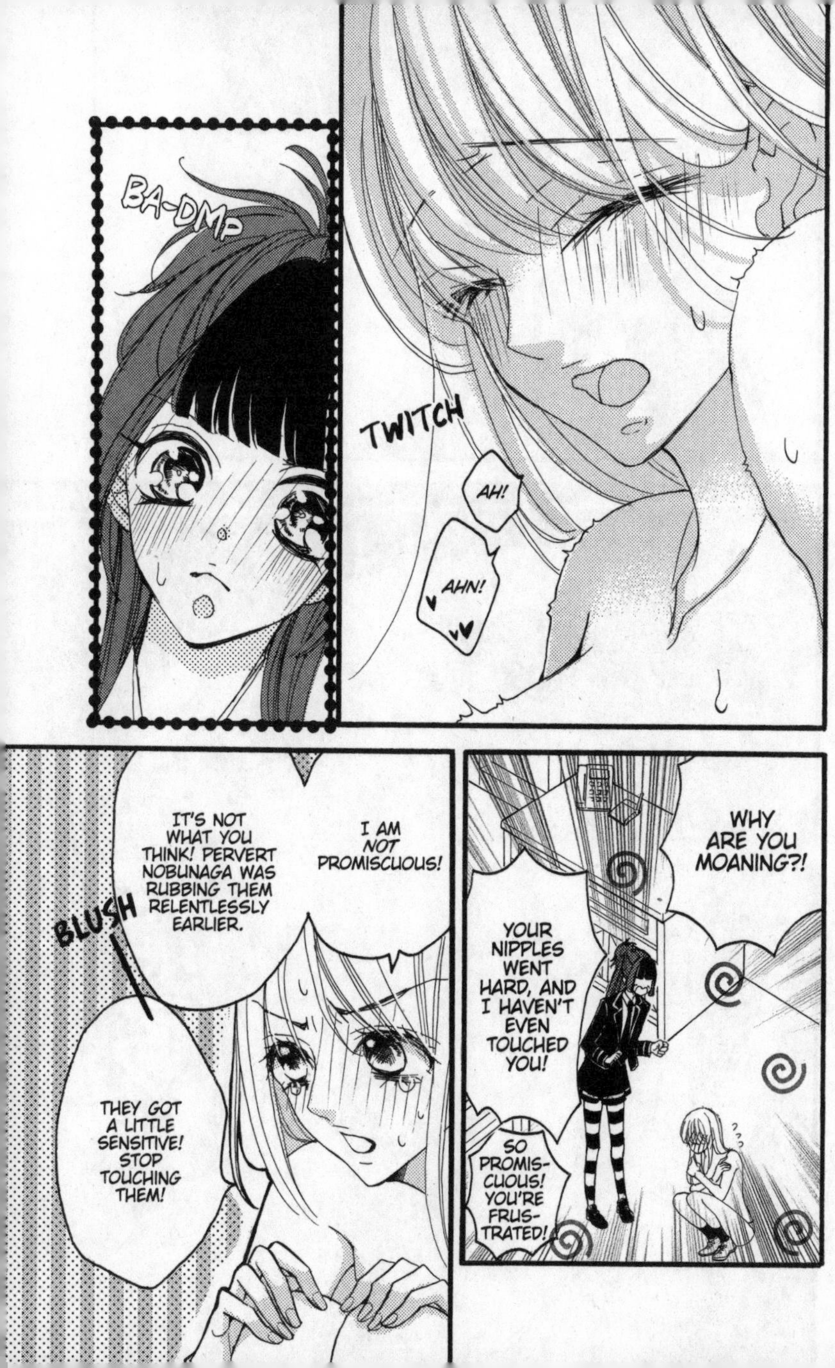

TWITCH
AH!
AHN!
BA-DMP
WHY ARE YOU MOANING?!
YOUR NIPPLES WENT HARD, AND I HAVEN'T EVEN TOUCHED YOU!
SO PROMIS-CUOUS! YOU'RE FRUS-TRATED!
I AM NOT PROMISCUOUS!
IT'S NOT WHAT YOU THINK! PERVERT NOBUNAGA WAS RUBBING THEM RELENTLESSLY EARLIER.
BLUSH
THEY GOT A LITTLE SENSITIVE! STOP TOUCHING THEM!

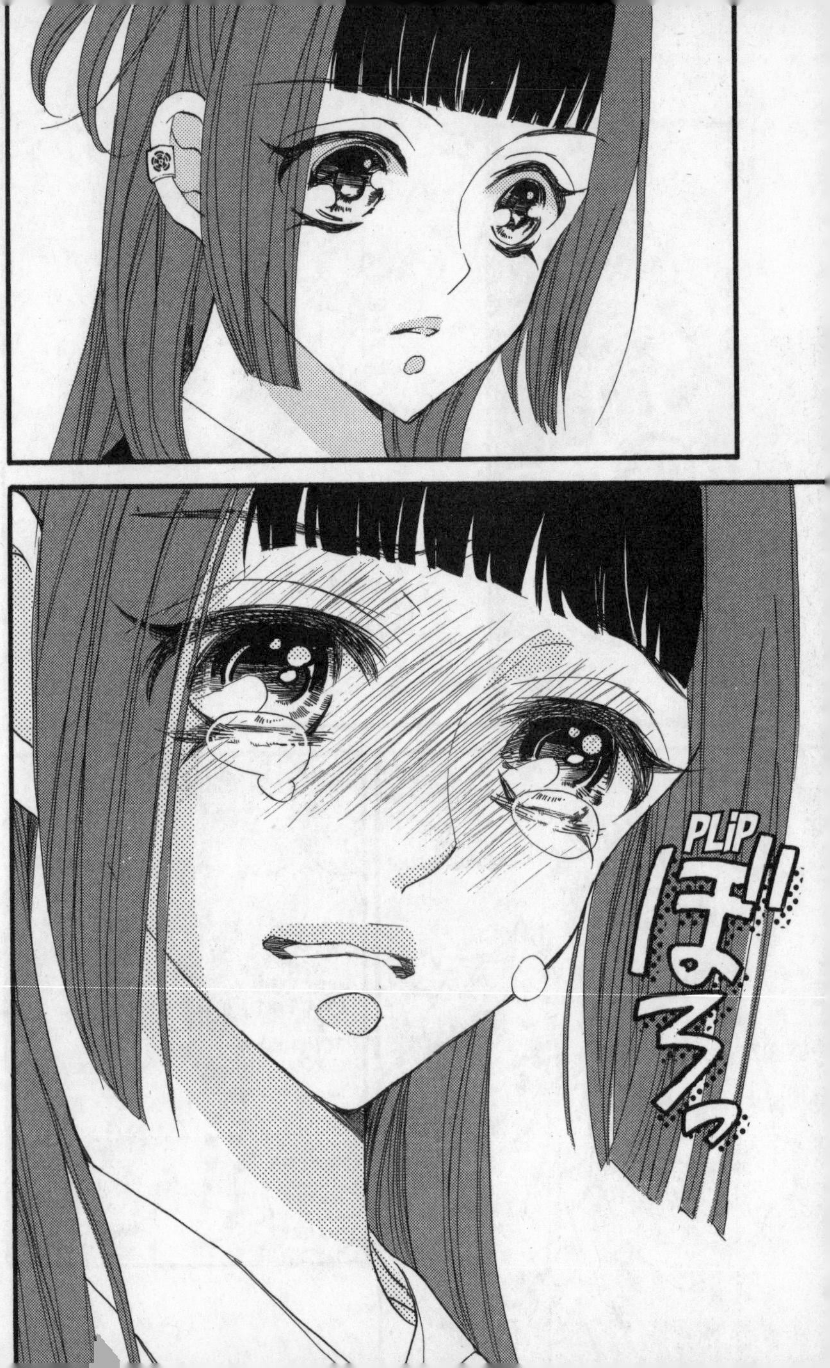
PLIP
ぽろっ

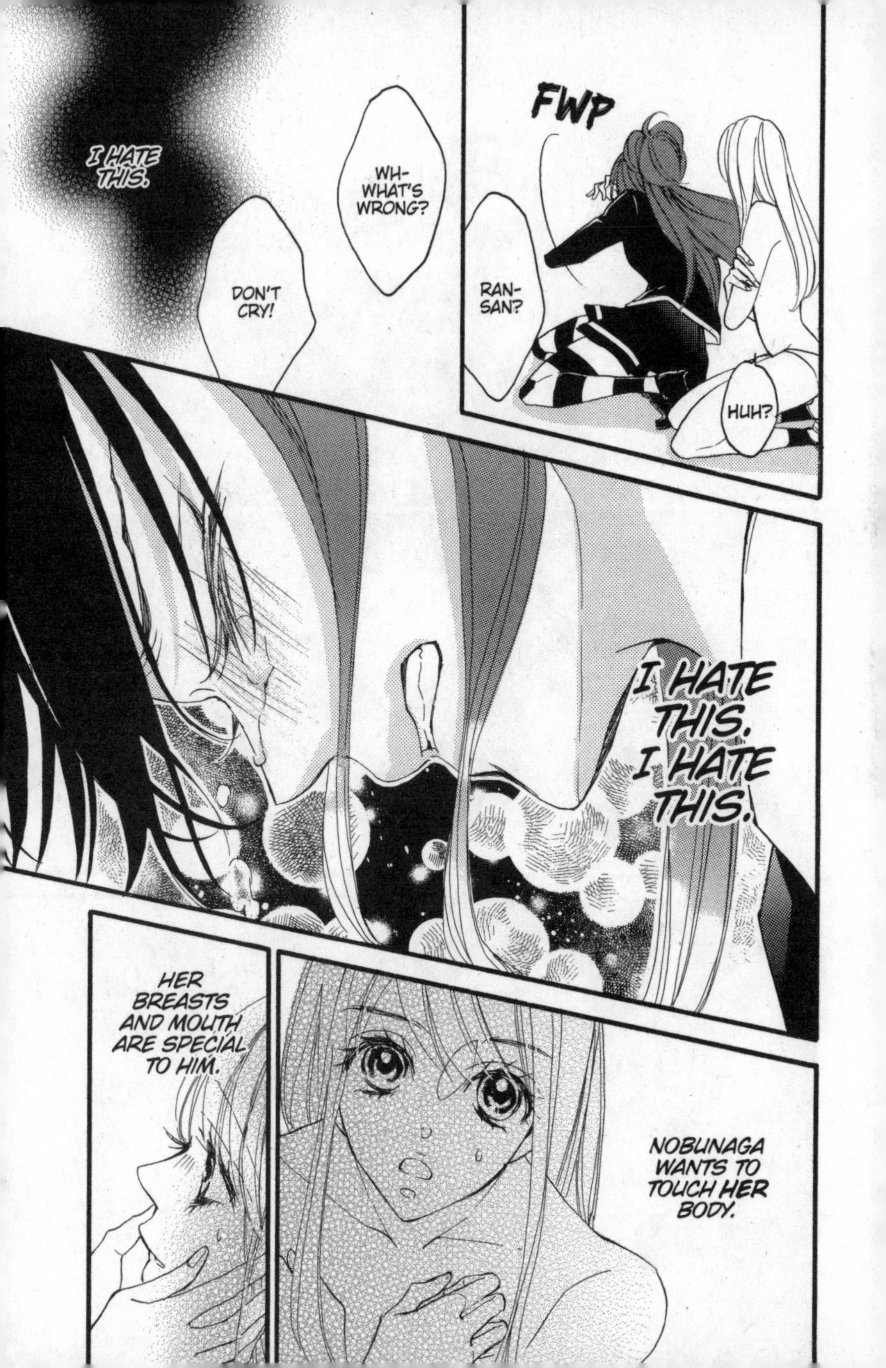
FWP
RAN-SAN?
HUH?
WH-WHAT'S WRONG?
DON'T CRY!
I HATE THIS.
I HATE THIS. I HATE THIS.
NOBUNAGA WANTS TO TOUCH HER BODY.
HER BREASTS AND MOUTH ARE SPECIAL TO HIM.

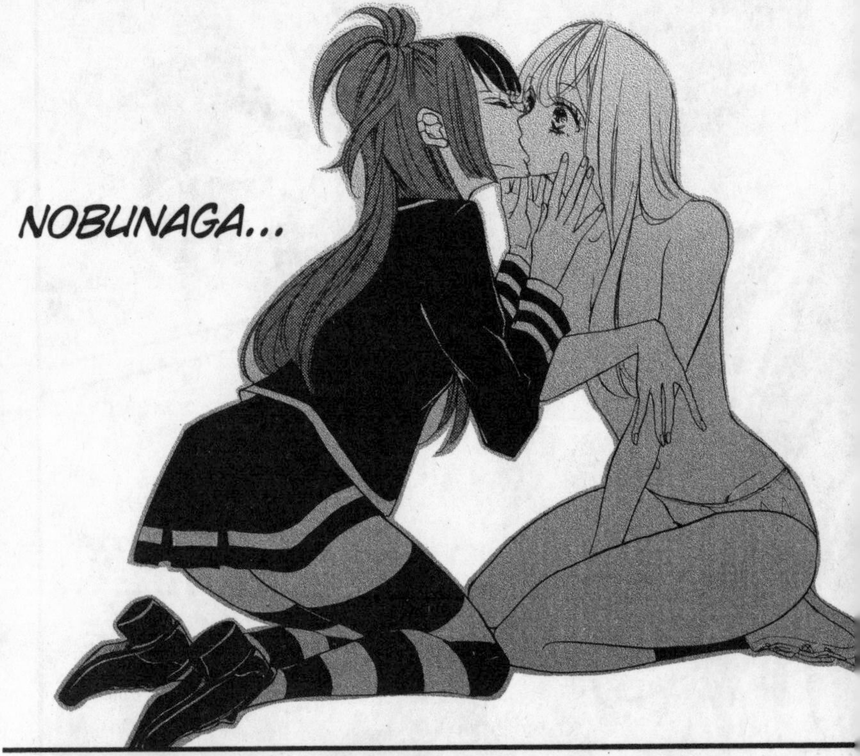
NOBUNAGA...

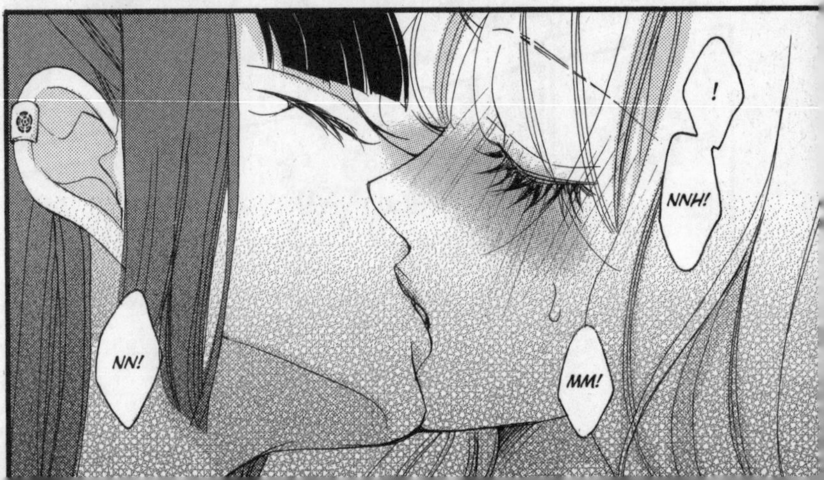
!
NNH!
MM!
NN!

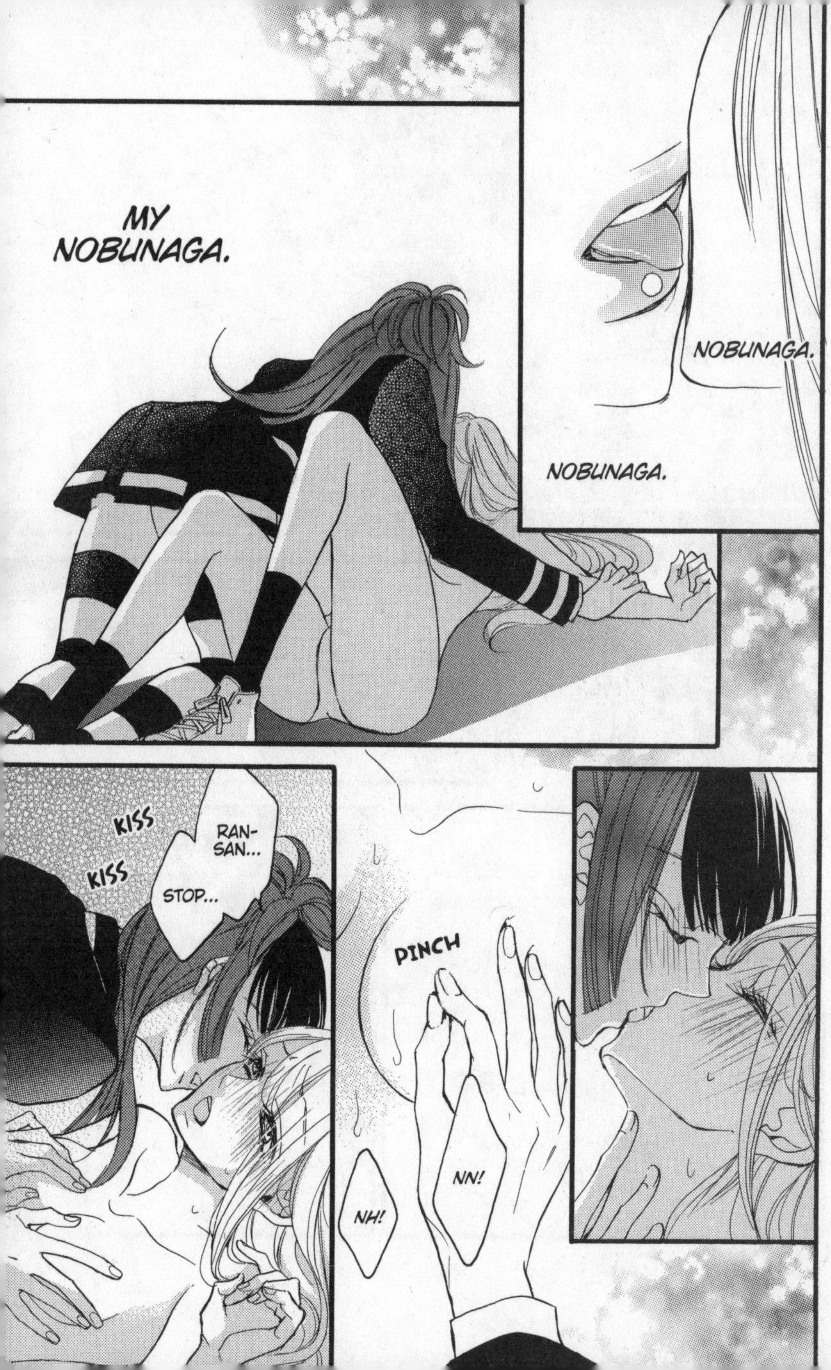
NOBUNAGA.
NOBUNAGA.
MY NOBUNAGA.
PINCH
NN!
NH!
RAN-SAN... STOP...
KISS
KISS

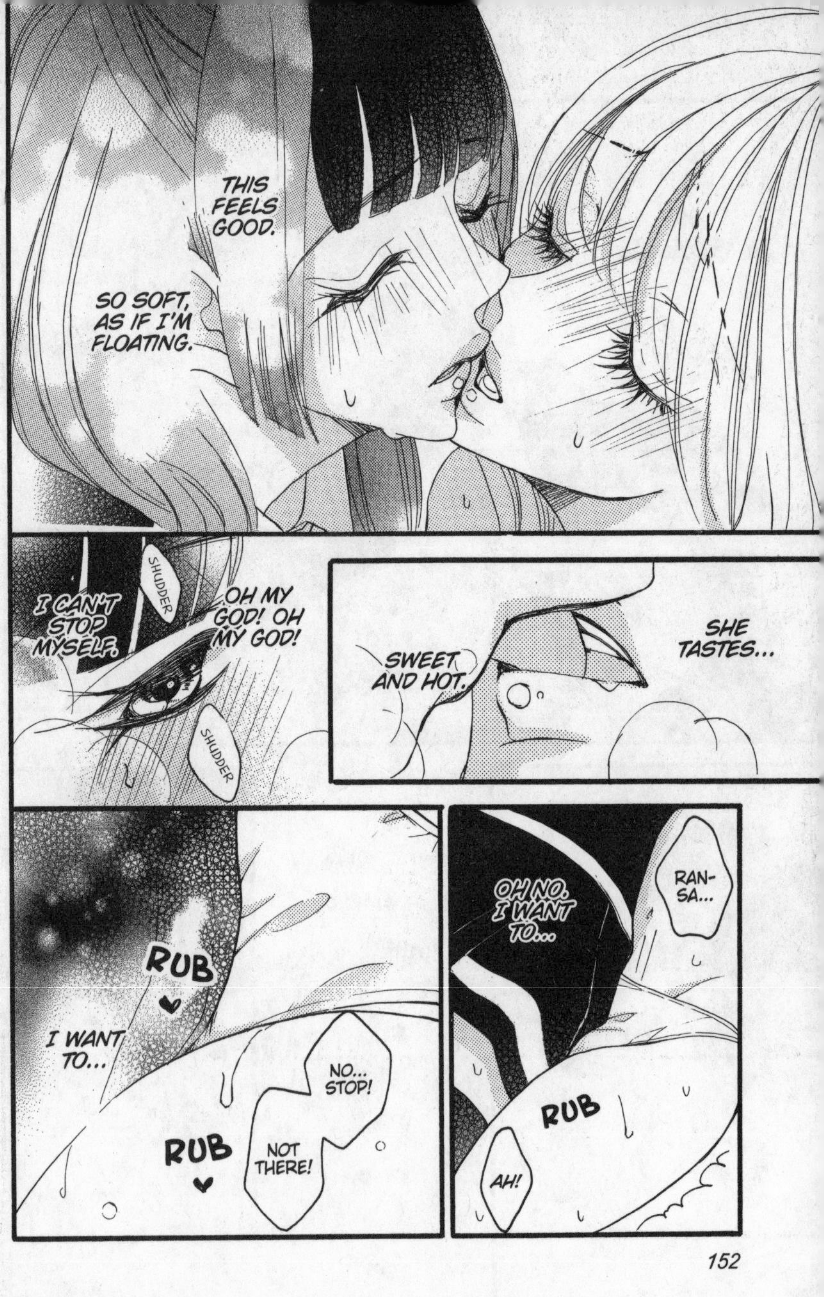
THIS FEELS GOOD.
SO SOFT, AS IF I'M FLOATING.
SHE TASTES...
SWEET AND HOT.
OH MY GOD! OH MY GOD!
SHUDDER
I CAN'T STOP MYSELF.
SHUDDER
RAN-SA...
OH NO. I WANT TO...
RUB
AH!
RUB
NO... STOP!
NOT THERE!
I WANT TO...
RUB

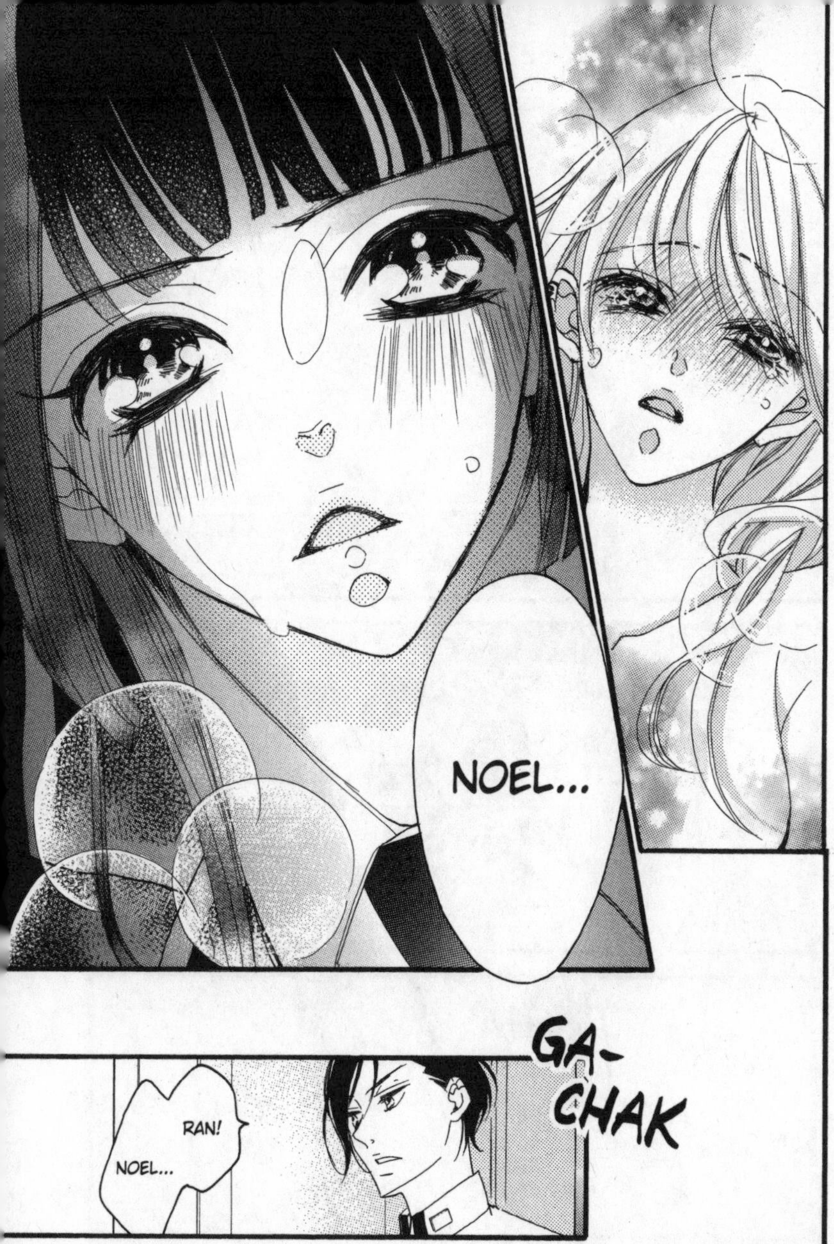
NOEL...
GA-CHAK
RAN! NOEL...

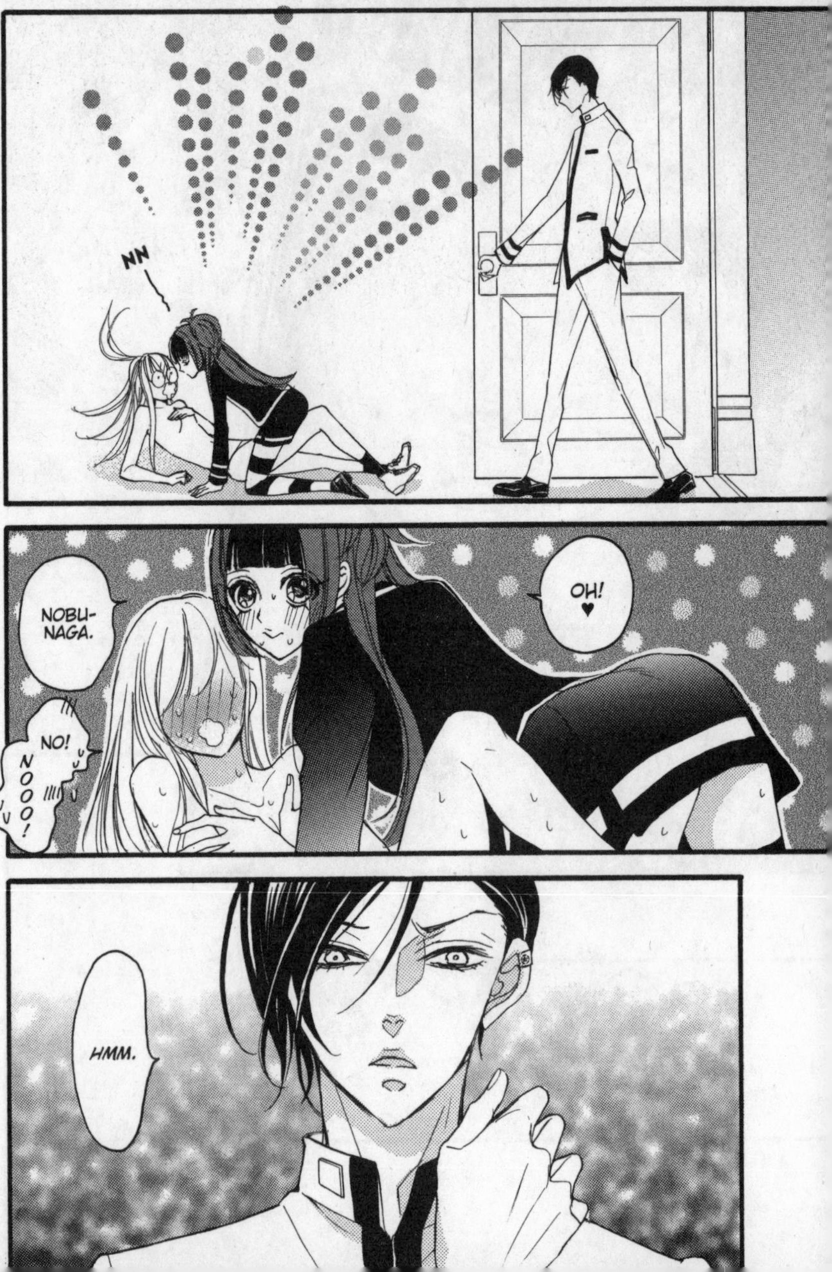
NN
OH! ♥
NOBU-NAGA.
NO! NOOOO!
HMM.

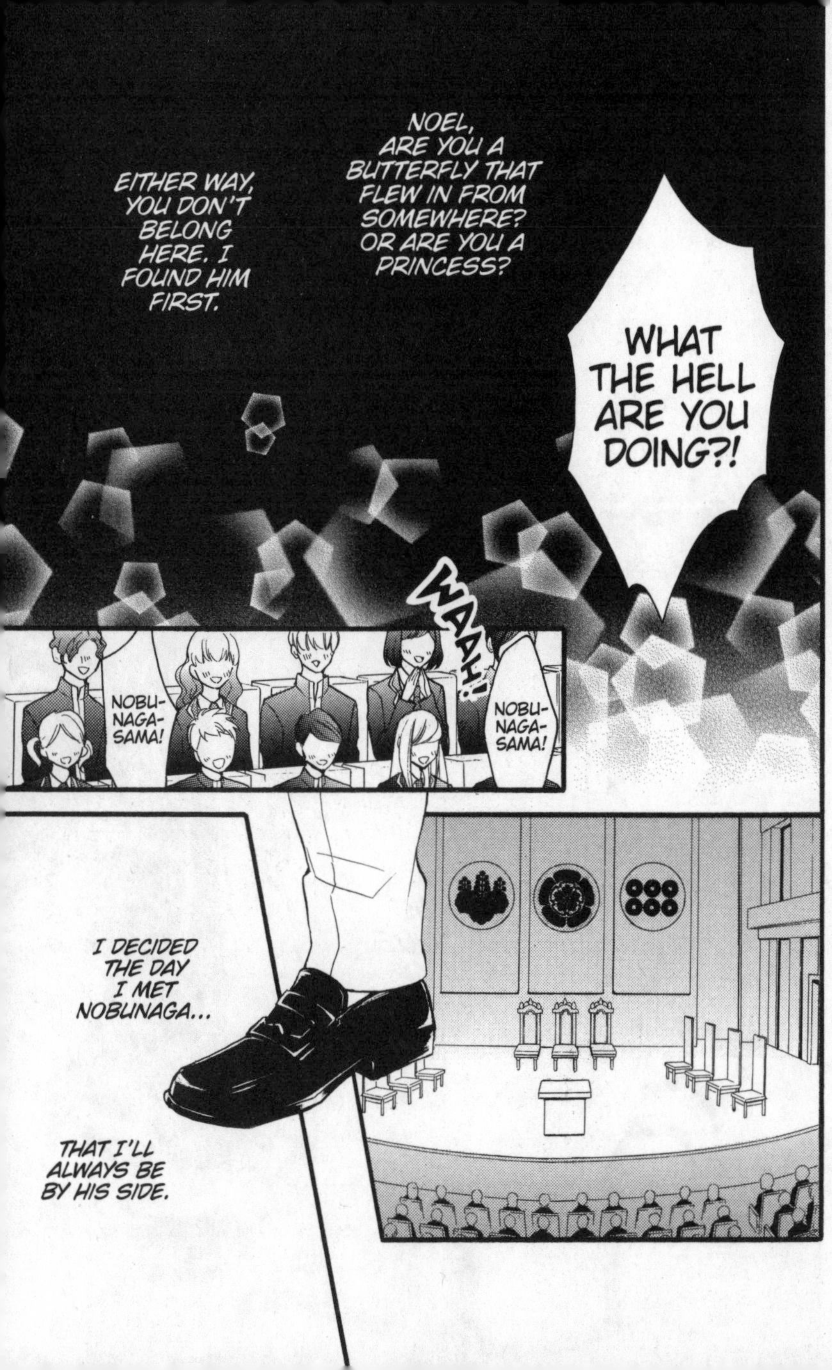
WHAT THE HELL ARE YOU DOING?!
NOEL, ARE YOU A BUTTERFLY THAT FLEW IN FROM SOMEWHERE? OR ARE YOU A PRINCESS?
EITHER WAY, YOU DON'T BELONG HERE. I FOUND HIM FIRST.
WAAH!?
NOBU-NAGA-SAMA!
NOBU-NAGA-SAMA!
I DECIDED THE DAY I MET NOBUNAGA...
THAT I'LL ALWAYS BE BY HIS SIDE.

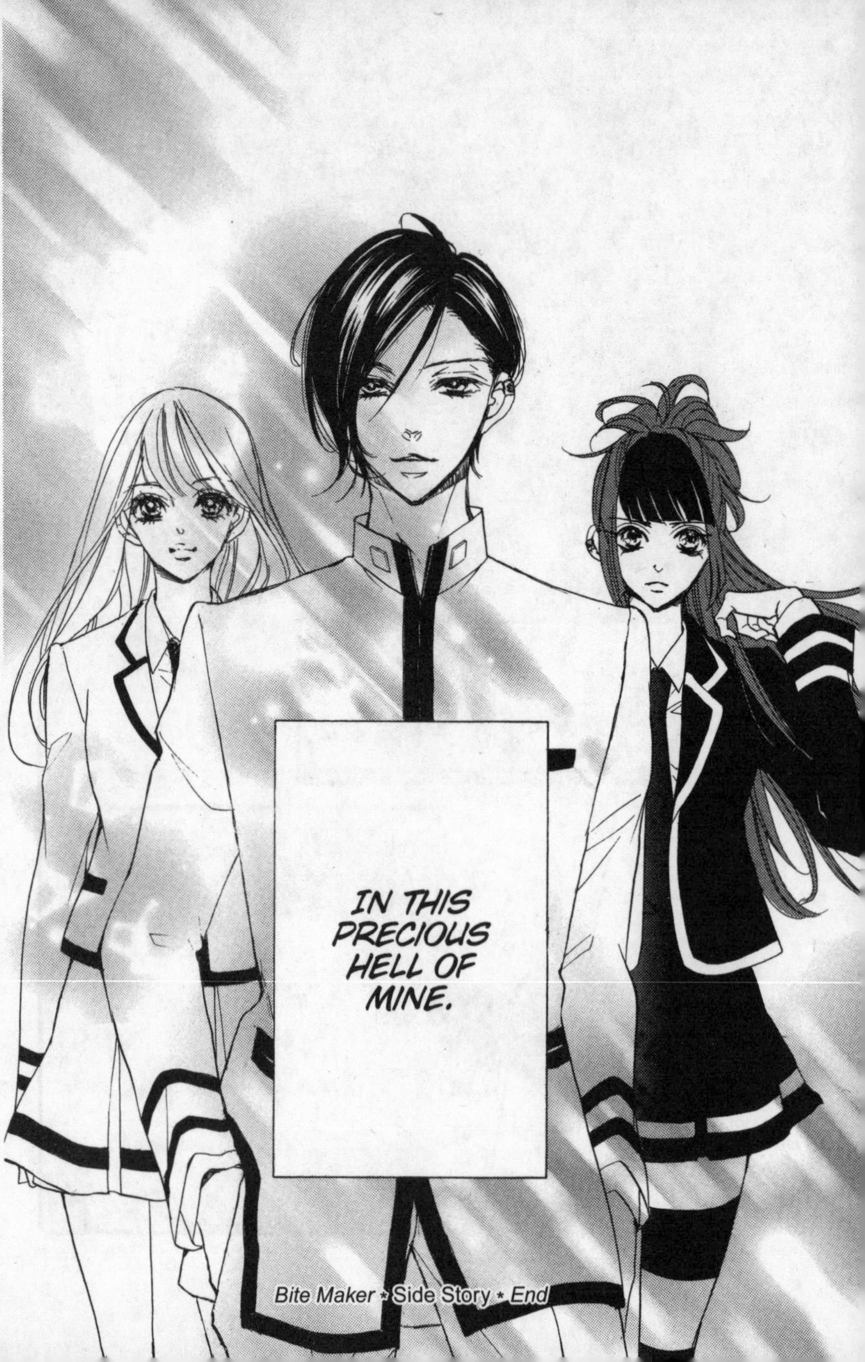
IN THIS PRECIOUS HELL OF MINE.
Bite Maker * Side Story * End

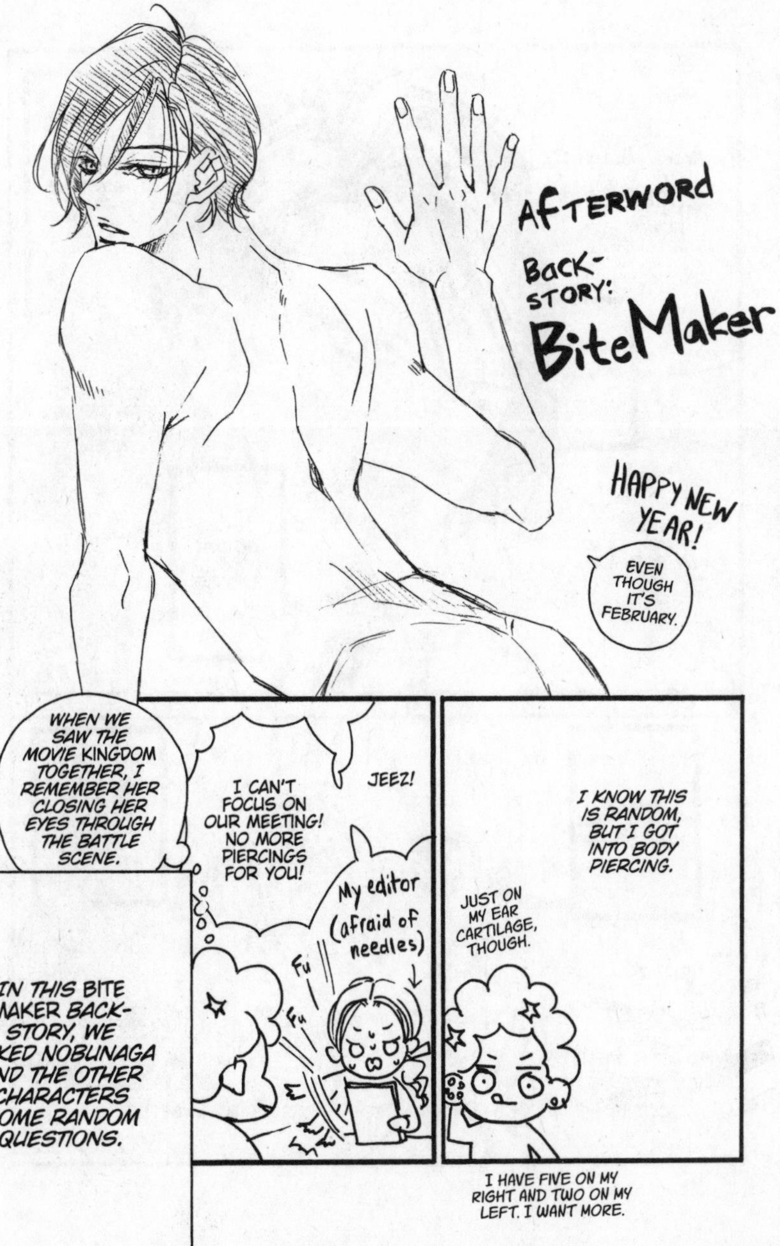
AFTERWORD
BACK-STORY:
BiteMaker
HAPPY NEW YEAR!
EVEN THOUGH IT'S FEBRUARY.
I KNOW THIS IS RANDOM, BUT I GOT INTO BODY PIERCING.
JUST ON MY EAR CARTILAGE, THOUGH.
I HAVE FIVE ON MY RIGHT AND TWO ON MY LEFT. I WANT MORE.
JEEZ!
I CAN'T FOCUS ON OUR MEETING! NO MORE PIERCINGS FOR YOU!
My editor (afraid of needles)
Fu
Fu
WHEN WE SAW THE MOVIE KINGDOM TOGETHER, I REMEMBER HER CLOSING HER EYES THROUGH THE BATTLE SCENE.
IN THIS BITE MAKER BACK-STORY, WE ASKED NOBUNAGA AND THE OTHER CHARACTERS SOME RANDOM QUESTIONS.

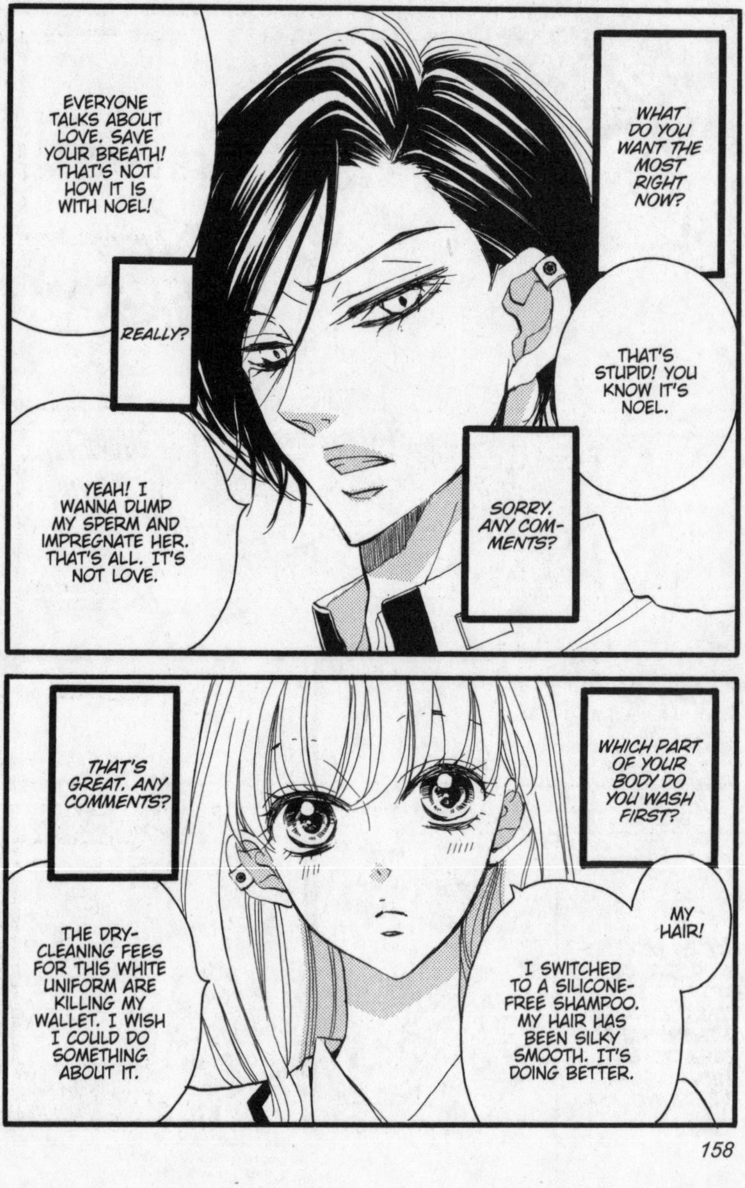
WHAT DO YOU WANT THE MOST RIGHT NOW?
THAT'S STUPID! YOU KNOW IT'S NOEL.
SORRY. ANY COMMENTS?
EVERYONE TALKS ABOUT LOVE. SAVE YOUR BREATH! THAT'S NOT HOW IT IS WITH NOEL!
REALLY?
YEAH! I WANNA DUMP MY SPERM AND IMPREGNATE HER. THAT'S ALL. IT'S NOT LOVE.
WHICH PART OF YOUR BODY DO YOU WASH FIRST?
MY HAIR!
I SWITCHED TO A SILICONE-FREE SHAMPOO. MY HAIR HAS BEEN SILKY SMOOTH. IT'S DOING BETTER.
THAT'S GREAT. ANY COMMENTS?
THE DRY-CLEANING FEES FOR THIS WHITE UNIFORM ARE KILLING MY WALLET. I WISH I COULD DO SOMETHING ABOUT IT.

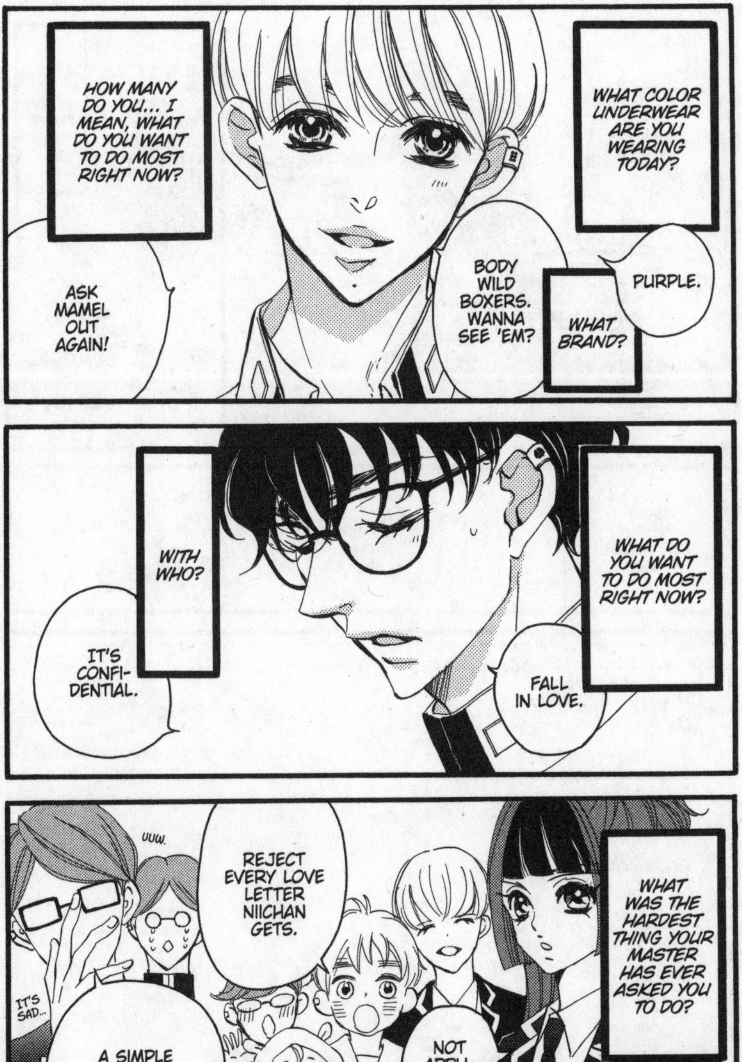
WHAT COLOR UNDERWEAR ARE YOU WEARING TODAY?
PURPLE.
WHAT BRAND?
BODY WILD BOXERS. WANNA SEE 'EM?
HOW MANY DO YOU... I MEAN, WHAT DO YOU WANT TO DO MOST RIGHT NOW?
ASK MAMEL OUT AGAIN!
WHAT DO YOU WANT TO DO MOST RIGHT NOW?
FALL IN LOVE.
WITH WHO?
IT'S CONFIDENTIAL.
WHAT WAS THE HARDEST THING YOUR MASTER HAS EVER ASKED YOU TO DO?
NOT APPLICABLE.
REJECT EVERY LOVE LETTER NIICHAN GETS.
UUW.
TEA?
IT'S SAD...
A SIMPLE "DON'T DO ANYTHING."

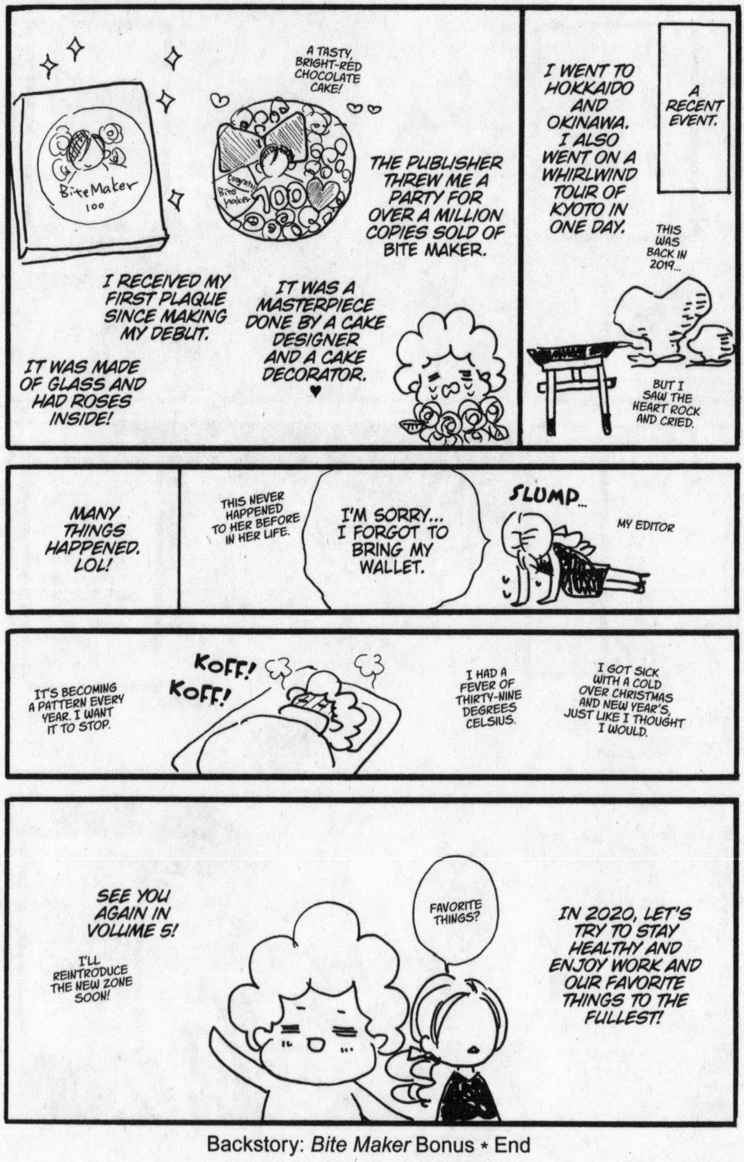
A RECENT EVENT.
I WENT TO HOKKAIDO AND OKINAWA. I ALSO WENT ON A WHIRLWIND TOUR OF KYOTO IN ONE DAY.
THIS WAS BACK IN 2019...
BUT I SAW THE HEART ROCK AND CRIED.
THE PUBLISHER THREW ME A PARTY FOR OVER A MILLION COPIES SOLD OF BITE MAKER.
A TASTY, BRIGHT-RED CHOCOLATE CAKE!
Congrats! Bite Maker 100
IT WAS A MASTERPIECE DONE BY A CAKE DESIGNER AND A CAKE DECORATOR. ♥
Bite Maker 100
I RECEIVED MY FIRST PLAQUE SINCE MAKING MY DEBUT.
IT WAS MADE OF GLASS AND HAD ROSES INSIDE!
MY EDITOR
SLUMP...
I'M SORRY... I FORGOT TO BRING MY WALLET.
THIS NEVER HAPPENED TO HER BEFORE IN HER LIFE.
MANY THINGS HAPPENED. LOL!
I GOT SICK WITH A COLD OVER CHRISTMAS AND NEW YEAR'S, JUST LIKE I THOUGHT I WOULD.
I HAD A FEVER OF THIRTY-NINE DEGREES CELSIUS.
KOFF! KOFF!
IT'S BECOMING A PATTERN EVERY YEAR. I WANT IT TO STOP.
IN 2020, LET'S TRY TO STAY HEALTHY AND ENJOY WORK AND OUR FAVORITE THINGS TO THE FULLEST!
FAVORITE THINGS?
SEE YOU AGAIN IN VOLUME 5!
I'LL REINTRODUCE THE NEW ZONE SOON!

Backstory: *Bite Maker* Bonus * End

Bite Maker
—The King's Omega—

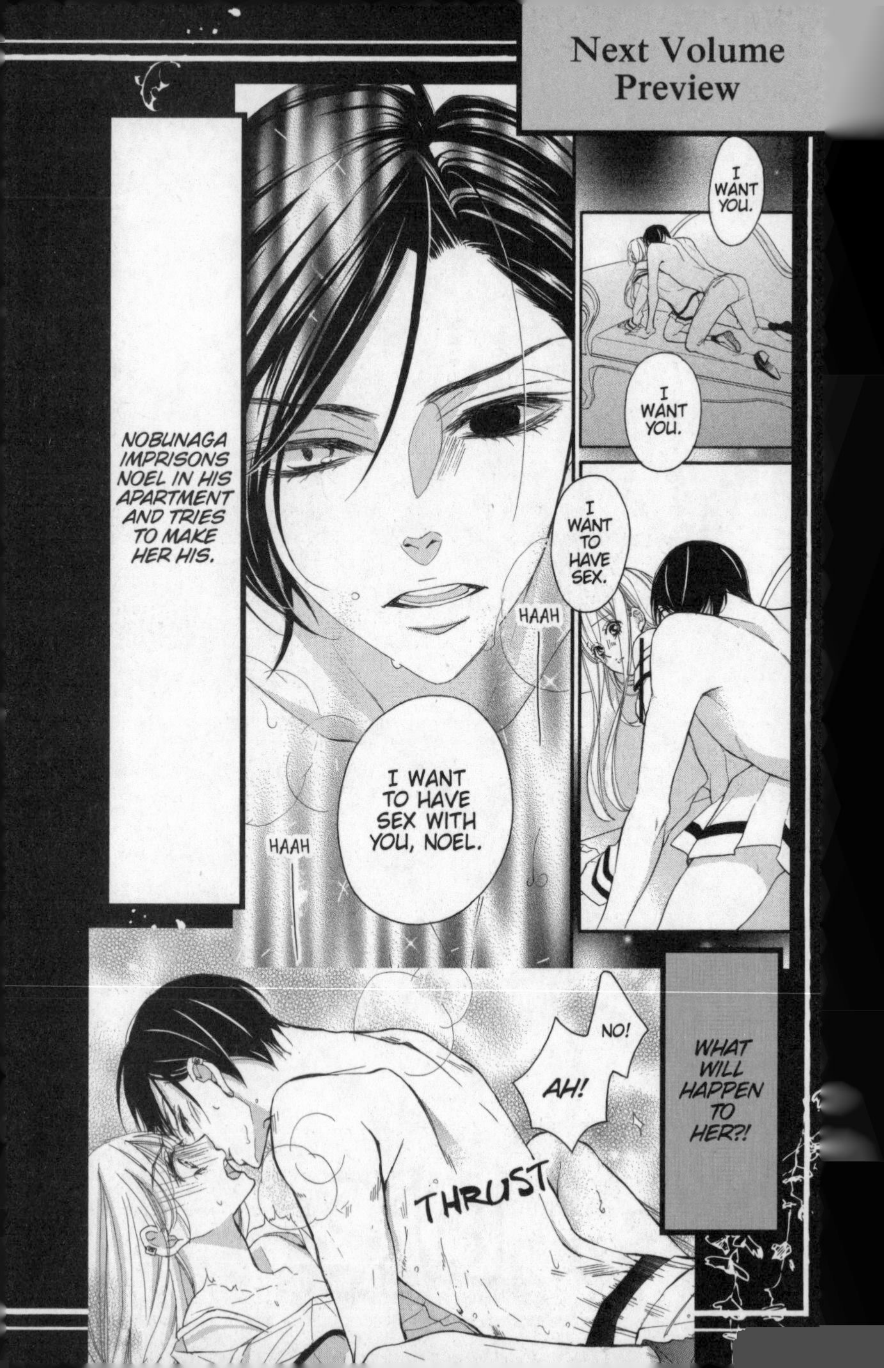
Next Volume Preview
I WANT YOU.
I WANT YOU.
I WANT TO HAVE SEX.
HAAH
I WANT TO HAVE SEX WITH YOU, NOEL.
HAAH
NOBUNAGA IMPRISONS NOEL IN HIS APARTMENT AND TRIES TO MAKE HER HIS.
WHAT WILL HAPPEN TO HER?!
NO!
AH!
THRUST

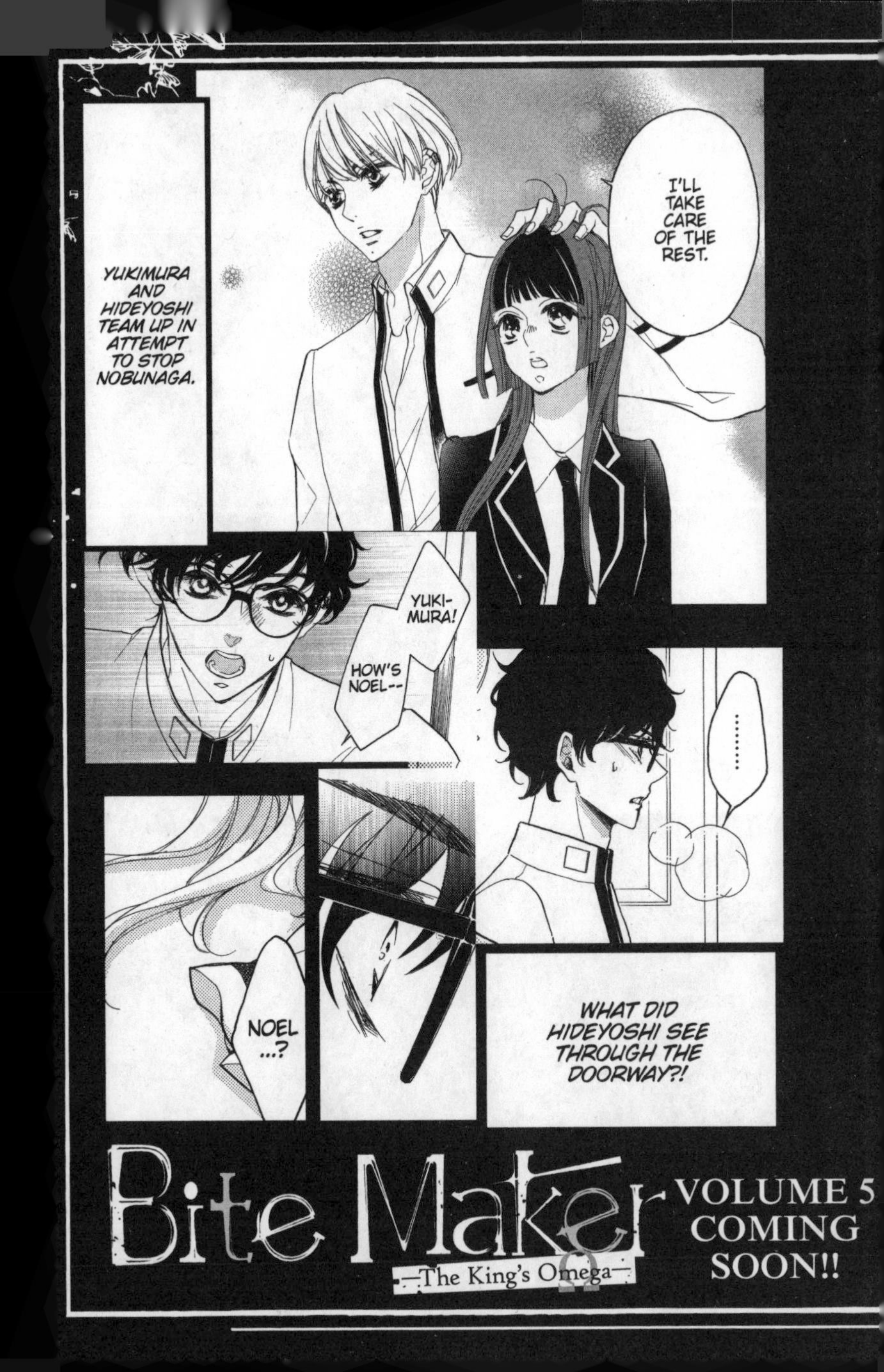
I'LL TAKE CARE OF THE REST.
YUKIMURA AND HIDEYOSHI TEAM UP IN ATTEMPT TO STOP NOBUNAGA.
YUKI-MURA!
HOW'S NOEL--
......
WHAT DID HIDEYOSHI SEE THROUGH THE DOORWAY?!
NOEL ...?

Bite Maker
—The King's Omega—

VOLUME 5
COMING
SOON!!

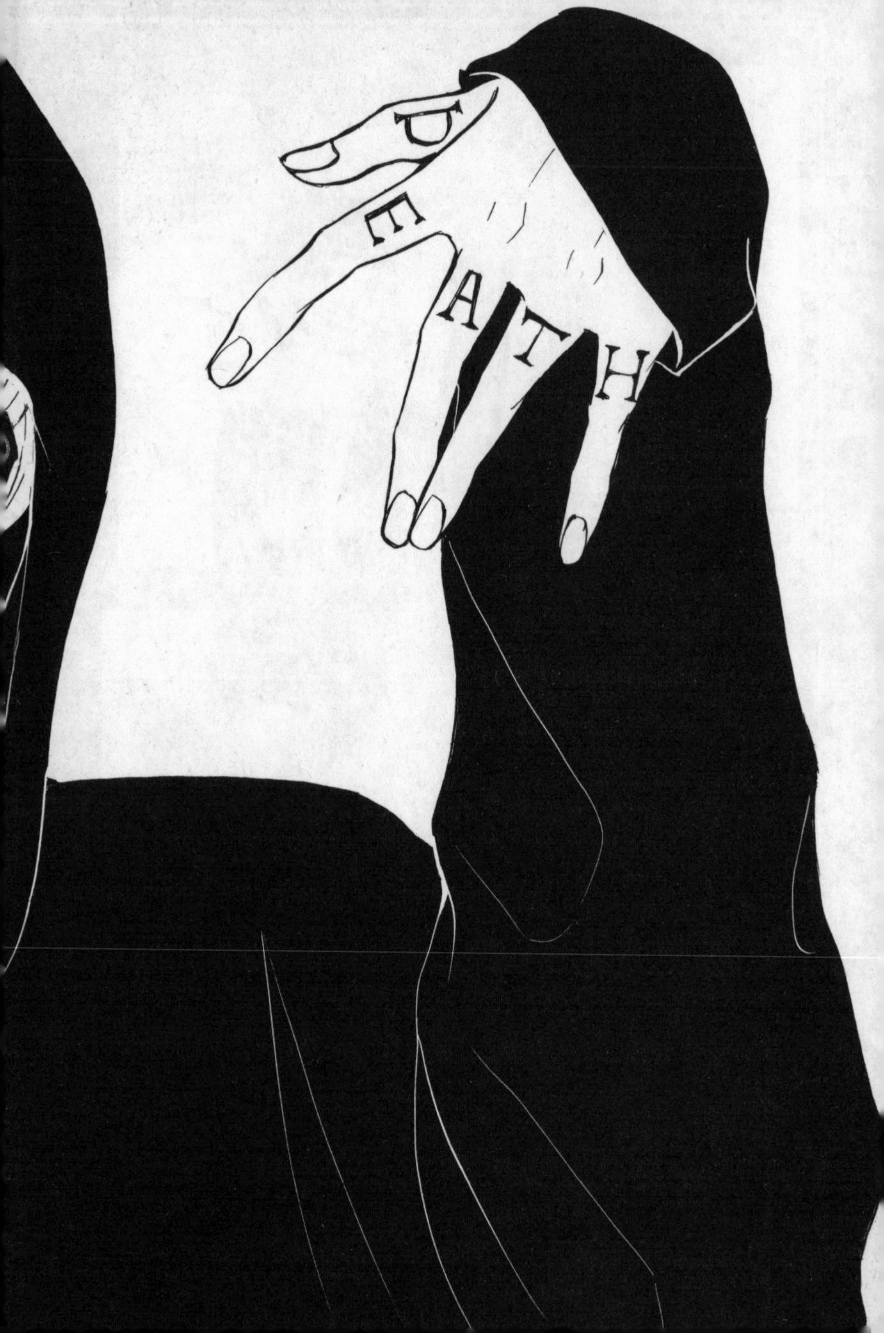
DEATH

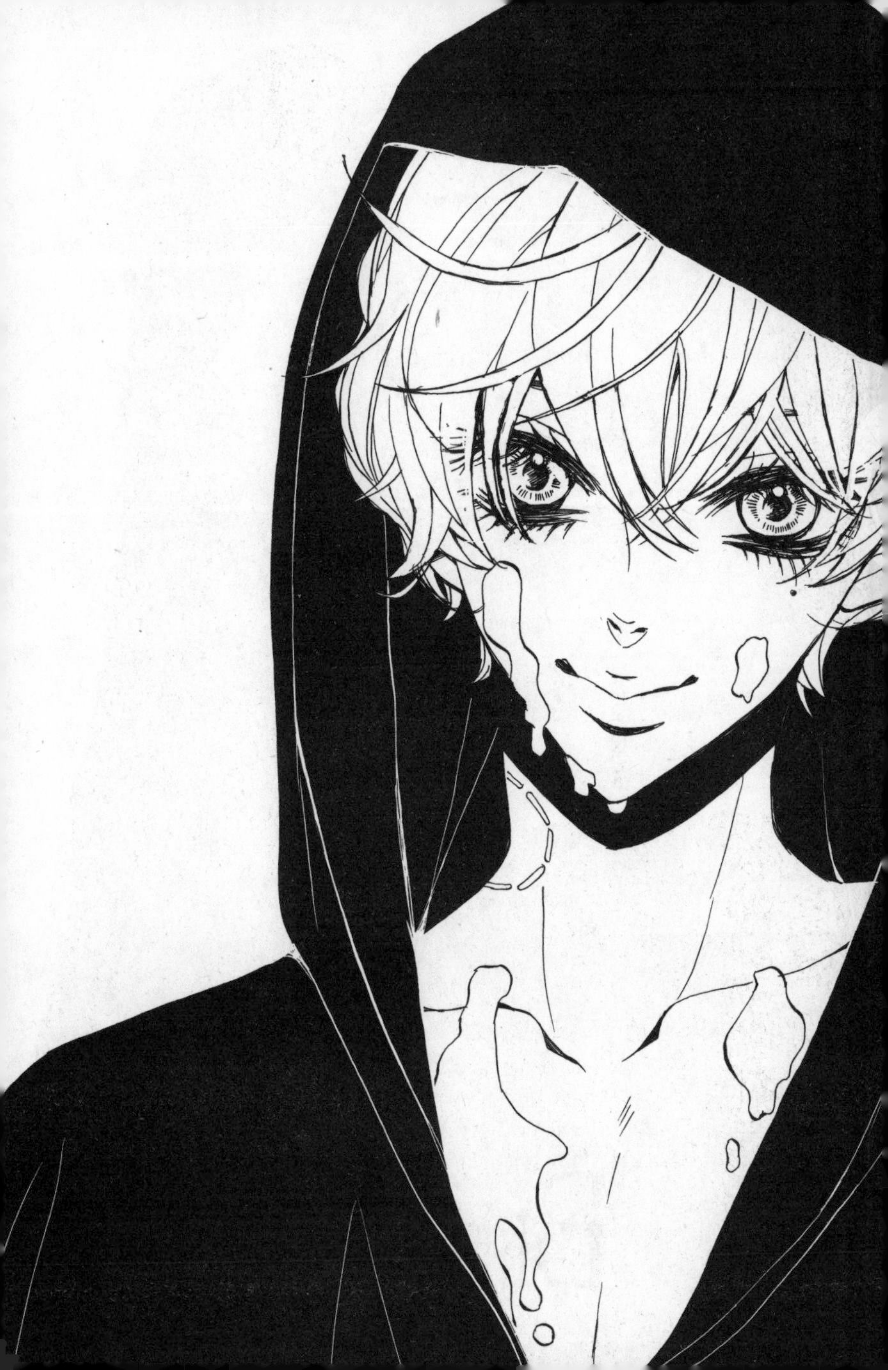

Bite Maker
-The King's Omega-